MW01105664

The Politics of Cultural Mediation

Baroness Elsa von Freytag-Loringhoven and Felix Paul Greve

Edited by Paul Hjartarson and Tracy Kulba

The Politics of

Baroness Elsa von Freytag-Loringhoven

Cultural Mediation

and Felix Paul Greve

The University of Alberta Press

Canadian Review of Comparative Literature/
Revue Canadienne de Littérature Comparée

Published by
The University of Alberta Press
Ring House 2
Edmonton, Alberta, Canada   T6G 2E1
    and
Canadian Review of Comparative Literature/
Revue Canadienne de Littérature Comparée
347 Arts Building
University of Alberta
Edmonton, Alberta, Canada   T6G 2E5

NATIONAL LIBRARY OF CANADA
CATALOGUING IN PUBLICATION DATA

Main entry under title:

The politics of cultural mediation : Baroness
Elsa von Freytag-Loringhoven and Felix Paul
Greve / edited by Paul Hjartarson and
Tracy Kulba.

    Includes some text in German.
    Co-published by: Canadian Review of
    Comparative Literature.
    Includes bibliographical references
    and index.
    ISBN 0-88864-412-4

    1. Freytag-Loringhoven, Elsa, Baroness
von, 1874-1927—Criticism and interpretation.
2. Grove, Frederick Philip, 1879-1948—
Criticism and interpretation. 3. German
literature—20th century—History and
criticism. 4. German American authors—20th
century. 5. Culture conflict in literature.
I. Hjartarson, Paul Ivar. II. Kulba, Tracy, 1969–
III. Title: Canadian review of comparative
literature.
PT2611.R49Z86 2003   831'.912
C2003-910586-5

NOTICE TO LIBRARIANS: The Politics of
Cultural Mediation, is co-published with the
Canadian Review of Comparative Literature/Revue
Canadienne de Littérature Comparée and is also the
Canadian Review of Comparative Literature/Revue
Canadienne de Littérature Comparée 29.1 (2002)
(ISSN: 0319-051X)

Copyright © Canadian Review of
Comparative Literature/Revue Canadienne de
Littérature Comparée 2003
Volume 29, Issue No. 1 (2002)
ISSN 0319-051X
ISBN 0-88864-412-4

Printed and bound in Canada by Houghton
Boston Printers, Saskatoon, Saskatchewan.
First printing, 2003

All rights reserved.

No part of this publication may be produced,
stored in a retrieval system, or transmitted in
any forms or by any means, electronic,
mechanical, photocopying, recording, or
otherwise, without the prior written consent
of the copyright owner or a licence from The
Canadian Copyright Licensing Agency (Access
Copyright). For an Access Copyright license,
visit www.accesscopyright.ca or call toll free:
1-800-893-5777.

The University of Alberta Press is committed
to protecting our natural environment. As part
of our efforts, this book is printed on stock
produced by New Leaf Paper: it contains 100%
post-consumer recycled fibres and is acid- and
chlorine-free.

The University of Alberta Press gratefully
acknowledges the support received for its
publishing program from The Canada Council
for the Arts. In addition, we also gratefully
acknowledge the financial support of the
Government of Canada through the Book
Publishing Industry Development Program
and from the Alberta Foundation for the Arts
for our publishing activities.

Contents

VII List of Illustrations

IX Foreword

XV Preface

XVII Acknowledgements

XIX **Introduction**
"Borne Across the World": Else Plötz (Baroness Elsa von Freytag-Loringhoven),
Felix Paul Greve (Frederick Philip Grove), and the Politics of Cultural Mediation
PAUL HJARTARSON & TRACY KULBA

PART I — The Baroness and the Politics of Cultural Mediation

3 **Limbswishing Dada in New York**
Baroness Elsa's Gender Performance
IRENE GAMMEL

25 **Baroness Elsa and the Aesthetics of Empathy**
A Mystery and a Speculation
RICHARD CAVELL

41 **Two Glimpses of the Baroness**
KLAUS MARTENS

PART II — FPG and the Politics of Cultural Mediation

69 **"Il me faut forger une arme de la littérature"**
Felix Paul Greve among the Magazines
JUTTA ERNST

85 **Of Life and Art**
FPG and the Writing of Oscar Wilde into Settlers of the Marsh
PAUL MORRIS

107 **"Out of the Wastage of All Other Nations"**
"Enemy Aliens" and the "Canadianization" of Felix Paul Greve
PAUL HJARTARSON

PART III — Translation and Mediation

133 **Randarabesken zu Oscar Wilde/Oscar Wilde: Marginalia
in Arabesque**
FELIX PAUL GREVE, Translated by PAUL MORRIS

189 Works Cited
203 Contributors
205 Index

List of Illustrations

FIGURE 1 (p. 4): Elsa von Freytag-Loringhoven. *Portrait of Marcel Duchamp.* c. 1920. Assemblage of miscellaneous objects in a wine glass. Photograph by Charles Sheeler. Francis M. Naumann Collection, New York.

FIGURE 2 (p. 12): Elsa von Freytag-Loringhoven. *Limbswish.* c. 1920. Metal spring, curtain tassel. 21 11/16 in. Mark Kelman Collection, New York.

FIGURE 3 (p. 13): Elsa von Freytag-Loringhoven. "Perpetual Motion." c. 1923. Visual Poem. Special Collections, University of Maryland at College Park Libraries.

FIGURE 4 (p. 17): Theresa Bernstein. *Elsa von Freytag-Loringhoven.* 1916–17. Oil. 12 x 9 in. Francis M. Naumann Collection, New York.

FIGURE 5 (p. 26): Richard Boix. *DA-DA (NEW YORK DADA GROUP).* 1921. Brush, pen and ink. 11¼ x 14½ in. (28.6 x 36.8 cm). Primary Inscription: Signed L.R. "Boix." The Museum of Modern Art, New York. Katherine S. Dreier Bequest.

FIGURE 6 (p. 26): Richard Boix, detail.

FIGURE 7 (p. 27): Alexander Archipenko. *Seated Woman (Seated Geometric Figure).* 1920. Plaster, painted Venetian red and burnt sienna. Signed: "Archipenko." 57 cm. Gift of the Goeritz family, London. Tel Aviv Museum of Art Collection, Israel. © Estate of Alexander Archipenko/SODRAC (Montreal), 2002.

FIGURE 8 (p. 32): August Endell. Exterior façade (Elvira Photographic Studio, Munich). 1897–98. Bildarchiv Foto Marburg, Germany.

FIGURE 9 (p. 33): August Endell. Interior stairwell (Elvira Photographic Studio, Munich). 1897–98. Bildarchiv Foto Marburg, Germany.

FIGURE 10 (p. 34): Elsa von Freytag-Loringhoven (with Morton Livingston Schamberg). *God*. 1917. Philadelphia Museum of Art. The Louise and Walter Arensberg Collection.

FIGURE 11 (p. 37): Man Ray. Letter to Tristan Tzara, postmarked 8 June 1921. Bibliothèque Littéraire Jacques Doucet, Paris. © Estate of Man Ray/SODRAC (Montreal), 2003.

FIGURE 12 (p. 48): View of the Hotel Goldener Ring (second building from the left).

FIGURE 13 (p. 48): The "Old Theater" in the Hotel Goldener Ring. View of the Stage (*Zwanzig Jahre* 21).

FIGURE 14 (p. 50): Advertisement in the *Cottbus Anzeiger* for Max Walden's company with "Elsa Plötz."

FIGURE 15 (p. 50): Unsigned review of Schiller's *Don Carlos*, naming "Miss Plötz" (excerpt).

FIGURE 16 (p. 55): Else Lasker-Schüler. Else Lasker-Schüler's drawing of herself as "Prince Yussuf" ("Selbstbildnis im Sternenmantel"). Schiller Nationalmuseum, Deutsches Literaturarchiv, Marbach Germany.

FIGURE 17 (p. 58): Else Lasker-Schüler with flute, 1909–10. Schiller Nationalmuseum, Deutsches Literaturarchiv, Marbach Germany.

FIGURE 18 (p. 121): Great War Veterans Association Parade, Winnipeg 4 June 1919. Archives of Manitoba. N12295

FIGURE 19 (p. 121): Great War Veterans Association demonstration at City Hall, Winnipeg 4 June 1919. Archives of Manitoba. N12296

Foreword

THERE IS SOMETHING ABOUT movement and migration that has long been a part of human life. What the industrial and technological revolutions have done has been to allow more people to move faster and farther afield. The world of art—of literature and visual representation in the case of this collection—has embodied this longstanding experience and this changing dimension of an ancient practice and concern. Else Plötz (Baroness Elsa von Freytag-Loringhoven) and Felix Paul Greve (Frederick Philip Grove) were—as the editors, Paul Hjartarson and Tracy Kulba observe in their Introduction—"borne across the world." The travels of Plötz and Greve led them to embody and take part in the politics of cultural mediation. The coming together, translation and interpretation of culture are as much about the creation and dissemination of art as about the work of historians, political theorists and anthropologists. Being borne across the world, these two artists were born into a new world, which Europeans explorers called the New World. This typology between the Old World (Germany) and the New World (Canada and the United States) is part of that mediation for Greve and Plötz (as I shall call them even if they are referred to in many ways inside and outside this collection). Miranda's "O brave new world" in Shakespeare's *The Tempest* (1611) was new to her, as Prospero said, but was, in other ways, new to every other European who ventured generation after generation and century after century to the shores of the Americas. The story of these artists, then, like that of their predecessors, is one of displacement and disguise, representation and misrepresentation, reproduction and innovation, settling and unsettling, making and unmaking. The fashioning of identity and misidentification became, for artist and audience alike, a telos in the horizon as Europeans tried to make sense of or respond to the New World that they had so transformed and continued to change for better and worse.

In the early 1970s, I first read in school someone called Frederick Philip Grove and no one seemed to have, in Canada at least, much of an idea of a secret or previous life of this author. Grove's work was becoming part of a forging of a Canadian literature that was being developed for curriculum in schools and for national and international consumption. This interest in Grove/Greve remained with me when I had the good fortune of introducing to University of Alberta Press a book by Klaus Martens, whose focus was on unraveling the Old and New World identities of Greve. The connection between Greve and Plötz was another fascination that Irene Gammel and other scholars were illuminating while also concentrating interest in the accomplishments of Plötz herself. It was my pleasure to attend a session on these two artists in Edmonton that included some of the leading scholars in the field. I approached one of these scholars, Paul Hjartarson, to edit a special issue/collection in the *Canadian Review of Comparative Literature/Revue Canadienne de Littérature Comparée* Library and happily he agreed and later brought Tracy Kulba on board to strengthen the work further. The anonymous assessors made some constructive recommendations and also deserve our thanks. In time Linda Cameron and Mary Mahoney-Robson at the University of Alberta Press became involved in copublishing the collection and brought to bear once more the editorial and design expertise of Press to a book involving Grove. Glenn Rollans, Leslie Vermeer, Alan Brownoff and others at the Press had been committed to Grove before and it was a privilege to have a new director and editor and the same designer, among others there, now involved in this project. This partnership between the University of Alberta Press and the *Canadian Review of Comparative Literature*, of which I am the editor, has been a pleasure and is something that we hope to continue to build. The University of Alberta Press takes great care with its authors and books and the excellence of its list and of its design make it a privilege for the journal to be in such a partnership. Over the years it has also been pleasant to discuss Grove and other literary matters with E.D. Blodgett and with Christian Riegel and I thank them as well for their wisdom and support and also my colleague at the journal, Irene Sywenky, for her contributions to the making of this volume.

A distinguished group of scholars from Germany and North America have come together to tell a marvellous story about two innovative artists on the move and in disguise or role. By placing these two artists side by side, the tale is even more fascinating, and their different arts enrich each other the more. The collection begins with a wide-ranging Introduction by Paul Hjartarson and Tracy Kulba on Plötz and Greve (the Baronness and Grove) and cultural mediation. The first section includes ground-breaking essays on Plötz by Irene Gammel, Richard Cavell and Klaus Martens; the second section germinal essays on Greve by Jutta Ernst, Paul Morris and Paul Hjartarson; the third section an important work in German on Oscar Wilde by Greve and Paul Morris's recent translation of it.

The politics of cultural mediation is a complex topic worth the exploration in relation to these two figures. Briefly, I would like to highlight a few aspects of this intricate and suggestive collection. In the Introduction Paul Hjartarson and Tracy Kulba build on the notion of translation as spatial and cultural movement, foregrounding the zones of cultural contact produced by the migrations of two German-born artists: Else Plötz (1874–1927) (also known as Baroness Elsa von Freytag-Loringhoven or, simply, as the Baroness), Dada poet and artist; and Felix Paul Greve (1879–1948), also known as Frederick Philip Grove, the writer and translator. Hjartarson and Kulba argue that both Plötz and Greve learned languages beyond German, their mother tongue, moved between geographic and cultural worlds, produced cultural works in their adopted countries (the United States and Canada), and, even through their double and doubling names, translated themselves into new contexts. Plötz, known as the Baroness among the international avant-garde in New York and Paris in the second and third decades of the twentieth century, was a performance artist, model, sculptor, and poet who, according to Irene Gammel, was part of the rejection of conventional Victorian views of sex. Before coming to New York, Plötz, as Gammel notes, had undergone an apprenticeship amongst the *Kunstgewerbler* avant-garde in Munich and Berlin from around 1896 to 1911 before following her spouse Felix Paul Greve to Kentucky. After Greve's desertion, she went to New York, where she married Baron Leopold von Freytag-Loringhoven. Richard Cavell calls attention to the reasons for the shifts in Dada that allowed Plötz to emerge from the shadows of male dadaists. As Cavell points out, the increasing recognition of the historical importance of women in Dada (as in the anthology edited by Naomi Sawelson-Gorse); feminist theory, which has criticized the idea of Dada as a masculinist activity; the centrality of sexuality in the culture and in Plötz's memoirs (which Paul Hjartarson and Douglas Spettigue brought out under the title *Baroness Elsa*); poetry, prose and created artefacts, contribute to the renewed interest in the Baroness's work. There is also, as Cavell notes, a growing realization that the work of Plötz and Greve constitutes a significant intellectual collaboration. Klaus Martens stresses some detective work over the movement of Plötz: she left Germany in 1910, arriving in New York after she had been deserted by Greve in the hinterland of Kentucky. From June 1910 to late 1913, according to Martens, she did not become acquainted with or was not influenced by dadaists. Martens maintains that by assuming her German stage name "Elsa" in America, Plötz emphasized the interaction between high and low culture and the movement from an old to a new order in the arts, in which the artist and the art became inextricable.

New reconsiderations of Greve have borne significant new interpretations. Jutta Ernst asserts that Greve sought power and influence through literature, that he became a mediator who translated writers like Oscar Wilde, H.G. Wells, George Meredith, Gustave Flaubert, and André Gide into German while attempting to write and promote his own texts. Ernst focuses on one important context—the role periodicals played in this mediation—and says that Greve's first publications were a review of Stendhal's novel *Lucien Leuwen* and a commentary on volumes eleven and twelve of Friedrich Nietzsche's complete works, both appeared in 1901 in the supplement to the Munich *Allgemeine Zeitung*, a well-known daily newspaper founded in the late 1700s. For Paul Morris, Oscar Wilde constituted one of the central influences in Greve's writing and life. To investigate this influence, Morris concentrates on Greve's understanding of Wilde through his translation of Wilde's *Fingerzeige* (*Intentions*) and his critical assessment of Wilde and provides an interpretation of Greve/Grove's first Canadian novel, *Settlers of the Marsh*, and a reading of how Wilde's ideals provided Greve with key ideas in his later life and writing. Paul Hjartarson focuses on the historical circumstances surrounding Greve's settlement in Canada and resumption of a life as a writer. Hjartarson argues that when Greve came to Manitoba, relations with immigrants in the west of Canada were strained and that, early on in Canada as a teacher and writer, Greve considered himself as a mediator caught between these non-English immigrants and British-Canadians. This role, in Hjartarson's view, shaped both Greve's role as a writer in Canada and *Settlers of the Marsh* and *A Search for America*.

This volume—as the Introduction, the essays and translation attest—raises many more issues about these two intriguing artists and about the making and reception of art itself. If Plötz and Greve played many roles and haunted while they were haunted, they gesture beyond their gestures to new interpretations. The editors and contributors have produced a work that breathes life into two historic figures that time has obscured. Perhaps, as Greve wrote in his *Randarabesken zu Oscar Wilde* which Paul Morris translates for this collection, "Oscar Wilde — can that be you, returning from the grave once again in search of sacrifice from me?" Paul Hjartarson and Tracy Kulba, their contributors and all those who made this book possible might ask the same question of Plötz and Greve: all of them have made their sacrifices, and for this we should all give thanks.

JONATHAN HART, Editor
Canadian Review of Comparative Literature/
Revue Canadienne de Littérature Comparée

Preface

THE POLITICS OF CULTURAL MEDIATION began as two sessions on the Baroness Elsa von Freytag-Loringhoven and Felix Paul Greve as cultural mediators organized by Irene Gammel and Klaus Martens for the Canadian Comparative Literature Association annual conference held in Edmonton, Alberta in May of 2000. The idea for the panels grew, in part, out of the dialogue fostered among researchers by two different but related developments, both underwritten by the increasing globalisation of literary and cultural studies in the 1990s. One was the renewed interest in New York Dada—particularly the role and representation of gender in that contact zone of cultures—and in the Baroness as the embodiment of New York Dada and herself a cultural mediator. Signs of that interest include the publication of at least four books—*New York Dada* (Kuenzli 1986), *Baroness Elsa*, the Baroness's autobiography (Hjartarson and Spettigue 1992), *New York Dada 1915–23* (Naumann 1994), and *Women in Dada: Essays on Sex, Gender, and Identity* (Sawelson-Gorse 1998)—and the mounting of a major exhibition on New York Dada at the Whitney Museum of American Art titled "Making Mischief: Dada Invades New York." (The exhibition was curated by Francis M. Naumann and Beth Venn and ran from November 21, 1996 to February 23, 1997.) The book *Making Mischief: Dada Invades New York* (Naumann and Venn 1996) was published in association with the exhibition and took as its cover image Baroness Elsa's *Portrait of Marcel Duchamp* (figure 1). Irene Gammel's *Baroness Elsa: Gender, Dada and Everyday Modernity: A Cultural Biography* (2002), the first book-length, scholarly biography of the Baroness's life, is the latest contribution to this strand of the dialogue and another sign of the strong, continuing interest in both New York Dada and the Baroness.

The other development was a renewed interest in Felix Paul Greve not as the canonical English-Canadian author Frederick Philip Grove but as a

German translator and cultural mediator. Klaus Martens, Chair of North American Literature and Culture and Director of the Centre for Canadian and Anglo-American Cultures, and his colleagues at the Universität des Saarlandes have been central to this work.[1] The renewed interest in Greve's work was apparent in a series of events organised in 1998 to mark the fiftieth anniversary of FPG's death. These included a session for a conference held at the Universität des Saarlandes in April, the proceedings of which were subsequently published under the title *Pioneering North America: Mediators of European Literature and Culture* (Martens 2000); a joint session of two associations for a conference at the University of Ottawa in May; and a conference, *In Memoriam FPG: An International Symposium*, held at the University of Manitoba in September. By 1998, the year in which *Women in Dada* appeared and FPG's life was commemorated, Klaus Martens had published his *Felix Paul Greves Karriere: Frederick Philip Grove in Deutschland* (1997), a translated and updated version of which appeared as *F.P. Grove in Europe and Canada: Translated Lives* (2001); he and his colleague Jutta Ernst were completing *"Je vous écris, en hâte et fiévreusement": Felix Paul Greve-André Gide: Korrespondenz und Dokumentation* (1999); Richard Cavell had just published his essay "Felix Paul Greve, the Eulenburg Scandal, and Frederick Philip Grove" (1997); and Irene Gammel was in the midst of work on her biography of the Baroness. It was within the dynamics of this cultural production that the CCLA panels were organized and the present volume conceived.

NOTE

1   See the website for the Canadian and Anglo-American Cultures at the Universität des Saarlandes <http://www.klausmartens.com>.

Grove fascinating
not for his work but as
a figure.

Acknowledgements

JONATHAN HART, editor of the *Canadian Review of Comparative Literature*, first proposed that the essays on cultural mediation presented at the Canadian Comparative Literature Association meetings become the nucleus of a special issue of the journal; he also initiated the joint release of *The Politics of Cultural Mediation* as a book in the Library of the *Canadian Review of Comparative Literature/Revue Canadienne de Littérature Comparée*, co-published by the University of Alberta Press. Without his initiative and encouragement, this volume would not have been possible. While it was Jonathan Hart who made *The Politics of Cultural Mediation* possible, it was the contributors themselves who made it a reality: they agreed to revise and expand their papers for the volume; they patiently responded to our many questions; and they offered us their advice and encouragement throughout this project. A special thanks to Irene Gammel and Klaus Martens who organized the CCLA sessions and who thus gave *The Politics of Cultural Mediation* its original shape, and to Paul Morris for permitting us to include his translation of *Randarabesken zu Oscar Wilde* in the volume. We are indebted to Irene Sywenky, CRCL's editorial consultant, for her assistance. Many people at The University of Alberta Press have contributed to this project, especially Alan Brownoff and Mary Mahoney-Robson. We also wish to acknowledge the work of two anonymous assessors chosen by the *Canadian Review of Comparative Literature* to assess the manuscript; we benefited from their careful scrutiny.

For granting permission to use copyright material, we would like to thank: the Archives of Manitoba; the Bildarchiv Foto Marburg, Germany; the Cottbus Stadtarchiv; the Cottbus Theaterarchiv; the Estate of Alexander Archipenko; the Estate of Man Ray; A. Leonard Grove; Mark Kelman; the Museum of Modern Art, New York; Frances M. Naumann; the Philadelphia Museum of Art; the Schiller Nationalmuseum, Deutsches Literaturarchiv,

Germany; the Tel Aviv Museum of Art; and the University of Maryland at College Park Libraries. The cover and title page photograph of Baroness Elsa was taken from *The Little Review* (Sept.-Dec. 1920) and used with permission. A special thank you to Jeannine Green at Bruce Peel Special Collections, University of Alberta, for locating and lending it to the Press. Every attempt has been made, where appropriate, to trace the copyright holders of material reproduced in *The Politics of Cultural Mediation*; the editors and publishers would be pleased to hear from any interested parties.

Introduction

"Borne Across the World":
Else Plötz (Baroness Elsa von Freytag-Loringhoven),
Felix Paul Greve (Frederick Philip Grove),
and the Politics of Cultural Mediation

The word 'translation' comes, etymologically, from the Latin for 'bearing across'. Having been borne across the world, we are translated men. It is normally supposed that something always gets lost in translation; I cling, obstinately, to the notion that something can also be gained.

— SALMAN RUSHDIE, *Imaginary Homelands*

◆ Conceptualising Cultural Mediation

DRAWING OUT the etymological roots of the word, Salman Rushdie describes translation as an act of "bearing across" that marks a doubled space of loss and possibility. Nuances are lost, nuances are gained; layers overlap, meanings accrue. In Rushdie's passage, however, the process of translation includes, but goes beyond, the textual register to encompass also a more subjective, cultural process. Just as texts are translated across linguistic and cultural divisions, acquiring different imaginative dimensions in that process, Rushdie suggests that the diasporic individual who is "borne across the world" is equally translated, representing a contact zone between cultures.[1] In these terms, translation involves a movement between cultures and contexts, a movement simultaneously away from and toward an imaginary homeland. Building on this notion of spatial and cultural movement, The Politics of Cultural Mediation foregrounds the cultural contact zones produced by the migrations of two German-born cultural figures: the Dada poet and artist Else Plötz (1874–1927), better known as Baroness Elsa von Freytag-Loringhoven or, simply, as the Baroness; and the writer and translator, Felix Paul Greve (1879–1948), also known as the Canadian author Frederick Philip Grove.[2] Both the Baroness and FPG negotiated languages beyond their mother tongue (German); both figures moved between geographic and cultural worlds; both produced cultural works in their adopted countries (the United States and Canada); and, as their dual names make obvious, both 'translated' themselves into new contexts.[3] However, the Baroness and FPG were also both positioned within overdetermined fields of influences—in Europe and in North America—that nuanced the contexts within which they produced their works and within which those cultural objects and performances were received. Thus, where Rushdie's concept of translation makes obvious a kind of movement between cultures, The Politics of Cultural Mediation focuses also on the dynamics of cultural production within a given social and institutional context to ask how that "thick" perspective might complicate or be complicated by the contact zones of different cultures.[4]

To foreground this complex site of contact, exchange and overdetermined production, we have organised this volume around a central concept of cultural mediation. By titling the Introduction "Borne Across the World," we seek to convey the sense both that texts and people move from one place to another and that they are moved or repositioned by forces beyond themselves; moreover, following Salman Rushdie, we mean to suggest that the change in geographical, political and social location involves not just a loss but a gain, the reshaping of meanings and lives. Exploring the dynamics of that movement, the contributors in this collection engage the writings and performances of the Baroness and FPG in three key ways: by translating their texts; by examining the Baroness and FPG as 'cultural migrants'; and by analysing these two artist-producers as the subjects and objects of mediation in shifting social-institutional contexts. The first approach is manifest in Paul Morris's translation of a much discussed article, Randarabesken zu Oscar Wilde, published by Felix Paul Greve in Germany in 1903.[5] Greve was not only among the first to make Oscar Wilde's writing available to German readers but used Wilde to mediate his own entry into the literary field of production. Publishing this work in translation and in its original German text, we attempt to foreground and to invite discussion about issues of textual and cultural mediation. The second mode of analysis understands the Baroness and FPG as cultural migrants and mediators who travelled across oceans and between cultural worlds. Focussing on this movement between cultures, this approach examines the contact zones manifest in the works and performances of the Baroness and FPG. Lastly, contributors also investigate the different ways in which the Baroness and FPG mediated themselves within and were mediated by different social-institutional contexts. This approach examines how the Baroness and FPG worked to produce and legitimise themselves as artists and how their cultural status (and the works they produced in that context) was mediated by a broader social and institutional apparatus. These modes of analysis frequently overlap in contributors' papers to enable complex interrogations. What effects, contributors ask, did European influences have on the new North American contexts of the Baroness and FPG? How were those European influences reshaped in the face of new cultural and social fields of production? How did the Baroness and FPG practice cultural mediation in Europe and North America? How, in turn, were they mediated? How did their immigrant status position them in North American debates? And how did they position themselves? Exploring these and other questions, the contributors in The Politics of Cultural Mediation interrogate the contact zone of cultures and contribute to a more historicised understanding of the influences and innovations of the Baroness and FPG as artist-producers in shifting social-cultural-institutional fields of production.

To develop the concept of cultural mediation, we reflect on the three modes of cultural mediation outlined—mediation as translation, as migration, and within a social-institutional apparatus—exploring how different authors develop analyses of the Baroness and FPG in each mode. While we have organised the Introduction in this manner to elucidate the theoretical questions that connect the papers, we have grouped the essays themselves to foreground The Politics of Cultural Mediation's important contribution to historicizing FPG and the Baroness in cross-cultural contexts. Exploring collections in Germany, Canada and the United States, contributors bring a vast array of archival documents and historical contexts to their papers, offering readers new ways of thinking about cultural influences on FPG and the Baroness and about the social contexts within which they moved. To highlight this dimension of the volume and the consequent historical "thickness" it enables, we have grouped papers about the Baroness and FPG into separate parts. Although the relation between these two artists and cultural migrants spanned a decade (1902–1911) and led to their marriage in 1907, they spent most of their creative lives apart and, following their separation in 1911, moved in very different worlds: the Baroness in the avant-garde art circles of Greenwich Village; and FPG in post-war Canadian literary circles. In Part III, the volume presents Paul Morris's translation— "Oscar Wilde: Marginalia in Arabesque"—of FPG's important critical study, *Randarabesken zu Oscar Wilde* (1903). This part, including here FPG's original German text and Morris's translation of that study, will appeal not only to scholars interested in FPG, but also to scholars interested in translation theories and practices. As editors of this collection, we elaborate a framework within which to think about processes, contexts and effects of cultural mediation. We anticipate, however, that the volume's juxtaposition of papers will further nuance the overlaps and interplays between modes, hopefully facilitating grounds for future work.

◆ Cultural Mediation: Translation

THE POLITICS OF CULTURAL MEDIATION organises itself around the concept of mediation to facilitate and complicate analyses of cultural contact zones. One manifestation of that concept is represented in Paul Morris's translation, "Oscar Wilde: Marginalia in Arabesque." A critical analysis of Wilde's aesthetics, the article contains important insights into Greve's artistic development. It marks an early attempt by Greve to articulate his sense of aesthetic value, and it manifests Greve's self-mediation in the distinguished periodicals and publishing houses of Munich's literary culture; that is, the 1903 article resonates strongly with Jutta Ernst's analysis—"'Il me faut forger une arme de la littérature': Felix Paul Greve among the Magazines"—of FPG's efforts to make a name for himself as a translator and critic so as to advance his own status as an artist and influential literary figure in Munich circles. Published during Greve's German years, the article was a central document in Douglas O. Spettigue's attempt, in *FPG: The European Years* (1973), to piece together the life of

Greve/Grove and has not lost its fascination for scholars.[6] Beyond those parameters, the text is an intriguing experiment in voice, evincing E.D. Blodgett's assertion that "[FPG] could translate himself as well as his authors" (Foreword x); that is, like Greve's translations of Wilde, *Randarabesken zu Oscar Wilde* marks Greve's ability to "[insinuate] himself into Wilde so as to imitate the merest gesture, his way of using his eyes, perhaps his turn of phrase. It is evident that Greve had such skills and that his abilities to translate worked in two directions" (Foreword x). Alternately a critical interpretation and a rhapsodic invocation, the article suggests that Wilde was a complex figure for Greve, in personal and in professional registers.

As a critical study of Wilde distributed to a German public, *Randarabesken zu Oscar Wilde* attests to Greve's own cultural and institutional mediations; as a translation, however, the article makes obvious the mediation of Greve by later academics. In a textual 'bearing across', Morris translates Greve's article into a different language and cultural medium, making it accessible in another register and to another audience. At the same time, *The Politics of Cultural Mediation* also includes the German text of *Randarabesken zu Oscar Wilde* (1903), to represent Greve's study in its original form. Printed on parallel pages, the two texts invite discussion about the difficulties and possibilities of translation as a site of textual mediation, contact and exchange. Interrogating the grounds on which we engage that site of contact, however, is crucial. Measured against the original, Morris engages in the always impossible task of invoking and approaching a spectral authenticity of meaning at which he can never arrive. The original marks the site of authenticity; the translation can only be a mediated version. Within that framework, however, the translator risks becoming, in Eric Prenowitz's words, "authoritarian if not authoritative":

> [...] in translation the text itself is presented without being present: it is here and yet there. A translation is irresponsible, unreliable, deceptive. Yet imposing. Authoritarian if not authoritative. It inevitably inflicts an irresistible covenant. Whereas a foreign text in the *original* leaves the reader free, because the reader is not a reader, the text being foreign and thus legibly illegible for those who have not domesticated the other mother tongue. It does not suppose and impose a *we*, because to begin with it says "we" differently, that is, it literally does not say

saying + understanding are different.

"we." Rather, and precisely because translation always remains possible, it inscribes the limits, the singularity or the extra-ordinary common to any *we*. And so a translation does violence at once to the text to which it offers an ambiguous hospitality, both becking and balking, and to the reader: it takes something foreign and makes something familiar, readable at least, and thereby imposes the indubitable community of a homolinguistic, a homonolinguistic *we*. (106)

In the logic of authenticity suggested by Prenowitz, the translation is dislocated from authoritativeness; however, trapped in that structure of desire, the translation becomes "authoritarian" in its transmutation of otherness into the imposed familiarity of a "homonolinguistic *we*." Articulated against the foreign-ness of the original and repressing the otherness within, translations produce familiarity as a structure of dominance through a type of policing: they write for an imagined "homonolinguistic" community. This act of imagining community marks then the social policing that Prenowitz names "authoritarian." It is worth noting, however, that translators move between languages and cultures, often occupying the spaces 'in between', and that, although they are structured in dominance, communities are not homolinguistic. Translation marks not only a movement from one site to another, but also an overlapping of cultural systems of signification. Raised in Canada but living and working in Germany, for instance, Morris translates from a position between cultures. How, one might ask, does that nuance the "homonolinguistic *we*" for whom he translates the text? Is it an either/or? What kinds of effects might be produced from translating the 'in between' space?

In printing the original against the translation, we encourage analyses of mediation on a textual level to suggest that—as a cultural contact zone—translation has multiple effects which register contextually and that the meanings that accrue from the process of 'bearing across' attach themselves to the original as well as to the translated text. The desire for authenticity assumes that the translation mimics the original, that the translation registers the effects of cultural movement in its dislocation from authenticity. However, structuring Greve's original and Morris's translation in parallel, we imagine that the effects of the cultural contact zone move in both directions. In reprinting the original, we do not, as Prenowitz suggests, think to "[leave] the reader free." The very terminology of foreignness already establishes an imagined community's boundaries of inclusion and exclusion. Yet, while marking relationships of linguistic dominance with complex effects and within which different readers are differently situated, translations also bring cultures and communities into contact. Moving away from the discourse of authenticity, we suggest rather that the translation marks an(other) version of the text: a site of lost authenticity but also a site of possibility. Further, while the translation makes obvious a primary dynamic of mediation—that of Morris as the textual translator—the doubled German/English text marks also a broader problematic: a site of seduction wherein one might seek to identify an 'original' that is prior to and beyond the mediation at hand. *The Politics of Cultural Mediation* hopes not only to invite responses to the textual mediation of Greve's text but also to problematize simple notions of authenticity that might construct the original article as an unmediated work. In multiple registers, Greve's article and Morris's translation thus ask: what are the politics of translation as a form of mediation? How is Greve being here mediated in English? How did Greve, in turn, mediate Wilde and himself to a German audience? What has been lost and what has been gained through this process? What has been assumed and what has been left out?

◆ Cultural Mediation: Migration

CONTINUING THIS EXPLORATION of cultural contact zones, the articles by Klaus Martens and Paul Morris in this volume investigate the cultural influences the Baroness and FPG carried with them to North America to examine these artist-producers as cultural migrants and mediators. In "Two Glimpses of the Baroness," Klaus Martens intervenes into constructions of the Baroness as a "kind of unchaste Athena Parthenos" who sprang "somehow fully made into Dada existence" in two ways: first, by revealing new evidence regarding the Baroness's early theatrical experiences in Cottbus, Germany; second, by positing the German poet and novelist, Else Lasker-Schüler, as a possible mediator of the Baroness's later New York persona. Martens attempts to historicise the Baroness's Dada and to situate it in broader social movements of the period. His discovery of her theatrical training in Cottbus offers another perspective on the historical picture developed by Irene Gammel in her recent biography of the Baroness. His portrayal of Else Lasker-Schüler asserts the importance of the 'oriental vogue' in Germany as a performative phenomenon that may have influenced the Baroness's later persona in New York. Martens's paper opens the field for future work examining the ways in which von Freytag-Loringhoven's Dada poems, performances and *objets d'art* might have contributed to or destabilised hegemonic constructions of the orient. Given the market value of cultural orientalism, for instance, what did it mean for Western European women to mobilise this discourse in the service of gendered transgressions and financial advancement? How did this inflect the Baroness's Dada performances? And how might it have shaped her reception? Arguing for an orientalist reading of the Baroness's poetry and performances in New York, Martens's paper bridges the gap between Else's Dada in North America and her life in Germany to set up several important extensions, premised on the idea of cultural mediation. As noted, it contributes to a more historicised understanding of Baroness Elsa von Freytag-Loringhoven's radical Dada. It interrogates the myth of the autonomous artist-genius to reconfigure that narrative in a more socially and historically engaged methodology. And it participates in and resonates with Martens's wider commitment to mapping the movement and re-configuration of cultural paradigms in different locations. In the preface to *Pioneering North America*, Martens argues that:

> [...] much of America's modernist and post-modernist international cultural and literary impact has its origins, after all, in the diversity of European literatures and cultures. We feel, therefore, that the time has come to rediscover and reexamine those influences, to see what has happened to some European cultural "goods" in their transatlantic transfer and, how, in several instances, they have come back home in different guises. (12)

Challenging the idea that the new world marked a site of rebirth for European artists of the period, Martens insists instead on recognizing the Baroness as a cultural migrant and mediator, who approached a new imaginary 'homeland'—here manifested in Dada—by translating her earlier life into her new environment.

A similar approach to the idea of cultural mediation informs Paul Morris's "Of Life and Art: FPG and the Writing of Oscar Wilde into *Settlers of the Marsh*." Morris's paper builds on Greve's critical study of Wilde, *Randarabesken zu Oscar Wilde*, to trace the aesthetic influence of Oscar Wilde on Greve as a writer. Wilde was an important touchstone for Greve, if only because in the early stages of his career as a writer in Germany, Greve produced multiple translations of and critical works on Wilde who, in England, was closely associated with the avant-garde Decadent movement and who, after his trial in 1895, was widely condemned as a degenerate. In the face of this wide public condemnation, FPG's mediation of Wilde as a critic and translator is itself a fascinating moment, which one might understand as a personal moment of sympathy and identification (given Greve's own prison time and his struggles to be considered an artist); as a strategic self-positioning in a cultural field (given Wilde's currency in certain avant-garde circles); or as the manifestation of FPG's aesthetic response to and engagement with Wilde's theory of artistic production and value. Concentrating here on Wilde as an aesthetic influence Greve embraced and interrogated, Morris argues that, through his translations of and critical work on Wilde, Greve clarified the vision of artistic value that informs his novel, *Settlers of the Marsh* (1925), and his autobiographical works, *A Search for America* (1927) and *In Search of Myself* (1946). In particular, Morris elaborates the distinction between "life" and "art" that underwrites Greve's critique of Wilde to posit a dialectic that structures Greve's later works and nuances his commitment to realist writing. Supporting his argument with further reference to *Randarabesken zu Oscar Wilde*, Morris locates a second structuring principle that becomes central to FPG's writing in Canada: the theory of the artist as *entwurzelt*, an uprooted wanderer who is "no longer at home in either his native or adopted environment." FPG identifies this "uprooted wanderer" as an artist-figure who has the potential to become many-rooted—and thus more attuned to the life-nerve of humanity—but who also has the potential to become a degenerate criminal. Reading FPG as an example of the uprooted individual who idealises a commitment to art as a universal human expression and locating this aesthetic theory in Greve's response to Oscar Wilde, Morris explores the aesthetic influences that crossed the ocean with Greve, mediating his later cultural works as Frederick Philip Grove in Canada.

◆ Cultural Mediation: Institutional and Social

COMPLEMENTING THE ANALYSIS of cultural migrancy as a type of mediation, other papers in this volume examine the mediation of FPG and Baroness Elsa von Freytag-Loringhoven by institutional and social factors. For papers such as Jutta Ernst's "'Il me faut forger une arme de la littérature': Felix Paul Greve among the Magazines," this last approach to the theme of cultural mediation is usefully informed by Pierre Bourdieu's theory of culture as a field of production in which participants compete for symbolic power. A field with relative autonomy—evidenced in its inverse logic of symbolic as opposed to financial capital—cultural production is considerably bound up with the production and mediation of value. Hence, the mediation of 'artists' by secondary producers—gallery owners, publishers, and critics—importantly determines how cultural producers are legitimised or delegitimised, but always positioned in the field. Demystifying what he calls the "charismatic ideology" of artistic production, the notion of the artist as a genius who composes great, universal works of art in isolation, Bourdieu points instead to an apparatus of production:

> The 'charismatic' ideology which is the ultimate basis of belief in the value of a work of art and which is therefore the basis of functioning of the field of production and circulation of cultural commodities, is undoubtedly the main obstacle to a rigorous science of the production of the value of cultural goods. It is this ideology which directs attention to the *apparent producer*, the painter, writer or composer, in short, the 'author', suppressing the question of what authorizes the author, what creates the authority with which authors authorize. (76)

This focal shift from the charismatic artist to an apparatus of production that distributes legitimacy thus describes another way of conceptualising cultural mediation: as a process of determination within the field in which 'artists' struggle to acquire legitimacy and symbolic capital. This background frame usefully informs Jutta Ernst's article on Felix Paul Greve, charting his frustrated efforts to legitimise himself as an artist among the poets and publishers of Munich's literary elite.

Foregrounding his desire to acquire and exert "influence" through literature, Ernst points to Greve's early attempts to establish himself as a member of the poet Stefan George's avant-garde circle. His endeavours were designed to land an elite publisher for his own poetry; however, toward that end, Greve mediated his own unrecognised name by translating and publishing critical studies of other recognised artists such as Oscar Wilde and André Gide. With reference to the many sites in which Greve advertised and interpreted his own work, and largely informed by his correspondence with Gide and with various editors, Ernst carefully details Greve's efforts and difficulties. He was compelled to abandon the George circle because he needed to earn money from his cultural work; he successfully landed work with other publishing houses but only by mediating others; translations that he published anonymously were, on more than one occasion, attributed to his rival contemporaries (sometimes under suspicious circumstances); and, repeatedly, he was frustrated in his efforts to legitimise his own literary endeavours. Eventually he abandoned his career as a writer in Germany and relocated in North America. However, as Ernst describes it, he found even greater challenges in this new context. Concentrating primarily on FPG's early publishing in Germany, his concerted efforts and frustrated struggles to produce himself as an artist in his own life, Ernst's paper situates Greve in a broader apparatus of production to explore his mediation by institutional factors and his attempts to mediate himself in that context.

Paul Hjartarson's "'Out of the Wastage of All Other Nations': 'Enemy Aliens' and the 'Canadianization' of Felix Paul Greve" also discusses the mediations of FPG; however, it takes as its focal point Greve's positioning in the context of a developing surveillance state in Canada after World War One. Without erasing the fact that FPG was a cultural migrant who brought European ideas with him into Canada, Hjartarson complicates the picture of the field into which FPG stepped as an immigrant from Germany. That is, Hjartarson argues for a thicker reading of existing social debates in Canada so as to understand the context of surveillance that FPG negotiated as a German immigrant and within which he re-established himself (and was received) as a writer. Charting a broad shift from the opening of the West to its closure, Hjartarson details the effects of a nexus of historical events—including Canada's entry into World War One (1914), the Russian Revolution (1917), and the Winnipeg General Strike (1919)—on debates about immigration and assimilation. The tensions created by these historical events registered in a series of Orders in Council (which created new categories of 'enemy aliens' and gradually legislated their surveillance, internment and disenfranchisement); in changes to Canada's immigration and naturalization legislation; and in debates over education and 'Canadianization'. Within this larger framework, Hjartarson situates the production and reception of FPG's first Canadian novel, *Settlers of the Marsh* (1925), and he examines the public promotion of Grove as a prototypical 'new Canadian' with reference to a series of lecture tours undertaken by Grove at the behest of Graham Spry, executive secretary of the Association of Canadian Clubs. FPG's positioning in these debates—and particularly his ability to represent himself as a 'new Canadian' as opposed to an 'enemy alien'—mediated not only his access to the speaker's platform but also his reception by the audience. That said, while pointing out FPG's mediation within this social context, Hjartarson simultaneously notes that FPG used his 'new Canadian' lecture platforms to advocate counter-hegemonic ideas of limited cultural pluralism and tolerance. Thus, while FPG's attempts to re-signify himself in Canada have been well-documented, Hjartarson contributes to a thicker description of how—in the social-institutional context of post-World War One debates about immigration and Canadianization—FPG mediated himself to safe-guard his civil liberties within Canada's developing surveillance state and to accrue value and legitimacy as a 'new Canadian' writer.

Similarly examining the social-institutional contexts of mediation but with a specific focus on gender and embodiment, Richard Cavell and Irene Gammel analyse Baroness Elsa's experimental poetry, assemblages and performative practices to explore how 'the body' and gender function as mediated and mediating aspects of the Baroness's Dada. Specifically, Richard Cavell posits the *Jugendstil* movement in Germany—a school that elaborated an empathic theory of artistic production and reception—as a possible informing context for Elsa's performative Dada in New York. As with other papers in *The Politics of Cultural Mediation*, Cavell attempts to historicise the Baroness's later art practices in America with reference to the aesthetic influences that she might have brought with her across the Atlantic, understanding the Baroness as a cultural migrant and mediator. However, his paper goes beyond that initial concept of mediation to examine also how the empathic theories that he explores as German influences on the Baroness themselves effected an interrogation of visual art as a mediated practice.

These theories of empathic production and reception challenged traditional art with an "anti-retinalist" focus that made the body and processes of embodiment central to artistic practice. Hypothesizing that the body projected and objectified itself in spatial forms, empathic theorists such as Robert Vischer enabled art practices that decentred the site and the subject of traditional art. Cavell thus quotes Visher's editors: "[t]he phenomena that we encounter in the world ... become analogies for one's own bodily structure." Empathic theory shifted visual art's traditional focus on the eye to a production and response mechanism grounded in the body and its practices. In turn, this shift facilitated a move outside the gallery, informing the Baroness's Dada as an engagement with the phenomena and practices of daily life.

Informed by his work on Marshall McLuhan and the production of cultural space, Cavell's article works with densely overlapping concepts of mediation:[7] he understands the Baroness as a migrant who mediates between cultural worlds; conversely, he explores the challenges posed by empathic theories to the retinalist focus of traditional visual art to examine the production of culturally mediated spaces and practices. What remains implicit in Cavell's article, but which is explicit in his work on McLuhan, is the way in which "space" is a social and historical construct produced, in part, by an institutional and material apparatus. In his broader work, Cavell builds on McLuhan's argument that media function as extensions of the body—for example, extending the capacity to see and to hear—and that within these visual and acoustic spaces, communication happens. The production and mediation of space as a cultural construct is thus importantly connected to communication as a mediated practice, a complex mode of production and reception that occurs within social and institutional frameworks. The material and social apparatus that mediates communication in a given context stands as the background against which Cavell weighs the Baroness's Dada interventions. In these terms, Cavell examines empathic theories of embodiment as a latent element of the Baroness's performative Dada that disrupts spaces traditionally designated for the cultural exchange of visual art (the gallery), and modes of cultural production and reception that privilege the visual. The body, for Cavell, is thus not a site of unmediated experience. Rather, empathic theory becomes a point of disruption making obvious the mediation and production of the body in social spaces and practices. Informed by theories of empathic embodiment, the Baroness practiced a highly sexualized performative art— flaunted on the street and in public spaces—in which her body became her canvas. It is in these terms, Cavell suggests, that she emerges as a central figure in New York Dada, which rejected traditional art in favour of nonsense, non-art and the ready-made object.

Describing the Baroness's performative Dada as acts of 'everyday modernity,' Irene Gammel complements Cavell's analysis of embodied performance with an examination of gender as performative social practice. In this frame, Gammel reads the Baroness's performative Dada as interventions into gender practice. While disrupting the gallery as a privileged site, these performances, suggest Gammel, also disrupted the everyday, ordinary practices and performances of gender that defined femininity and masculinity in this moment. Shaving her head and painting it vermilion, costuming her body with tea-balls and tomato cans, decorating her apparel with gilded vegetables, dangling bird cages containing live birds from her neck as jewellery, the Baroness appropriated objects of everyday life and divested them of their utilitarian functions. However, where early commentators were frequently bemused, confused or even revolted by the Baroness, Gammel argues that Elsa appropriated these objects and harnessed them to her performances so as to re-signify them as objects and to re-signify herself through them. Referencing a wide swath of contemporary commentators as well as representations of the Baroness by later critics, Gammel's article offers a wealth of research. It contextualises and theorises visual poems, assemblages of objects and little-known *objets d'art* created and worn by the Baroness (figures 1–3), and it explores how the Baroness has been legitimised and delegitimised by others. Lauded as an avant-garde radical or described as a curious oddity, Freytag-Loringhoven was alternately celebrated and disavowed by contemporaries such as Jane Heap, Ezra Pound, William Carlos Williams and Mary Butts; in the wider context of modernist studies, she was denied the recognition granted to male Dada artists such as Marcel Duchamp until feminist critics began to examine women's contributions to and representation within modernism. The theme of mediation thus informs a number of compressed issues in Gammel's paper. Reframing the Baroness's performances and self-productions as interventions into highly mediated gender practices, Gammel's paper participates in a feminist interrogation and recovery project. Simultaneously, however, she gestures toward a broader methodological problematic: if performance art is by nature ephemeral and situational, how are we to understand it from a later historical moment? What does it mean for our understanding of the Baroness's performances to be so highly mediated through contemporary commentary? Can the material traces of those performances—that is, the objects with which she adorned herself—themselves illuminate our interpretation of her cultural interventions? Rather than commenting on the Baroness's mediation from an external perspective, Gammel implicitly signals her own participation and implication in that social-institutional complexity.

◆ Towards a Thick Description: Scholarly Mediations

OFFERING DIFFERENT ENGAGEMENTS with the theme of cultural mediation in relation to Baroness Elsa and FPG, the papers in *The Politics of Cultural Mediation* complement one another on multiple levels. Examining their lives in Germany and in North America, their productions as authors, translators, critics and avant-garde artists, this volume explores the similarities and differences of the Baroness and FPG's parallel trajectory. To highlight the theme of cultural mediation, we have drawn out three broad, thematic categories of analysis: mediation as an aspect of translation; mediation as cultural migrancy; and mediation as a site of determination and negotiation in a given social-institutional context. *The Politics of Cultural Mediation*, however, organises itself in three different parts. Clustering papers about Baroness Elsa and about FPG and including a translation part, we hope to thicken the reader's engagement with these two artist-producers and to heighten the overlaps among the three thematic approaches outlined above. That is, this volume nuances mediation as a site of determination and production, of intervention and agency. It explores cultural contact zones—in which overlapping 'structures of signification' made meaningful the Baroness's and FPG's cultural productions—and it contextualises those sites in broader debates, processes and practices. For scholars interested in the works of Baroness Elsa von Freytag-Loringhoven, this volume includes images of her assemblages, visual poems and performative apparel. It explores how European art-movements and discourses conditioned her

North American Dada, and it thickens that analysis with socio-historical perspectives. Similarly, readers interested in the writings of FPG will find new European and North American contexts in which to appreciate and understand his attempts to produce himself as an artist within existing socio-cultural fields. Moreover, as a cultural contact zone itself, representing an international array of voices, *The Politics of Cultural Mediation* attempts to articulate a model of intellectual engagement capable of and committed to thinking across borders. Recognizing that criticism—like translation—is a political act, this issue holds to Rushdie's insistent idea "that something can also be gained" in that work of bearing across.

NOTES

1   The idea of the "contact zone" has been theorised by Mary Louise Pratt to mark colonial sites of encounter, interaction and improvisation occurring within "radically asymmetrical relations of power" (7). Here, the term is invoked in a looser sense to examine the movement of Plötz/Freytag-Loringhoven and Greve/Grove between worlds and their production of cultural objects and performances from those sites of encounter, but also to suggest a dynamic process wherein texts are resignified in new contexts, marking a site of cultural contact. In both instances, Pratt's term, borrowed from its postcolonial context, helps to foreground "asymmetrical relations of power" that determine and nuance those exchanges, even while allowing for the possibility of "improvisation." See Mary Louise Pratt, *Imperial Eyes: Travel Writing and Transculturation.*

2   Two recently published biographies are available for readers unfamiliar with the lives of these cultural migrants: for an account of Baroness Elsa's life, see Irene Gammel's *Baroness Elsa: Gender, Dada, and Everyday Modernity: A Cultural Biography* (2002); for a biography of FPG, see Klaus Martens's *F.P. Grove in Europe and Canada: Translated Lives* (2001).

3   Scholars of Plötz/Freytag-Loringhoven and Greve/Grove invariably confront the problem of how to name these two individuals, especially when speaking of their entire life and work: on the one hand, Plötz/Freytag-Loringhoven and Greve/Grove are awkward formulations; on the other, it can be misleading to refer to them under simply one name. Greve/Grove, for instance, published under "Greve" in Germany and "Grove" in Canada; identifying him exclusively as "Greve" or "Grove" can cause confusion. That said, Greve/Grove is actually the easier of the problems to solve: since in transforming himself from "Felix Paul Greve" into "Frederick Philip Grove," Greve retained the initials FPG, scholars tend to follow Douglas O.

Spettigue's example and refer simply to "FPG." Regarding Plötz/Freytag-Loringhoven, the problem is more complex. First, there is the gender issue: Else Plötz became Else Endell, then Else Greve, and finally Baroness Else von Freytag-Loringhoven. Second, as an artist she is known predominantly for her Dada in New York, produced under the name of Baroness Elsa von Freytag-Loringhoven. Finally, there is the issue of the Baroness's first name: German scholars refer to her as "Else" while North American scholars (following the Baroness's American contemporaries) tend to use "Elsa." Richard Cavell refers to Plötz/Freytag-Loringhoven as "Else" when speaking of her in the German context and "Elsa" when speaking of the North American context. Klaus Martens, in "Two Glimpses of the Baroness," develops another perspective on this split, linking the Else/Elsa shift to the Baroness's adoption of a theatrical stage name. Since this issue of naming marks one index of what is lost and gained in the cultural contact zones produced by migration, the editors of this volume have attempted to foreground the problem rather than standardising usage between papers. In the Introduction, however, we refer to Plötz/Freytag-Loringhoven and Greve/Grove most commonly as "the Baroness" and "FPG."

4   We build here on Clifford Geertz's idea of anthropological "thick description." Through the term, Geertz advocates a methodology that recognises within cultural exchanges a "multiplicity of complex conceptual structures, many of them superimposed upon or knotted into one another, which are at once strange, irregular, and inexplict, and which [the ethnographer] must contrive somehow first to grasp and then to render" (10). We adapt this concept to signal multiple, contextual, overlapping structures of signification that made meaningful the texts, objects, and performances of the Baroness and FPG. For those who, like the Baroness and FPG, are "borne across the world," these structures and processes are particularly complicated and rewarding to analyse. At the same time, we highlight Geertz's representation of the anthropologist as an "ethnographer" to indicate problems within his interpretive method; that is, Geertz does not acknowledge his own implication in a nexus of power/knowledge that constructs the object of which it speaks. We say this not to foreclose the possibility of 'bearing across' cultural divides; rather, we suggest that such acts are politically charged and also require interrogation. See Geertz's chapter "Thick Description: Toward an Interpretive Theory of Culture" in The Interpretation of Cultures: Selected Essays.

5   For the provenance of Randarabesken zu Oscar Wilde see Paul Morris's Introductory Note to the essay included in this volume.

6   Concerning Randarabesken zu Oscar Wilde, Spettigue writes in FPG: The European Years (1973): "It is precisely because Felix models himself so closely on Wilde, and then draws on his own experiences and emotions to elucidate Wilde, that we come closer to him in this pamphlet than in any other of his European writings" (117).

7   See Richard Cavell, McLuhan in Space: A Cultural Geography (2002).

PART I

The Baroness
and the Politics of Cultural Mediation

Limbswishing Dada in New York
Baroness Elsa's Gender Performance

With me posing [is] art—aggressive—virile—extraordinary—
invigorating—antestereotyped—no wonder blockheads by
nature degeneration dislike it—feel peeved—it underscores
unreceptiveness like jazz does.

THE BARONESS to PEGGY GUGGENHEIM, 1927

Felix Paul Greve [...] hat intellektuellen Ehrgeiz—Aber er will
'Originalität'—von der ist er *strikter Antipod. Ich bin das*—was er
nicht ist. So musste er mich hassen—lassen.

THE BARONESS, "Seelisch-Chemische Betrachtung"[1]

CELEBRATING her *posing* as *virile* and *aggressive art* in the first epigraph,
the Dada artist Elsa von Freytag-Loringhoven, née Plötz (1874–1927) summed
up her remarkable life and work just months before her mysterious death
in Paris. Known as the Baroness amongst the international avant-garde in
New York and Paris of the teens and twenties, the German-born performance artist, model, sculptor, and poet was a party to the general rejection of
sexual Victorianism, launched with the 1913 International Exhibition of
Modern Art, the so-called Armory Show, in Manhattan. Before coming to
New York, the Baroness had undergone a picaresque apprenticeship amongst
the *Kunstgewerbler* avant-garde in Munich and Berlin from around 1896 to
1911, before following her long-time spouse Felix Paul Greve (aka F.P.

FIGURE 1: Elsa von Freytag-Loringhoven. *Portrait of Marcel Duchamp*. c. 1920. Assemblage of miscellaneous objects in a wine glass. Photograph by Charles Sheeler. Francis M. Naumann Collection, New York.

Grove) on a quixotic immigration adventure to Kentucky. After Grove's desertion, she made her way to New York and promptly married the impecunious (but sexually satisfying) Baron Leopold von Freytag-Loringhoven. Soon a titled war widow (the Baron was incarcerated by the French in 1914 and committed suicide in 1919), the Baroness claimed her new spiritual home amidst an energetic and international group of vanguard artists—

many of them exiles from Europe. From 1913 on, she threw herself with abandon into New York's experimental ferment, quickly becoming the movement's most radical and controversial exponent.[2]

Perhaps it is appropriate to begin by commenting on the irony of F.P. Grove and Elsa von Freytag-Loringhoven's diverging trajectories. Just as the Baroness never tired of contrasting their antithetical artistic personalities, so their shifting cultural value follows opposite trends. In examining Canada's settler literature and Grove's vital importance for the Canadian canon of literature during the 1920s and 1930s, Paul I. Hjartarson has noted the "steady decline of interest, both academic and public, in Grove's novels in the past two decades" ("Staking a Claim" 19; see also 28–29).[3] In contrast, as I have noted with respect to the Baroness, after decades-long obscurity, her cultural value has surged over these past years ("Transgressive Body Talk" 73–74), with recent citations of her work in the *New York Times* and *Time* magazine (Kimmelman; Hughes) following the prestigious Whitney exhibition *Making Mischief: Dada Invades New York*, in which her sculpture *Portrait of Marcel Duchamp* photographed by Charles Sheeler was prominently featured on the cover of the exhibition catalogue (figure 1).[4] An exhibition curated by Francis Naumann in New York City was dedicated exclusively to the Baroness's art work (April 2002). In addition, there have been extensive scholarly discussions (Naumann, *New York Dada*; Sawelson-Gorse); her auto-biography and letters have been published (Hjartarson and Spettigue, *Baroness Elsa*); and last but not least, her art work has made important forays into university curricula in Modernism and Art History courses.

In his pioneering *New York Dada, 1915–23*, the American art historian Francis M. Naumann has championed the Baroness amongst a motley international crowd of Americans and Europeans fleeing the war in Europe: Gabrielle Buffet-Picabia, John Covert, Jean and Yvonne Crotti, Charles Demuth, Marcel Duchamp, Katherine Dreier, Albert Gleizes and Juliette Roche, Mina Loy, Louise Norton Varèse, Edgar Varèse, Man Ray, Henri-Pierre Roché, Francis Picabia, Charles Sheeler, Morton Schamberg, Joseph Stella, the Stettheimer sisters, Clara Tice, and Beatrice Wood. They gathered in the salon of the American art collector and poet Walter Arensberg, as Buffet-Picabia recalls: "The Arensbergs showed a sympathetic curiosity, not entirely free from alarm, towards the most extreme ideas and towards works which outraged every accepted notion of art in general and of painting in particular" (260). Amongst this richly diverse group of artists, the Baroness represented the most extreme and radical exponent.

Indeed, the Baroness's work belongs to the most aggressively iconoclastic expressions of the era. During unsettling war times, she collaborated with the American sculptor Morton Schamberg to produce *God* (1917), a sculpture sacrilegiously made of plumbing fixtures and designed to dismantle the supreme signifier of the western sign system itself (figure 10). *God* was "so powerfully iconoclastic that it came to represent the single purest expression of Dada sensibilities in New York," writes Naumann, who attributed this work to the Baroness (*New York Dada* 126, 129, 172). Today a canonised work of art, *God* is a sister piece to Duchamp's *Fountain*, the infamous urinal proclaimed a sculpture at the 1917 Independents Exhibition in New York, an art work in whose conception the Baroness probably also had a hand, as I have argued in detail elsewhere (Gammel, *Baroness Elsa*, chapter 8). The Baroness was also a poet with radical experimentations in sexual subject matter, as reflected in such poetic (or unpoetic) titles as "Orgasmic Toast," "Orgasm," "Subjoyride," and with irreverent references to "spinsterlollypops," "celluloid tubes" ("A Dozen Cocktails Please") and to "koitus" ("Literary Five O'Clock"), references that blasted to shreds the conventions of traditional love poetry. She was championed by the period's most avant-garde literary journal, *The Little Review*, which launched her controversial and emotionally intensive poetry including "Mineself—Minesoul—and—Mine—Cast—Iron Lover," although a great deal of her controversial poetry has remained unpublished (see Gammel, "German Extravagance"). By 1921 she was so in/famous that she became the object of parody in Charles Brooks's *Hints to Pilgrims*.

What, then, is the meaning of Dada, in which the Baroness gained such flashy prominence? According to the literary scholar Richard Sieburth, "Dada functioned as an infantile parody of the *logos*, a babbling *Urwort* aimed at echoing and cancelling the name of the Father and the authority of his Law" (46). Born in the midst of war, Dada was an anti-art, fed in New York by the influx of an international group of artists trying to escape the horror of war in Europe. As a nonsense art, its goal was to reveal the corrupt world by slashing all systems of order with abandon. Today, art historians and literary historians see the Baroness as "the epitome of Dada anarchy, sexual freedom, and creativity," as the American comparatist scholar Rudolf E. Kuenzli ("Baroness Elsa" 442) describes her. The feminist art historian Amelia Jones has placed her alongside Marcel Duchamp, arguing that "these artists' confusions of gender and over sexualizations of the artist/viewer relationship challenged post-Enlightenment subjectivity and aesthetics far more pointedly than did dadaist paintings and drawings" ("'Women' in Dada" 144).

In *Baroness Elsa: Gender, Dada, and Everyday Modernity*, the first book-length biography exploring the life and work of Elsa von Freytag-Loringhoven, I have traced the psychological roots of the Baroness's visceral Dada to her traumatic childhood and to the subsequent armouring of her body and self in a wild sexual odyssey through Berlin, Italy, and Munich. As I have argued, the trauma—which would coincide with the trauma of a whole generation during the World War I period—was inscribed on the Baroness's body (her non-feminine looks and militant aggressiveness, which included a boxing match with the poet William Carlos Williams and other altercations), and was articulated through her shocking art (her scatological humour, her acting out, her militant revenge on male misogyny in publicly performed gender acts). Her work was always uncompromisingly radical, routinely unleashing fierce controversy, even as the Baroness pioneered highly original art forms that effectively anticipated proto-punk, body art, and performance art (see also Gammel, "Mirror Looks").

Focusing in particular on her radical gender crossing in performances of erotically charged androgyny, I propose to trace the Baroness's performative trajectory from Europe, through New York and back to Europe. Her investment of herself, her living Dada, what she called "posing as art" in the earlier epigraph, must be seen as her most innovative contribution, one that makes her profoundly modern today, for her innovative art ultimately compelled the urbanite viewer to see city spaces and urban life in a new way. By shocking viewers, always taking them by surprise, by making sudden apparitions in quotidian spaces, her eroticized art created a profound affect in the viewer, making the viewer remember the event decades later. This art form grew out of her own personal history, as well as fermenting with the myriad of avant-garde movements and impulses in Europe and New York, impulses that she inscribed on her body. That her contemporaries felt deep discomfort with the Baroness had to do with what she described as the "aggressive" and "virile" quality of her art, as well as with her chosen format, eroticized performance art, which often filled her audience with a deeply threatening mixture of desire and repulsion. Ultimately, performance was the Baroness's most remarkable and most original contribution, but it also placed her at the outermost edge of the movement, representing its most avant-garde and most risky expressions.

———

AS EARLY AS 1915, the Baroness began to parade the streets of New York in strange costumes. She adorned her body with bizarre and often utilitarian objects: vegetables, stamps, teaspoons, teaballs, electric taillights, tomato cans, lead toys, wastepaper baskets as hats, parrot feathers as accessories, and so on. Her performances regularly included the parading of live animals: canaries worn in a small cage around her neck and dogs on long leashes. She even paraded a fake penis once. She shaved her head and lacquered it vermillion. She wore yellow make-up and painted her lips black. Picked up from the streets or purloined from Woolworth or Wanamakers, these items reflected America's consumer culture, utilitarian objects morphing into objects of strange beauty on the Baroness's living body, a form of *dadamerique* that mirrored America's contemporary culture in strangely decontextualized form. Just as in her poem "Subjoyride," the speaker travels along modern-day advertisement signs and records "Philadelphia Cream Cheese" and "Bologna" as objects of poetic beauty, poetic ready-mades of sorts, so the material consumer items displayed on her body became objects of art that compelled the viewer to contemplate this work in a new way. The effect was part of Dada's *Lachkultur* (Korte 42), but it was also Dada's way of de-automatising the public by mirroring its culture in strangely skewed forms.

Briefly consider the biographical roots of this art, as registered in some of the memory pictures in her letters and autobiography. As early as 1896, Elsa Plötz had dressed up as a Renaissance Madonna for her lover Melchior (Mello) Lechter (1865–1937), one of the leading *Kunstgewerbler* (arts and crafts movement) in Berlin, who injected art into life by creating artistic furniture, book covers, and stained glass art work (Hjartarson and Spettigue 123–30). Likewise, the Baroness's first husband, August (Tse) Endell (1871–1925), was a *Kunstgewerbler* in Munich and Berlin, "making decorations and furniture" (Hjartarson and Spettigue 72) and systematically crossing the boundaries of art and life, as discussed in detail by Richard Cavell in "Baroness Elsa and the Aesthetics of Empathy: A Mystery and a Speculation." The French scholar Thierry de Duve has effectively linked Duchamp's innovations, including the ready-made, to the *Kunstgewerbler* movement in Munich (41–63); for the Baroness, too, this movement was a profound influence. At the turn of the century, she witnessed the pagan cross-dressing that was an integral part of Munich's avant-garde circle, as they made an active effort to inject Eros into everyday life by celebrating androgynous models based on their reading of gynocritic treatises (Gammel, "No Woman Lover" 451–67). In addition to these early male gender-benders, the cross-dressing poet Else Lasker-Schüler may have been an influence, as discussed by Klaus Martens in this volume.

Yet the most profoundly affective influence, I propose, takes us back even further to the Baroness's Prussian home in Pomeranian Swinemünde on the Baltic sea (today the Polish bordertown of Swinoujscie). For the Baroness remembers vividly the events coinciding with her mother Ida-Maria Plötz's diagnosis of cancer in the early 1890s: her mother rebelled against her tyrant-husband, as described in Greve's *Maurermeister Ihles Haus* (1907). What Greve does not tell us is that she also began transforming *useful* fabrics into *useless* objects, "spoiling elegant materials with cheap trash [for] she was tired of doing 'fine handiwork.'" The Baroness later dramatized this memory picture in a letter to her most loyal friend during the Berlin years, the American writer Djuna Barnes. Of her mother she writes:

> [S]he was speculating about—maybe—putting [the golden fried squares] with "such and such a stitch"—some velvet of special tint—or silver braid—or lace—on it—to make [a] "handkerchief holder" [whose] "usefulness" had ceased to interest her. ("Djuna Sweet—If you would know")

As the Baroness describes it, Ida-Marie Plötz "felt revolutionary." Her "flashing smile—illuminating face—her giggle and untouchable aloofness" establish a likeness with "'Marcel' [Duchamp]," as the Baroness asserts, the comparison marking her mother as an artistic inspiration for the daughter ("Djuna Sweet—if you would know"). Just as her mother suddenly refused to create functional decorations for her bourgeois home, so her daughter now actively marshalled her mother's memory. In New York, she used innocuous domestic objects including tea-balls and ice-cream soda spoons for her anti-bourgeois art, purposefully stripping them of their domestic usefulness to proclaim her Dada message. Yet where Ida-Marie Plötz's scandalous rebellion had been confined to the privacy of home and sanatorium, dismissed, silenced, and ridiculed as madness, the Baroness took her strangely beautiful attires to the public street as deliberate acts of art. Her acts were born out of memory's deep affect, and her performance, in turn, would create strong emotional responses in her viewers. But if Ida-Marie Plötz's rebellion was ultimately constrained by patriarchal and bourgeois norms, the Baroness aggressively struck out at the very institutions that wished to impose those constraints.[5]

Indeed, the fiercely anti-bourgeois panache at the heart of Dada, as she tells us in her memoirs, was born in her passionate rejection of the "bourgeois harness" of her parental home, imposed by her father and new step-mother (Hjartarson and Spettigue 42). Her Dada has a Mephistophelian edge, as the young Elsa Plötz grew up with an intimate familiarity of Johann Wolfgang von Goethe's work through Ida-Marie Plötz's interest in the Romantics. Mephistopheles—or Mefu, Mefi as the Baroness calls him in her poems "Mefk Maru Mustir Daas" and in "Clock"—is the anti-thesis to "The Lord" in Goethe's philosophical drama Faust (1790–1833) and is key to understanding her entry into Dada.[6] As a demonic tempter, Goethe's figure of chaos, evil, and destruction is a roguish mischief maker, who uses theatrics, artifice, costuming, play, but also bodily and material pleasures to dismantle static systems of order. In Goethe's view, and the Baroness's appropriation of it, such chaos is only seemingly destructive, for the rogue as anarchic spirit of negation and antithesis (der Geist, der stets verneint [Goethe, Faust 82]) ultimately produces spark, energy, movement, drive, joy, and life (Leben). Here, in this focus on life and kinetic movement, then, lies a second important entry point into her distinctive form of Dada.

Indeed, most remarkable about the Baroness's art is the kinetic and erotic charge inherent in her body images, which tell a story fundamentally different from the male machine paintings and sculptures exhibited by Francis Picabia and Marius de Zayas in the Modern Gallery, works that marked the advent of modernity in New York, as documented in Naumann's

How, When, and Why Modern Art Came to New York: Marius de Zayas. Picabia's spark plug, provocatively titled *Jeune fille américaine dans l'état de nudité*, in particular, appears to encapsulate the catalyst spark of the Dada period, while Duchamp's *Large Glass* and *Bicycle Wheel* ready-mades likewise celebrated the perpetual motion of the new machine age with a focus on technological images (Naumann, *New York Dada* 61 and 38–39, 40). Typical, too, of the image of New York Dada are the sleek machine paintings and mechanical abstractions by Morton Schamberg (Naumann 126–29).

Most recently, feminist art historians have taken these male representations as a comparative springboard for a gender approach that points to the distinctive differences in the works of female dadaists. The American art historian Amelia Jones has theorized the Baroness's streetwalking as a revolutionary new art form within New York Dada ("Practising Space"; see discussion below) and has highlighted the gender effects of her art ("Eros, That's Life"; "'Women' in Dada"). In Naomi Sawelson-Gorse's edited volume *Women in Dada: Essays on Sex, Gender, and Identity*, the Baroness is featured prominently, with several essays arguing that her work is distinctively different from that of her male colleagues. Barbara Zabel, for instance, discusses the Baroness's work as a "recovery of the human in the machine-age portraiture" (36). Likewise, in the *Women's Art Journal*, the cultural historian Eliza Jane Reilly notes the "formal and iconographic contradictions between [Freytag-Loringhoven's] highly personal and sensual art, which incorporated human and animal forms, organic materials, and her own body, [on the one hand] and the deliberately machine-centred, anti-humanistic, and masculinist stance of much of the art classified as Dada [on the other]" (26–27).

In contrast to the steely immortality of the male machine gadgets, the Baroness's gilded vegetables are no longer extant, their demise a testimony to the precariously ephemeral nature of performance art. Modern performance theorists like Peggy Phelan remind us that this art form makes a dramatic impact precisely because it does not survive (146–53 *passim*). The Baroness's art consisted in parading her body as a living art museum in a contemporary quotidian urban space. As she perambulated along inner city streets, her art objects—including the long earrings, the hanging belt ornaments, the metal springs and tassels—were vibrating in movement, scripting kinetic energy onto her body. A few important items of the Baroness's performa-

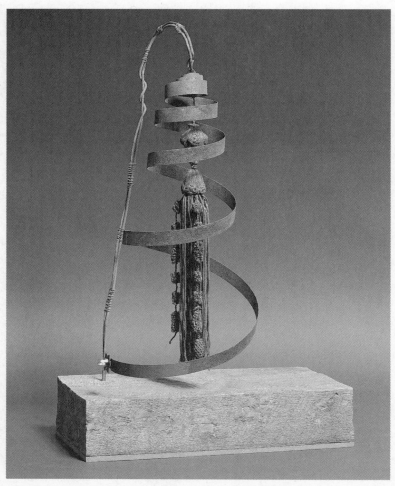

FIGURE 2: Elsa von Freytag-Loringhoven. *Limbswish*. c. 1920. Metal spring, curtain tassel. 21 11/16 in. Mark Kelman Collection, New York.

tive gear have survived and are held today in private collections and museums, as *Oggetto (Object)* in the Peggy Guggenheim Collection, Venice, a belt with ornaments loosely attached and swinging with the movement of the Baroness's body (reproduced in Schwarz 121). These surviving objects, then, provide a rare glimpse at an extraordinary art form.

The spirit of the Baroness's art is, perhaps, best epitomized in *Limbswish* (figure 2), held in Mark Kelman's collection in New York, along with *Enduring*

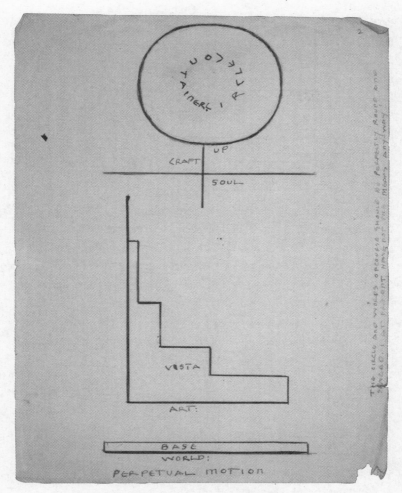

FIGURE 3: Elsa von Freytag-Loringhoven. "Perpetual Motion." c. 1923. Visual Poem. Special Collections, University of Maryland at College Park Libraries.

Ornament, an iron ring; *Earring-Object*, an earring; and *Cathedral*, a wood splinter (reproduced in Gammel, *Baroness Elsa*, chapters 6, 7 and 8). While our access to the Baroness's performative costumes is often mediated through textual testimonials and personal impressions provided by her contemporaries, these rare objects allow us some uniquely unmediated glimpses into the Baroness's body art and sculptures. These objects, therefore, are invaluable in recapturing the Baroness's art today. *Limbswish* was worn attached to her belt and consisted of a long curtain tassel surrounded by a metal spiral, the tassel and the metal's swirling shape thematizing and accentuating kinetic movement. The title is an erotically charged pun on limbs wish and limb swish, the latter evoking the sound of the object's swishing movement as the Baroness paraded her body in full gear. The Limbswish body ornament is large, about eighteen inches high, and worn on her belt; it makes the mannish Baroness a dominatrix of sorts. The reader familiar with her autobiography may easily imagine her handling of the object, intimidating her reluctant artist-lovers including Duchamp, Williams, and the "Cast Iron Lover."[7]

The Baroness's consistent focus on erotically charged movement is also found in her kinetically charged poetic experimentations. The visual poems "Perpetual Motion" (figure 3) and "Matter, Level, Perspective," for instance, compel the viewer's eye to move up the stairs, using treadmills and spirals, always climbing and circling without allowing the eye to come to a final resting point. "Read from down up," the Baroness instructs her viewer/ reader in "Matter, Level, Perspective," but even as the viewer's eye arrives in the uppermost section, the gaze is immediately propelled further in spirals of movement. Similarly, "Appalling Heart" creates a kinetically vibrant city space by featuring verbally swishing limbs:

> City stir—wind on eardrum—
> dancewind: herbstained—
> flowerstained—silken—rustling—
> tripping—swishing—frolicking—
> courtesing—careening—brushing—
> flowing—lying down—bending—
> teasing—kissing: treearms—grass—
> limbs—lips.
> City stir on eardrum—.
> In night lonely
> peers—:
> moon—riding!
> pale—with beauty aghast—
> too exalted to share! (47)

The long catalogue of action-charged participles "tripping—swishing" creates the city as a space of "perpetual motion." The reader careens with the speaker in a whirlwind ride through the moonlit metropolis, in which the city's body is rendered strangely skewed ("with beauty aghast"), like a cubist painting, with limbs grafted in entirely new ways, creating hybrid bodies and compelling new ways of seeing the city and the body.

In an essay entitled "Practicing Space: World War I-Era New York and the Baroness as Spectacular Flâneuse," Amelia Jones has applied Walter Benjamin's theory of flânerie and Michel de Certeau's urban theory to discuss the Baroness as "a quintessential New Woman/flâneuse" whose performative body scripted non-normative codings during the teens and twenties and who "perfected a rhetoric of walking, moving throughout the city to produce an alternative 'space of enunciation'" (6). In the second part of her essay, Jones proceeds to impersonate the Baroness, re-enacting her Dada ravings against male machine art:

> I ask you why I am mad—ruthlessly lonely by inner rendering of outer circumstance—within commonplace life mesh—while they cavort scrupulously making machine sex dolls. (8)

Jones's brilliant ventriloquising of the Baroness revives early twentieth-century gender dissidence in the metropolis with a striking immediacy for the twenty-first century reader. For those interested in gender issues, the Baroness's flashing memory bits often create a drive toward recreating and resurrecting this artist.

Indeed, much of the Baroness's modernity today has to do with her stunning gender acts that are bound to dazzle postmodern viewers and readers schooled in Butlerian theories. These gender theories stipulate that the material body repeats and reproduces socio-cultural constructs, and that daily performed gender acts can be used to trouble, disrupt, and parody the categories of body, gender, sexuality, and identity (Butler). The premise behind this theory is that political and social power no longer resides primarily in traditional centres of power such as the state apparatus or political parties but works at the microcosmic level of social relations. Consequently, political work and social change, in particular in the realm of gender relations, rely on microcosmic parodic performance and subversive repetition of conventional gender roles. Since it is believed that a parodic repetition will effectively change society from the microcosm up, the theatrical emerges as a political category, and costuming becomes an enactment of gender identities. It is within this context that the Baroness's gender acts achieve their ultra-modernity for the twenty-first century viewer and reader.

A key to the Baroness's performative trajectory into the postmodern era, then, is her radical androgyny, which publicly disrupts the binaries of conventional gender codes. The Baroness had begun modelling in her twenties, posing in 1896 for her lover, Melchior Lechter. During the teens and twenties, the Baroness still supported herself and her art through modelling, yet she had also begun to use her profession as a creative anchor for inscribing her diaristic personality experiments, critically commenting on the use painters had made of her body. The American painter George Biddle remembers such a performance in his memoirs. In 1917, when she was in her early forties, the Baroness presented herself as a model in his Philadelphia studio. Biddle recalls in his memoirs:

> Having asked me [Biddle], in her harsh, highpitched German stridency, whether I required a model, I told her that I should like to see her in the nude. With a royal gesture she swept apart the folds of a scarlet raincoat. She stood before me quite naked—or nearly so. Over the nipples of her breasts were two tin tomato cans, fastened with a green string about her back. Between the tomato cans hung a very small birdcage and within it a crestfallen canary. One arm was covered from wrist to shoulder with celluloid curtain rings, which later she admitted to have pilfered from a furniture display in Wanamaker's. She removed her hat, which had been tastefully but inconspicuously trimmed with gilded carrots, beets and other vegetables. Her hair was close cropped and dyed vermilion. (137)

In this self-display as model, the Baroness's body draws attention to the sexual signifiers: the breasts with the tomato cans as bra satirize the fetishizing of these sexual signifiers in visual representations. But perhaps most importantly, feminist art historians have shown that generations of

FIGURE 4: Theresa Bernstein. *Elsa von Freytag-Loringhoven*. 1916–17. Oil. 12 x 9 in. Francis M. Naumann Collection, New York.

male painters have represented themselves in self-portraits with their nude female models, enacting the hierarchical boundary male/female, active/ passive in the model/artist representation. The Baroness's autobiograph-ical self-display dismantles this traditional binary: when she throws opens her scarlet raincoat, the male painter Biddle is forced to reconfigure his model as an artist. Biddle's account is emblematic of the way in which the Baroness flashes through the memoirs and autobiographies of modernists, as well as appearing in photography and painting, as in the painting by Theresa Bernstein, which shows the nude Baroness with a thick shadow surrounding her body, as if she had wrapped herself in an Achilles-like armour of sorts (figure 4).[8]

The Baroness routinely shocked her viewers with her desexed body, her radical androgyny, as when she modelled for a film project in which the American photographer Man Ray and Duchamp collaborated in 1921. One still from the film has survived in Man Ray's 1921 letter to dadaist Tristan Tzara in Paris (figure 11), the startling pose highlighting the Baroness's radical gender fluidity: with the masculine, shaved head, slim boyish body in angular positioning, she displays herself as America's androgyny, her legs posing in shape of the letter A. With this self-representation, the model presents us with a physical diary picture, highlighting her aggressive rejec-tion of feminine shame, and her simultaneous ability to avoid the voyeuristic male gaze: the pose baffles and shocks the viewer in a Dada gesture, but does ultimately not serve titillating ends. The Baroness is in charge, not the photographers behind the camera. In 1921, the Baroness was prominently featured in the only *New York Dada* issue which was edited by Man Ray and featured contributions by Duchamp and the Romanian dadaist Tristan Tzara. Alongside her Dada poem, "Yours with Devotion," the Baroness was featured in profile—her head shaved, her breast nude—and in frontal view with feathery head-gear and heavily bejewelled hand—the performative gear and artistic armour with which she confronted bourgeois conventions and masculinist misogyny (reproduced in Naumann, *New York Dada* 206).

Given that the Baroness had been parading her shocking androgyny since at least 1915, one wonders whether Duchamp's famous pose as *Rrose Sélavy* (1921), photographed by Man Ray, as well as his later partial shaving of his head, might not have been inspired by the Baroness's cross-dressing and radical hair removal. As her extensive correspondence with *The Little Review* editors documents, Duchamp was her friend from 1915 and figured in several of the Baroness's art works including the sculpture *Portrait of Marcel Duchamp* (figure 1). Jones argues that Duchamp's pose as *Rrose* is central to New York's "performative Dada," the injection of eros into everyday life ("'Women' in Dada"); Naumann has compared it with Charlie Chaplin's cross-dressing in the movie *A Woman* (1915) ("Marcel Duchamp" 20–40); and Krauss has read *Sélavy* as *Levy* with Duchamp cross-dressing into Jewish identity (42–46). *Rrose Sélvay* is decidedly feminine, with Duchamp turning himself into art object, making new the conventional "rose" of poetry by autoerotically wrapping himself in feathers, big hair and soft clothing. *Rrose Sélavy* was the perfect male complement to the female Baroness who, disrobed and desexed, wrapped herself in her virile armour of shock performance.

In February 1921, Anderson and Heap strategically deployed the Baroness's photograph and writing in their activist fight against US obscenity legislation, using her as a literal figure-head in their legal battle against America's obscenity laws (Gammel, "German Extravagance"). Finding themselves in court for having serialized Joyce's sexually explicit *Ulysses* in *The Little Review*, they defended women's right to view and control sexual subject matter by displaying alongside their programmatic defence of *Ulysses*, "Art and the Law," not James Joyce's portrait, but the Baroness's, the Village's militant performance artist. The photograph of the Baroness, looking severe and austere with a few feminine necklaces, is vertically extended with her signature at the bottom, arranged in columns like a poem, and extended with a hand-drawn crown on top. The crown signals the Baroness's titled status, but is also a visual signifier for the bars of the jail that literally threaten to silence the women claiming their sexual rights, as Heap writes in her 1922 "Dada" article: "And then 'bars' for Dada, 'bars' for Else von Freytag—two sets of bars for the same thing!" (46). Just as Joyce's *Ulysses* was effectively silenced in the United States by 1922, so the Baroness found herself silenced. In New York, she literally lived at the borderline of American society, routinely stealing from department stores in order to support her art and life. "That is now—why I want to go away too—I am fed up with myself—my loneliness and memories———I must live—and not become a nervous freak. Here nobody wants me—I am respectfully—or—horrifiedly———avoided." So she wrote in a letter to Jane Heap, who helped organise her trip back to Germany.

———

YET WHEN THE BARONESS returned to Germany in 1923, her journey funded by donations made by Williams, Heap, and others, she found even more horrendous conditions in post-war Germany. Her father had disinherited her; her widow's pension was denied; and she was an aging woman during a time when a generation of younger women, most notably Marlene Dietrich, were conquering the stage with sexually charged androgyny that appealed to a mainstream viewership. Still, even while destitute and often suicidally desperate, the Baroness continued to perform herself aggressively. Denied an exit visa for Paris and caught in Germany, she presented herself to the French Consulate in Berlin. Presumably on her birthday on July 12, 1924, she flashed the French Consul in full performative gear, a memorable act she detailed in her letter to Barnes:

> I went to the consulate with a large—sugarcoated birthday cake upon my head with 50 flaming candles lit—I felt just so *spunky and afluent* [sic]—! In my ears I wore sugar plumes or matchboxes—I forgot wich [sic]. Also I had put on several stamps as beauty spots on my emerald painted cheeks and my eyelashes were made of guilded [sic] porcupine quills—rustling coquettishly—at the consul—with several ropes of dried figs [dangling] around my neck to give him a suck once and again—to entrance him. I should have liked to wear gaudy colored rubber boots up to my hips with a ballet skirt of genuine goldpaper white lacepaper covering it [in the margin: to match the cake] but I couldn't afford *that*! I guess—that my inconsistency in my costume is to blame for my failure to please the officials? (Hjartarson and Spettigue 216–17)[9]

The iconographic tale of this Dada performance is as personal as it is political. In this staged German/French confrontation, the fifty flaming candles on her head flash into tension-filled political relations and diplomatic stalemate, after Germany's suspension of reparation payments and France's subsequent retaliatory invasion of the Ruhr territory in the spring 1923, political events that were, in part, the cause for the Baroness's inability to leave Germany. Her performance is a peace offering of sorts, a seductive display of decidedly oral delights of cake and sugary figs—with the desired gaudy coloured rubber boots and ballet skirt poking fun at the officers' high booted military outfits, as well as ridiculing bureaucratic seriousness. Even though the consul still refused to issue a visa, the daring episode was commemorated by her contemporaries (Flanner 39).[10]

At the same time, there was an important (self-)destructive side to the Baroness and this side was explored, perhaps not entirely fairly, in a 1932 short story by Mary Butts, "The Master's Last Dancing," published only recently, in 1998 in *The New Yorker*. The red-headed British modernist writer and free-spirit Mary Butts used the Baroness's personality as raw material to comment on the decadence of the Montparnasse era: "There was a woman come lately to Paris, from somewhere in Central Europe by way of New York, who made her living by giving us something to talk about," writes Butts (111). In this barely veiled portrait of the Baroness, the Empress, as she is called in the story, dies her hair green, paints on her head a phallic sign and on her knees a skull, and wears a dustbin and hearthbrush for jewels. The satirical portrait is none too flattering, however, for the last dance functions, as Butts's biographer Nathalie Blondel has written, as Butts's farewell to her own wild life of decadence in Paris (Blondel 226–27, 327). In this story, the Dada Baroness retrospectively comes to encapsulate the pathology of the age, personifying the trauma that was the result of the war. As Butts writes, "we were the war lot. We had a secret" (110). This *roman à clef* made the Baroness its focus, as it critically engaged the wild parties organized by Ford during the twenties in Paris. Butts's party ends in a wildly grotesque and clearly fictionalized scene, in which the Baroness literally dances on Djuna Barnes's face, leaving a pool of blood, Butts thus exorcising her decadently destructive life by using the Baroness as a medium.

As for the Baroness's important legacy, she had launched an art form whose trajectory would span to the postmodern era, her "anti-stereotyped" posing anticipating, amongst others, the grotesque poses of the American performance artist Cindy Sherman. During the teens and twenties, the Baroness was far ahead of her time in paving the way for other 1920s and

1930s gender performers as seen with Anita Berber in Berlin and Claude Cahun in Paris. Indeed, in 1923, Anita Berber (1899–1928) continued the Baroness's trajectory, performing with monocle and cylinder in Berlin's Wintergarten and bars, with breasts nude, the nipples painted red, "like two drops of blood," the mouth "a bloody wound" (Lania 162). With her partner Sebastian Droste, Berber performed radical androgyny, enacting a state beyond conventional gender boundaries in in/famous nude performances. Droste was "more and less than a man, more and less than a woman—different," during a time when "nude dance was the fashion in 1922" (Lania 152). The titles of their performances—House of Madness (Haus der Irren), Cocaine (Kokain), Byzantinian whipping dance (Byzantinischer Peitschentanz), the latter evocative of the Baroness's Limbswish title—highlight the grotesqueness that coincided with the post-war atmosphere in Germany (Lania 156–57). The abandonment and self-destructiveness was an expression of the times of unemployment, post-war despair, and escape.

Meanwhile in France, the French photographer, surrealist poet, and performer Lucy Schwob, aka Claude Cahun (1894–1954), gave herself an androgynous identity that, like the Baroness's, was reflected in a stunning mutability of gender identities recorded in her photographs. It is intriguing to speculate how well the Baroness and Cahun knew each other. When in 1926, the Baroness arrived in Paris, she settled in the Hôtel Danemark on rue Vavin, just a short walk from 70 rue Notre-Dame-des-Champs, where Claude Cahun lived from 1922 on. Moreover, Cahun and the Baroness shared some friends: Heap, Anderson and Georgette Leblanc. During the twenties and thirties, Cahun took photographs of herself in male costumes with her hair shaved off or dyed outrageous colours. She photographed herself as socially constructed sex doll, powerfully drawing attention to the gender imprisonment in daily life (Krauss 30–36). Cahun powerfully parodied the codes of gender conventions in a way that continued the Baroness's performative trajectory into the 1930s and 1940s, when Cahun, a Jew and lesbian, was incarcerated by the Nazis in 1944, and much of her work destroyed as decadent and perverted art.[11]

Ultimately, the Baroness had pioneered a new art with her virile "posing" as art. She had turned herself into an art object, producing flamboyant and provocative self-images that were controversial but also highly inspirational. "She is the only one living anywhere who dresses Dada, loves Dada, lives Dada," Jane Heap wrote in what was an impassioned defence of Dada from attacks launched from within the modernist camp (Harriet Monroe), who feared that Dada was going too far in assaulting traditional conventions of art and mores. Anderson and Heap judged her genius to be on par with that of James Joyce: they championed both as radical experimenters, publishing the Baroness's poetry and poetic prose alongside *Ulysses* from 1918 to 1921, while the poet Ezra Pound immortalized her by name in his *Cantos* for her "principle of non-acquiescence" (Canto 95: 646). The Baroness's performative spirit and radicalism are, perhaps, best encapsulated in Heap's proclamation in her editorial note "Full of Weapons," which appeared in the Picabia number in 1922, printed in capital letters that were reminiscent of the Baroness's loud upper case letters in the "Cast Iron Lover": "*The Little Review*," Heap shouted at her readers, "is AN ADVANCING POINT TOWARD WHICH THE 'ADVANCE GUARD' IS ALWAYS ADVANCING" (33). The Baroness lived and embodied that slogan. An uncompromising, androgynous Amazonian warrior, her sleek body armour a virile and aggressive tool, she was marching and fighting at the front line of the avant-garde. Like no other, she was ardently committed to her art—and ultimately willing to sacrifice herself for it.

NOTES

1   "Felix Paul Greve [...] is intellectually ambitious—he craves 'originality,' but is originality's *strict antipode. I am that*—which he is not. And that is why he hated me—and left me" ("Spiritual-Chemical Reflection"). My translation from the original German.

2   These events have been documented in a number of sources including Paul I. Hjartarson, "Of Greve, Grove, and Other Strangers" 269–84; "The Self, Its Discourse, and the Other" 115–29; Paul I. Hjartarson and Douglas Spettigue in the introduction to *Baroness Elsa* 9–35; Gammel, "Breaking the Bonds of Discretion" 149–66.

3   This important point should not, however, denigrate or gloss over the impressive number of recent scholarly studies, including special sessions as well as published revisionist and cultural approaches (feminist, gender, comparative, auto/biographical, and translation theory) that bring F.P. Grove into the modern-day scholarly discussion, as well as into the university classroom. In *Sexualizing Power*, introduc-

tion 1–12, I make a case for revisionist reading approaches to Grove, as a way of making this author accessible and relevant today. Grove has not achieved the enduring academic and public status of a Hemingway, but compared with Canadian contemporaries like Morley Callaghan, he has held his own.

4 My thanks to Francis M. Naumann for making available a photograph.

5 It is important to note that F.P. Grove drew at least in part on the same memory pictures of Ida-Marie Plötz when he created his temporarily resisting Canadian mother figures in *Settlers of the Marsh* (1925) and in *Our Daily Bread* (1928), figures that leave the reader with a haunting sense of quixotic female rebellion. Many of the Baroness's letters about Ida-Marie Plötz lend further credence to E.D. Blodgett's earlier argument that Grove's fictional characters always lash out but are eventually constrained by patriarchal systems; their rebellion and disruption "never leads to the advent of a new order, but is at best frustrated comedy" (Blodgett, *Configuration* 54); see also my *Sexualizing Power*, in particular chapter 12, "The Father's Seduction and the Daughter's Rebellion" 207–32.

6 In a circa 1924 letter to Barnes ("Dearest Djuna [...] It is marvellous how you love me"), she connects "Mefk" and "Maru" of her poem "Clock" with "Mephistopheles," as she writes: "I should have 'mefy' printed rather than 'mephy' and 'Mephistopheles'; Mefistofeles—with F too—in regard to 'mefk maru mustir dass' with which it pretends to be connected." She continues: "[m]efy—mefisto—mefistopheles—as he is variously called—that ph in German in derived from the Greek—I believe—it is not uncommon already to change it into 'f'."

7 My thanks to Mark Kelman for providing me with a photograph and ektachrome of *Limbswish* and for the rare opportunity of seeing this inspirational object in New York City, along with *Enduring Ornament*, *Earring-Object*, and *Cathedral*. I am also grateful to Mark Kelman for making available detailed and hard-to-access information on the provenance of *Limbswish*. My thanks to Francis M. Naumann for first drawing my attention to these art objects.

8 My thanks to Francis M. Naumann for sending me a photograph.

9 Although corroborating evidence is missing, the number of candles—fifty—suggests that the Baroness's performance act took place on July 12, 1924, her 50th birthday.

10 Interestingly, the British author Ford Madox Ford attributes to the Baroness a similar performance in the British Consulate in Paris, possibly in 1927. "I found the telephone bell ringing and a furious friend at the British Embassy at the end of it. He wanted to know what the hell I meant by sending them a Prussian lady simply dressed in a brassière of milktins connected by dog chains and wearing on her head a plum-cake!" (334).

11 It is important to note that, even though ahead of her time in breaking many bourgeois conventions, the Baroness remained caught in the anti-Semitism that was rampant during the teens and twenties even among avant-gardists. The Baroness's comments on Karl Wolfskehl's "oriental" sexuality, for instance, reveal anti-Semitic stereotyping (Hjartarson and Spettigue 138).

Baroness Elsa and the Aesthetics of Empathy

A Mystery and a Speculation

ON APRIL 1ST, 1921, *the Société Anonyme of New York, which was the first American society devoted to the presentation of modern art, held a session on Dada which was immortalized in a drawing by Richard Boix (figure 5). In this drawing we find a number of key figures within New York Dada, including Man Ray and Marcel Duchamp, all of whom are clearly identified by name. In the centre of the image, however, there is a figure resting on a pillar identified only as "La Femme," and it is around this figure that a mystery has grown up (figure 6). The New York Dada scholar Francis Naumann has suggested an identification with a sculpture by Archipenko (figure 7), while admitting that "no specific sculpture by Archipenko—nor, for that matter, any other artist from this period—exhibits the unusual details that can be found in this illustrator's flight of fancy" ("New York Dada" 14). Identifying the figure with Eve through the icon of the apple, Naumann notes contrariwise that from the "string attached to the woman's elbow (or is it a beaklike extension of her nose?) a cup dangles freely in space, a detail that makes the sculpture look less like the depiction of a woman and more like an organ-grinder's monkey 'gone Dada'" (14). In the mystery of this figure Naumann sees the very reason why "people keep asking 'what is Dada?'" (14).*

———

IN THE DECADE FROM 1986, when Rudolf Kuenzli published New York Dada, to 1996, when Francis Naumann issued Making Mischief: Dada Invades New York, the figure of Baroness Elsa von Freytag-Loringhoven has moved from the peripheries of New York Dada to occupy a central position,

FIGURE 5: Richard Boix. *DA-DA (NEW YORK DADA GROUP)*. 1921. Brush, pen and ink. 11¼ x 14½ in. (28.6 x 36.8 cm). Primary Inscription: Signed L.R. "Boix." The Museum of Modern Art, New York. Katherine S. Dreier Bequest.

FIGURE 6: Richard Boix, detail.

FIGURE 7: Alexander Archipenko. *Seated Woman (Seated Geometric Figure)*. 1920. Plaster, painted Venetian red and burnt sienna. Signed: "Archipenko." 57 cm. Gift of the Goeritz family, London. Tel Aviv Museum of Art Collection, Israel. © Estate of Alexander Archipenko/SODRAC (Montreal), 2002.

as the reproduction of her 1920 *Portrait of Marcel Duchamp* on the cover of Naumann's book tellingly indicates (figure 1). The reasons for this shift are many: one has to do with the increasing recognition of the historical importance of women in Dada (as in the anthology of articles recently edited by Naomi Sawelson-Gorse). Closely connected to this avenue of approach is that of feminist theory, which, by critiquing the notion of Dada as an exclusively masculinist activity, has opened up a space for important figures such as Elsa to emerge from obscurity. Another avenue along which Elsa studies have developed is that of sexuality: Elsa's memoirs, published by Paul Hjartarson and Douglas Spettigue under the title *Baroness Elsa*, remain among the most breathtakingly frank documents of this period, and we are now beginning to understand that sexuality was absolutely central to Elsa's art, be it her poetry, her prose or the artefacts she created. Finally, the growing interest in and research on Elsa's German partner, Felix Paul Greve, has been accompanied by the realisation that their work constitutes much more of an intellectual collaboration than was previously known to be the case.[1]

We are far from having answered all the questions raised by the *fin-de-siècle* stories of self-fashioning told by Felix Paul Greve and Else Plötz; my own research into Greve has highlighted the homosexual panic that infiltrated his early writings, influenced his flight from Germany in 1909, and shaped his subsequent "Canadian" writings.[2] The present article complements that research in its focus on Elsa (as the Baroness was known)[3] and her New York incarnation as the very embodiment of New York Dada, according to the current critical consensus. I agree with this assessment, and I do so with particular emphasis on this notion of *embodiment*: indeed, it can be said that the greatest work of art that Elsa produced in her New York period was herself (and this is another reason why she subsequently slipped into obscurity).

This paper contributes to one particular area of interest: the roots of Elsa's dadaism within a little known though profoundly influential aesthetic movement in late nineteenth-century Germany, a movement to which Elsa was directly connected.[4] This context requires that I recuperate one of the most vilified characters in Elsa's memoirs: August Endell, an architect very much in the *Jugendstil*[5] vanguard of his time. While at the end of her life Elsa remembers Endell for his "snivelling lack of backbone—bawling babyconduct—weeping impotence" (Hjartarson and Spettigue 131), Endell nevertheless

[handwritten in margin: "homosexual panic"]

played a very important role in Elsa's early artistic life, and, indirectly, in her aesthetic formation. It was during her Munich years (circa the 1890s–Elsa's memoirs contain few dates) that Else wrote to Endell, whom she had previously met socially, to ask him "how one may earn money in doing applied art.... I... really have no idea nor any art training. That is why I turn to you—because you seem to know so much about it" (Hjartarson and Spettigue 58). Endell accepted her proposal, and soon Else found herself working four to six hours a day on her art (Reiss 94). The rest of the story we can glean from Else's memoirs: how she and Endell marry, her discovery of his impotence, his encouragement of her affairs, and her entanglement, thus, with Greve. The complexities of this entanglement are brought out in an unforgettable passage of the memoirs, which detail Else's experiences in a sanatorium to which Endell had sent her "to be away from him and to have by-the-way, for his impotence my womb massaged–so that he should not look the only guilty one":

> So here I was–installed in a sanatorium having my womb twiddled by a bourgeois very married doctor–who for businessake with the silent consent of his spouse–silently suffered himself to be the more or less openly expressed desire for many a waning young lady's hysterically erring sexcall–that was under his care. And the man [Greve]–who was to be the first potent mate I ever possessed–with whom I also remained together the longest time I ever was with one man–about 10 years–was in Berlin–keeping my husband [Endell] company–I dreaming about him–but–also about my husband–whom I did not desire to abandon–not even for this miracle of a youth–if it was only possible and he came up to expectation after my wombsqueeze excursion. But he did not–and the matter ended with hairpulling and slipperhurling from my part. (61)

Despite Else's scorn for Endell as a lover, it was through him that she was exposed to an art-critical milieu that was concerned with developing an *empathic* theory of artistic production; the theory was psychologistic, and embraced notions of sensory development and psychic dynamism.

The empathic aesthetic grew up as part of a late nineteenth-century debate in Germany whose context was a post-1850s disenchantment with the notion of idealism; as such, it was concurrent with some of the most revolutionary movements of the late nineteenth century, movements that would subsequently be identified with the origins of Modernism. Drawing on the attention that Schopenhauer had given to the physiology of the perceptual act (Mallgrave 9), this debate increasingly turned to the question of content, as opposed to idealist and universalist notions of form, and to the subjectivity that encountered it. "Empathy" (Einfühlung, literally 'in-feeling') was the term coined in the early 1870s by Robert Vischer to describe that relationship.

Robert Vischer drew on the work of his father, Friedrich Theodor Vischer (one of the originators of this intellectual debate), who had argued that the 'artistic spirit' could animate form in such a way as to imply both the interrelationship of viewer and object, and the interrelationship of sensory apprehension in perceiving that object, through a form of "emotional transference" (Mallgrave 19). Robert Vischer further developed the notion of empathy (as he writes in On the Optical Sense of Form) as a specific attack on the strictures of idealist aesthetics (Mallgrave 21). Drawing on a proto-Freudian text by Karl Albert Scherner, Vischer writes: "Here it was shown how the body, in responding to certain stimuli in dreams, objectifies itself in spatial forms. Thus it unconsciously projects its own bodily form...into the form of the object. From this I derived the notion that I call 'empathy'" (Mallgrave 24). This dreamlike projection of the self characterized our everyday experiences as well, argued Vischer: "'an objective but accidentally experienced phenomenon always provokes a related idea of the self in sensory or motor form'" (Mallgrave 25). Thus, as Vischer's editors interpolate, "[t]he phenomena that we encounter in the world...become analogies for one's own bodily structure; in viewing a specific object, [as Vischer writes], 'I wrap myself within its contours as in a garment'" (25). As the editors further note, "Although the notion of empathy in English can suggest a simple projection of emotions or the emotional response we may feel toward an object, it denotes for Vischer a more radical and thorough-going transference of our personal ego, one in which our whole personality (consciously or unconsciously) merges with the object" (25). This emphasis on the physiological underpinnings of aesthetic response (as opposed to formalist or idealistic ones) is the key to understanding the aesthetics of empathy, and provides powerful linkages to Elsa's work, including the insistence upon the bodily and the sensual, the relationship between the sensual and the spatial, and the notion of projection, or extension, that issues in an empathic set of sensory relationships.

Vischer's notion of empathy remained attractive to aesthetic theorists such as Theodor Lipps, who sought to develop a psychologistic theory of empathic intermediation.[6] Lipps was particularly concerned with empathy in terms of architectural space and ornament, providing "[e]laborate dramatic accounts of the emotive character of the perception of lines" (Podro 107 n. 9). It was this aspect of Lipps's work that influenced August Endell, who wrote two articles in this connection (1897–98): one on the possibilities within the 'new' architecture; the other on decorative art. As a resident of and practitioner in Munich, Endell was particularly well placed in terms of the Jugendstil; as Stephen Escritt remarks, "In the 1890s and 1900s, pluralism was fostered in Munich, where there was a relatively liberal attitude towards the arts. It is in this context of local liberalism and confident authoritarian nationalism that Jugendstil flourished in the city" (117). The style was named after the journal with which it was most closely associated—Jugend—whose motto was Kunst und Leben: art and life (Escritt 119).

In his article on architecture, Endell espouses a sensuous, tactile aesthetic: "Seht das Einzelne, Linie für Linie, Fläche für Fläche, geht den Formen mit dem Auge nach, tastet sie ab, erlebt sie, geniesst sie, erst dann werdet ihr begreifen was sie uns sein können" (143).[7] Such an aesthetic should lead one to bold new insights: "Lasst euch ruhig anmassend und arrogant schelten, wenn ihr alte Berühmtheiten tadelt. Ihr sollt tadeln, sollt hassen, denn nur so lernt ihr lieben, lernt ihr mit ganzer Seele fühlen" (143).[8] The essay on decorative art is concerned with kinetic aspects of art and perception: "Während wir also beim Durchlaufen von krummen Linien immer ein Neues aufzufassen haben, bietet die Gerade fortwährend dasselbe Bild. Es wird somit die Wahrnehmung der Geraden sich rascher vollziehen, und zwar um so rascher, je länger die Gerade sich dehnt. Denn jeder neue Moment giebt ja nur der Art nach schon Bekanntes. Es wird aber ganz allge-mein das Bekanntere auch rascher aufgefasst und macht auch rascher anderem Platz; somit wird sich die Schnelligkeit im Auffassen der Geraden fortwährend steigern" (119).[9] Endell saw Jugendstil as embodying this new aesthetic based on tactile qualities and free forms, and sought to embody

FIGURE 8: August Endell. Exterior façade (Elvira Photographic Studio, Munich). 1897–98. Bildarchiv Foto Marburg, Germany.

these qualities in his own architectural and decorative work, particularly the Elvira photographic studio (1897–98; figures 8 and 9). Elsa's genius was to translate these elements into a personal, performative aesthetic.

This performative aesthetic was given its theoretical underpinnings in the work of another empathic theorist, Conrad Fiedler, who sought to develop empathic theory in the direction of the sensuous, arguing that the optical, for example, was not (only) an abstract sense. Fiedler is less known in his own right than as virtually the co-author of Adolf von Hildebrand's much better known work, the *Problem of Form*, which was based on the distinction between visual perception, that pertaining to the eye at rest taking in a distant view, and kinesthetic perception, that pertaining to the near view and the eye in motion. The implication of this theory was the rejection of three-dimensional representations of space in favour of kinesthetic, processual space.

Heinrich Wölfflin, one of the major figures within the history of art theory, took the empathic notion further, arguing, like Endell, that "it is in the applied arts that the signs of formal change first become manifest" (Mallgrave 47). For his own version of empathic theory, Wölfflin drew on

FIGURE 9: August Endell. Interior stairwell (Elvira Photographic Studio, Munich). 1897–98. Bildarchiv Foto Marburg, Germany.

the work of August Schmarsow, who suggested that the prime quality of architecture was not form but space (that is, not space as a container but space as something actively constructed through an interplay of sensory perception), and on Schmarsow's intellectual mentor, Carl Stumpf, and especially on his notion that "'the human body, rather than just vision, stands at the center of our spatial experience'" (quoted by Mallgrave 61). He

FIGURE 10: Elsa von Freytag-Loringhoven (with Morton Livingston
Schamberg). *God*. 1917. Philadelphia Museum of Art. The Louise and Walter
Arensberg Collection.

thus refused to valorize vision in terms of the fixed point of view, a notion
that was of crucial importance to the anti-retinalist art of Duchamp and
other New York dadaists—including the Baroness herself.

One of Elsa's first workings out of the notion of empathy is found in a
text that is arguably attributable to her as a collaboration, namely Greve's
Fanny Essler (1905). As the initials of the title itself suggests, this was a co-
production of Felix and Elsa, a notion confirmed by Elsa in the comment
published in her memoir that "He [Greve] had written *two novels*. They were
each dictated by me as far as *material* was concerned–it was *my life* and
persons out of my life–he did the executive part of the business–giving the
thing a conventional shape and dress" (65). While Elsa comments that she

"disliked the 'style' already *then*" (65–66) which Greve imposed on her material, there is in *Fanny Essler* a suggestion of the procedure through which Elsa would translate aesthetic theory into a form of psycho-sexual empathy,[10] a process that, as Gammel argues, would receive a further twist in the memoirs, where Elsa re-appropriates her life-story as originally appropriated by Greve. It was in *Fanny Essler*, however, that Elsa took her first major step towards the concept of empathic embodiment which characterized her New York persona. It is crucial, for this reason, to understand *Fanny Essler* as a collaboration. What I am suggesting is that the "autobiographical dialogue" ("No Woman Lover" 453), which Irene Gammel sees taking place between *Fanny Essler* and the memoir, is already present within *Fanny Essler* as an empathic dialogue in which the aesthetic becomes empathically sexualized through the details Else dictated from her autobiographical exploits.

The artworks that Elsa produced during her New York period demonstrate another form of her empathic aesthetic. Her 1917 work *God* (figure 10) at once "brilliantly [turns] the tables on the woman-as-machine trope," in the words of Amelia Jones, while offering a sexualized and scatological reading of Endell's musings on the relation of line to curve in decorative art ("Eros"). Her *Portrait of Marcel Duchamp* (1920) (figure 1) explores another dimension of empathic theory, taking the traditional portrait and making it into something tactile,[11] exploring thereby the sculptural space of anti-retinalist art—art that declared its independence from the fixed point of view.

The most important aspect of this aesthetic dialogue in Elsa's work, however, had to do with the notion of embodiment. This notion constituted an awareness that the mechanical era celebrated in the work of such artists as Francis Picabia and Fernand Leger was giving way to an increasingly organic notion of form; indeed, Elsa's description in *Baroness Elsa* (Hjartarson and Spettigue) of her lovemaking with Felix clearly indicates her sense of how the mechanical could become sexualized, and vice versa, a notion given classic expression in Duchamp's *Bride Stripped Bare By her Bachelors, Even*. It is this notion of sensual empathy that constitutes, in my view, the uniqueness of Elsa's art. In effect, she sought to embody her art, making herself into an artifact not so much in the Wildean sense that she might have imbibed from Felix's *Oscar Wilde*, but in a much more performative sense—the body as process rather than as product. Hence the descriptions of her Greenwich

Village appearances, which were almost Happenings in their own right: "she shellacked her shaven skull, colored it vermilion, wore an inverted coal scuttle for a cap, and applied to her body as decorative elements mechanistic implements such as metal teaballs" (Reiss 86); "'She wore also at times a black dress with a bustle on which rested an electric battery tail light.... Still another time on the street she had a wooden bird cage around her neck housing a live canary. The hem of her skirt was decorated with horse blanket pins, and she had five dogs on five leashes'" (Louis Bouché quoted in Reiss 87); "'She wore high white spats with a band of decorative furniture braid around the top. Hanging from her bust were two tea-balls.... On her head was a black velvet tam o'shanter with a feather and several spoons'" (quoted by Kuenzli, "Baroness Elsa" 442). Through such gestures, as well as through the performativity of her nude modelling (an active, rather than a passive, modelling; a modelling that took place inside and outside the art studio), Elsa represented her notion of the interface between the mechanical and the organic, the abstract and the sensual, the fixed point of view and multiple viewpoints. As she put it in her essay "The Modest Woman," "'America's comfort:—sanitation—outside machinery—has made American forget own machinery—body!'" (quoted by Kuenzli, "Baroness Elsa" 451), suggesting that body and machine are not oppositional but empathically interrelated.

Elsa's empathic aesthetics thus led her to a more interrelational notion of the mechanical and the sensual than that held to by her dadaist peers. These aesthetics also provide an enhanced context for comments which have recurred in the descriptions of Elsa's art: that "her whole life was Dada" (Reiss 86); that Elsa "dresses Dada, loves Dada, lives Dada," that she was "riding the line between woman and object" (Jones, "Eros" 244–45); that for the Baroness "life praxis and art were one" (Kuenzli, "Baroness Elsa" 450). Empathic theory thus allows us to understand more fully how, as Paul Hjartarson and Douglas Spettigue have put it, "Elsa was moving toward Dada before Dada was recognized" ("Introduction" 28).

———

IT IS THROUGH THIS NOTION *of empathic embodiment that Elsa lays claim to her centrality within New York Dada, and it is this observation that brings*

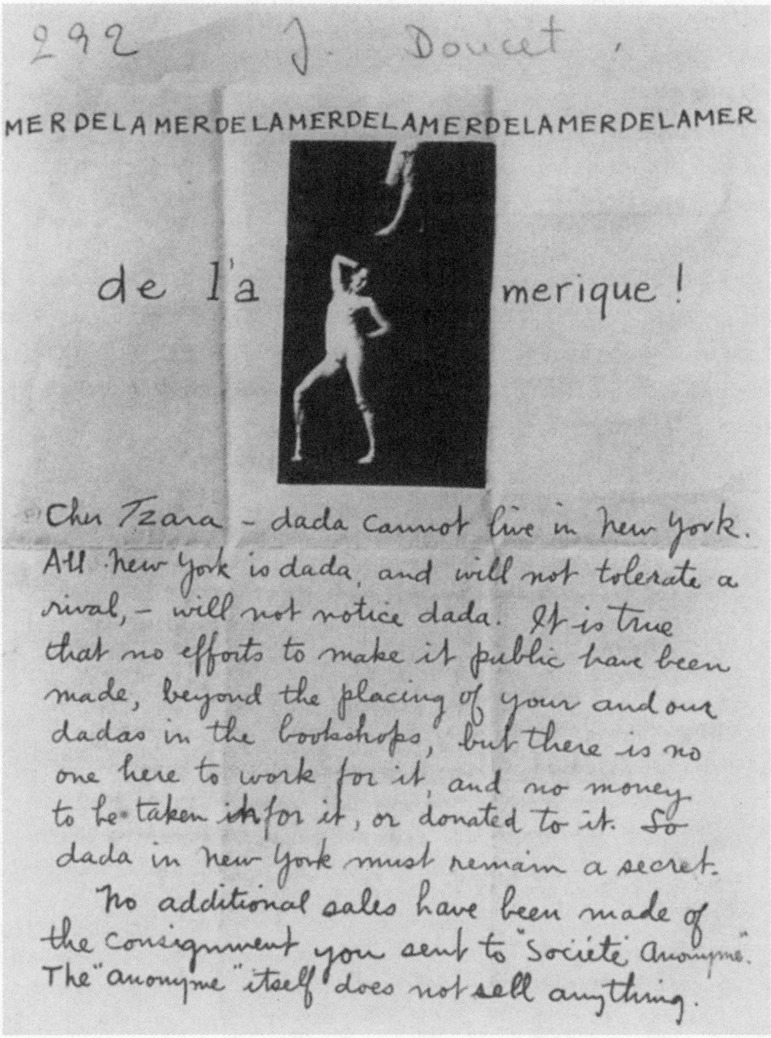

292   J. Doucet,

MERDELAMERDELAMERDELAMERDELAMERDELAMER

de l'a   merique!

Cher Tzara – dada cannot live in new York.
All new York is dada, and will not tolerate a
rival, – will not notice dada. It is true
that no efforts to make it public have been
made, beyond the placing of your and our
dadas in the bookshops, but there is no
one here to work for it, and no money
to be taken in for it, or donated to it. So
dada in new York must remain a secret.
No additional sales have been made of
the consignment you sent to "société anonyme."
The "anonyme" itself does not sell anything.

FIGURE 11: Man Ray. Letter to Tristan Tzara, postmarked 8 June 1921.
Bibliothèque Littéraire Jacques Doucet, Paris. © Estate of Man Ray/SODRAC
(Montreal), 2003.

me to my concluding speculation. Could it be that the identity of the artwork labelled "La Femme" in the drawing by Boix has remained a mystery for so long because it labels not an object at all, but, quite literally, a woman? In fact, I think it does, and I think that woman is Baroness Elsa herself, whose originary role in Dada is proclaimed by the apple she so boldly flaunts. Boix's drawing represents Elsa in one of her most famous poses (figure 11), captured thus by Man Ray in a still from the now-lost film, "Baroness Elsa Shaves her Pubic Hair." The drawing also represents one of Elsa's most famous forms of empathic objecthood, that of the metal teaballs hanging from her breasts. It is here, in this drawing, that Elsa finally escapes the strictures of critics who claim to know what "the depiction of a woman" (Naumann, "New York Dada" 14) should look like, and asserts her empathic identification with Dada itself, which proclaims her its central, if unnameable, figure.

NOTES

1   Chief among those researchers working in this area are Irene Gammel, whose cultural biography of Elsa was recently published by MIT Press (2002), and Klaus Martens, whose research into the early years of FPG has opened up highly productive terrain.

2   Richard Cavell, "Felix Paul Greve, the Eulenberg Scandal, and Frederick Philip Grove," Essays on Canadian Writing 62 (1997): 12–45.

3   The two spellings (Else/Elsa) of Freytag-Loringhoven's first name reflect the different periods of her life. In her early years in Germany, she circulated as Else; in New York, she assumed the anglicized version, Elsa.

4   Some dates: Elsa arrives in North America in 1909, meeting up with Felix, who had left earlier that year. In 1913, the two having split up, Elsa finds herself in New York and marries that year the Baron von Freytag-Loringhoven. In that same year, Marcel Duchamp, with whom Elsa was to be closely associated, begins producing his ready mades. New York Dada, however, is normally situated in the period from 1915–1924, although Hans Arp does not invent the term Dada until 1916, and he does so in Zurich, with the New York group adopting the term only circa 1921. Elsa's first New York publication was issued in 1918, and her artworks date from 1917–1920. See Hjartarson and Spettigue, Baroness Elsa, and Kuenzli, New York Dada.

5   This is the German equivalent of Art Nouveau, characterized by flowing, organic lines deriving from Nature.

6   One of the publication venues through which Lipps disseminated his theories was Die Zukunft, and it is indicative of the close interconnections within German artistic and critical circles of this time that this same journal was the central instigator of

the Eulenberg scandal that I have argued was one of the precipitating causes of Felix Paul Greve's sudden departure from Germany.

7   "See the detail, line by line, surface by surface, follow the forms with your eyes, feel them all over, experience them, enjoy them, only then will you comprehend what they mean." Passages from the German are translated with the assistance of Ilona Iatzli.

8   "Let them scold you as presumptuous and arrogant when you disapprove of old celebrities. You should disapprove, should detest, for you only learn to love, to feel with all your soul by doing so."

9   "While we constantly take in something new as our eyes pass over the curved line, the straight line continuously offers the same picture. The perception of the straight line will consequently happen faster [;] this is faster, the longer the straight line extends. Every new moment only shows something already familiar in a similar way. But the familiar, in general, is also perceived faster, and it too makes quicker space for something else, therefore the speed of perception of the straight line continuously increases."

10   Anna Freud uses the phrase "*völligen Sicheinsfühlens*" (complete empathy) to represent the culmination of a sexual fantasy she describes in a paper on "The Relation of Beating Phantasies to a Daydream." See the discussion in Darian Leader, *Freud's Footnotes* (London: Faber and Faber, 2000) 172, note 2.

11   Gammel remarks that "Elsa's writing takes pleasure in words...experiencing them in their physical materiality" ("No Woman Lover" 455).

Two Glimpses of the Baroness

RECENT ELSE VON FREYTAG-LORINGHOVEN (EFL) research has increasingly focused on her role as an independent actor on the literary stage of New York between, roughly, 1918 and 1923.[1] Most of what we know—and of what interests us so keenly—has emerged from the concentration on the fascinating role she played as a recognized figure in American Dada and Surrealist circles. During these years of her much-deserved rediscovery, however, why has she been exclusively categorized as a Dada author? As a maker of striking assemblages, herself the subject of art works, and as an artist who seems to have surfaced abruptly into Dada existence, somehow fully formed, EFL has been made to appear as a kind of unchaste Athena Parthenos sprung from the head of Zeus. There is no doubt as to her strong involvement in New York with such artists as Marcel Duchamp, Man Ray, and Morton Livingston Schamberg, and her prominent part in "The European Art Invasion."[2] Although EFL took part in many of the activities of the artists who came to New York from Europe before, during, and after the Great War, she did not, as Davidson writes in 1996, come to New York from Germany in 1913 (223). Davidson clearly follows an early remark (since corrected) that she had gone "from Cincinnati to New York and from there back to Germany," eventually returning, with the Baron, to New York (Hjartarson, "Of Greve" 283). But wherever she came from in the United States before she first surfaced in Pittsburgh, did she know of the Armory Show at the time? There is no indication of that or of her having met Duchamp at the scene of his earliest and greatest American successes. Meeting Duchamp then, and witnessing the scandal involving the Frenchman and his painting *Nude Descending a Staircase*, might indeed have caused her to turn towards an

41

art more experimental than that which she had known as Felix Paul Greve's (FPG) companion.

We do know for certain that Freytag-Loringhoven left Germany in 1910, finally drifting to New York after she had been deserted by her lover in the hinterland of Kentucky (Hjartarson, "Of Greve" 282; Martens, *F.P. Grove* 240–47). What deserves emphasis then is this: from June 1910 to late 1913 she had no way of becoming acquainted or influenced by Dada artists-to-be, including those whom she later joined in New York, were they Europeans or Americans. In fact, she could hardly have been in contact with those early Expressionists and Futurists who gathered around such leading Berlin publications as *Der Sturm* after 1911. Thus, she would not have known of Jean (Hans) Arp, Hugo Ball, Richard Huelsenbeck, Kurt Schwitters or Tristan Tzara, the earliest Dada artists to surface in Switzerland and Germany, in their very self-consciously played roles as "new" artists, roles that helped them achieve welcome notoriety. She certainly could not have been a harbinger of the good Dada news from Zürich and the Café Voltaire to New York, since the Swiss beginnings of Dada did not occur before February 5, 1916 at the first performance in the Café Voltaire, as recorded by Hugo Ball (Döhl 719). What Freytag-Loringhoven, in New York, did have in common, however, was the immigrant status shared by these artists from different nationalities in Zürich during the Great War: Ball and Huelsenbeck were Germans, Arp was a bilingual Alsatian, and Tzara was a Romanian. They were united in what they opposed: war, "ideas," the individual person, meaning. Regarding their art, they did not flaunt so much their outrageous artistic inventiveness as their collagistic restatement, exacerbation, and, finally, synthesis of existing trends in Expressionism, Futurism, and other isms of their day. "Dada zielte auf Provokation...Und das Medium seines Protests war die Kunst oder auch Anti-Kunst, aber nur, wenn man Anti-Kunst auf die traditionellen Vorstellungen von Kunst bezogen sieht" ["Dada aimed at provocation...and the medium of this protest was an anti-art, if anti-art is understood as reacting against traditional ideas of art"] (Döhl 727). Hugo Ball tried to pin down Dada's specific manner and *materia poetica*:

Was wir Dada nennen ist ein Narrenspiel aus dem Nichts, in das alle höheren Fragen verwickelt sind; eine Gladiatorengeste; ein Spiel mit den schäbigen Überbleibseln; eine Hinrichtung der posierten Moralität und Fülle. Der Dadaist liebt das Außergewöhnliche, ja das Absurde: Er weiß, dass sich im Widerspruche das Leben behauptet und dass seine Zeit wie keine vorher auf die Vernichtung des Generösen abzieht. Jede Maske ist ihm darum willkommen: jedes Versteckspiel, dem eine düpierende Kraft innewohnt. Das Direkte und Primitive erscheint ihm inmitten enormer Unnatur als das Unglaubliche selbst.

What we call Dada is a fool's game from nothingness in which are gathered all higher questions; it is a gladiator's gesture; a game with the worn out remnants; an execution of posed morality and bounty. The Dadaist loves the extraordinary, yes, the absurd. He knows that life survives in contradictions and that his own time, as no time before, aims at the elimination of the generous. Any kind of mask, therefore, is welcome to him. Any game of hide-and-seek that is inhabited by a power of deceit. The direct and primitive appear to him in the midst of such enormous non-nature as the incredible itself. (Döhl 725–26, my translation).

In addition, and maybe most importantly, these early dadaists shared a profound distrust of language which, at first, resulted not in a language of their own invention but in a recombination of traditional vocabulary, confronting "the nonsense of the time by art's no-sense" (Döhl 730). Only their performances of the *poème simultan* (simultaneous poem) and Ball's own invention of the *Klanggedichte* (sound poems) promised something new (732, 734). Ball turned away from Dada in 1917, the Zürich experiment ended in 1919, and new groups of artists sprang up all over Europe, interpreting Dada in their own ways.

Among these, it should be noted, was Kurt Schwitters who, from 1919, singlehandedly developed his own idiosyncratic version of Dada which he called "Merz." In a letter from Berlin to Djuna Barnes, Else von Freytag-Loringhoven calls one of Schwitters's pictures a "senseless truly idiotic— mimicking 'modern' picture" and finds the painter "mediocre." She adds: "Seldom have I seen anything so offensively impotent of any *inner necessity*— or *outside cleverness*—by him! It is shameful imitative—*nothing else*—without any flourish! Fi!"[3] Else was apparently not merely flattering her American correspondent to whom she always praised everything American to the skies and from whom she expected salvation from the depths in which she found herself after her return to Germany in 1923. It is important to note that while she was in Germany in the twenties she remained aware of developments in art in spite of her dire poverty and frequent depressions. She knew of Schwitters's work and she put it down (whimsically, because of Schwitters's homely first name, Kurt). Schwitters, however unfairly treated by her in her despair, is the only second-generation dadaist she mentions at any length. Freytag-Loringhoven, when still in New York, herself belonged to this second generation that surfaced towards the end of the Great War. John Rodger indirectly acknowledged this in *The Little Review* (1920), although his time-frame, too, was a little off: "Paris had had *Dada* for five years and we have had Elsa von Freytag-Loringhoven for two years" (Naumann, *New York Dada* 168). At the time of her writing to Barnes from Germany, Dada, in its many new incarnations, was all over Europe in what might be called a third wave. Was EFL's reaction to Schwitters merely the invective of a rival who had lost her (New York) audience? It was more than that, since she perceived a marked difference between Schwitters and herself: she castigates the other artist for his "outside cleverness," that is, his cleverness publicly displayed, and his lack of "flourish."

The lack she perceived in Schwitters helps us to characterize her own peculiar qualities in New York: her panache and the congruence of her striking costumes and appearance with her radical state of mind. In EFL, art and the person form a unity. That also marks the vast gap between her and the artists of the New York circles in which she moved. If, as her contemporary and acquaintance, the poet Wallace Stevens, was to note later, "the poem is the cry of its occasion," then EFL's artistic expressions as *objects d'art* or her own bodily appearance are, quite unmelodramatically, the artistically expressed *cri de coeur* of a woman left and lost and without the mastery of the language she needed. To express herself, she developed a language that rendered palpable that cry of hurt and protest. She may have turned her linguistic shortcomings in English to advantage by developing her own pointedly naive and stunned "da-da"—in contrast with and striking parallel to her European colleagues' crass protest against the even crasser horrors of the war—out of her own multilingual poetic being, her body language, and the language of art objects. The painting of the body, however, even though she may have arrived at it on her own, she cannot have witnessed in even a proto-Dada context in Europe at or before the time she developed as an artist in New York. DeVore, incidentally, is the only critic to claim that Else was in Europe after 1918 (and before 1923) and thus could have experienced European Dada at first hand (76).

How, then, did EFL arrive at the outrageous art, provocative outfits, and challenging presentations of herself that led to her acceptance as the New York Dada queen? The timing is not right. She may have absorbed a good deal, although unspecified, from those artists she first met in New York. However, I am going to argue that the transcendence of ordinary bounds of language, the use of masks and other striking features of her art had been practised by her in Germany prior to her arrival in the New World during the time she spent in Cottbus, Berlin, and Munich about which, also, not much is known.

◆ Baroness Else von Freytag-Loringhoven: Theatrical Beginnings

MUCH AS IN the German and Canadian novels and autobiographical writings of Frederick Philip Grove *aka* Felix Paul Greve, EFL's surviving autobiographical statements in her letters and the account of her early life written for Djuna Barnes contain fact and fiction in the form of fictionalised and highly selective autobiography. If FPG gave the heroines of his two German novels, *Fanny Essler* and *Maurermeister Ihles Haus*, numerous details from the career of his then life-partner, Else, using her early life as the pattern for his fictionalised elaboration of it, then EFL used the pattern of some of the years spent with FPG as the basis for her autobiographical account of these years from her perspective. The result is a surprising narrative both severely narrowed by her omissions, the limited viewpoint of the selections she made, and by the slant given by the writer's intentions, one of which, apparently, was 'to get even' with her most important implied reader, FPG, whom she correctly assumed was still living on the American continent. The ensuing fragmented narrative she wrote for Barnes was also meant to secure the American writer's help in obtaining a visa for France. EFL's memoirs were, then, emphatically, a narrative with more than one purpose.[4]

Compared to the relative wealth of material from and about the Baroness's activities during and after the period she spent in New York as an artist active among some of the outstanding figures of high modernism—Marcel Duchamp, Man Ray, William Carlos Williams, Wallace Stevens, and others— there is no published first-hand and little surviving second-hand evidence of her activities before her marriage to August Endell and the approximately nine years she spent in the company of FPG in Germany and the United States. There is only what she wrote in the memoir and letters to Barnes and what FPG used for his 1905 and 1906 German novels based on her youth in Swinemünde and her career in Berlin and elsewhere.

Thanks to Irene Gammel's research, apparently conducted parallel to mine, we now have a somewhat fuller, though still incomplete, account of Else's life in Germany. It, too, unavoidably draws on Else's own memoirs and letters, published since 1986, but it includes a good deal of new and original, on-site research that helps to narrow some of the previous gaps in our knowledge of that period of Else's life and of her development as a writer and performer. I have written elsewhere about some of the possible sources of the Baroness's Dada approach to writing poems and making art objects (Martens, *F.P. Grove* 215–20), also first pointing up the unavoidable parallels to Else Lasker-Schüler's career. Here, I am mainly concerned with the Baroness's beginnings as a performer. Gammel quite rightly points to circumstantial evidence of the young woman's role in Berlin as a model and her posing in variety shows of the "Wintergarten" kind (Gammel, *Baroness Elsa* 60–62). In this context, Gammel makes a case for Else's sexual adventures as a chorus girl, linking these to her thesis regarding the importance of such early encounters for the provocative later life of the artist in America. There is, however, little new evidence of other artistic activity on Else's part after her "work as a chorus girl at Berlin's Zentral Theater" (Gammel, *Baroness Elsa* 65–66). For the period 1896–98 we know that EFL met the artist Melchior Lechter and the writer Karl Wolfskehl. During the same period she may also have had an affair with the playwright Ernst Hardt before eloping in the "early summer...with Hardt's friend Richard Schmitz" and, a little later in the year, with Richard's brother, the writer O.A.H. Schmitz.

In Felix Paul Greve's 1905 novel *Fanny Essler*, a source text of the first importance for Else's biography (Martens, *F.P. Grove* 63, 94), the reader learns that Fanny/Else had been employed at the *Kleines Theater* in the city of Cottbus, a medium-sized town near the border of what today is the Czech Republic (FE 243). The year given is 1902. In 1902, of course, Else was married to the architect and designer August Endell and was living in Munich; she met Greve at the Wolfkehl's and had moved back to Berlin, ending the year in a sanatorium on the island of Föhr (Martens, *F.P. Grove* 130–32). The Cottbus trail seemed cold, after all, and my inquiries while I was at work on the German version of my FPG biography (1997) showed that there had been no *Kleines Theater* in that city (although there had been one in Berlin). Conversely, however, I have found that, as a rule, the large majority of FPG's fictionalised accounts in both his German and Canadian works usually rest on fact; that is, they were slightly 'doctored' and used in altered contexts. Since *Fanny Essler* also contains an account of time spent at a Berlin Acting School sometime between October 1894 and August 1895, since Greve's novel makes mention of an impressive array of plays she (Fanny) studied—by Ibsen, Goethe, Schiller, Hauptmann, and Richard Voss—I felt that EFL must have had some experience acting in real plays, outside an acting school or a hypothetical chorus line. Keeping that in mind, I again went to look for myself.

Cottbus today is a very lively city, proud of its many, freshly renovated *Jugendstil* buildings and fancy shopping malls. There is also an impressive art nouveau *Stadttheater* (municipal theater)—beautifully situated in a little park, and dedicated to "German Art," as the inscription reads—with its own archive, located elsewhere. No traces of Else could be found in either the splendid theater or in its archive. As it turned out, there had been no *Stadttheater* in Cottbus before 1908 (when FPG and Else were living in Berlin). However, during the last two decades of the nineteenth century, the city of Cottbus had indeed had places unofficially designated "*Stadttheater*" prior to the building of the 1908 edifice officially baptised with that name. During the 1890s, shows and theater performances by local and by travelling companies, directed by different personalities as the theater seasons changed, had been held at a large hotel and restaurant owned by the Hatrtmann family, the *Hotel Goldener Ring* (*Zwanzig Jahre* 32), located centrally on the south side of the *Altmarkt* (Old Market), number 21.

This hotel had been well known to citizens of Cottbus and its surroundings. It prided itself on a large and ornately decorated festival hall with a regular stage at one end. Around the end of the nineteenth century, it was familiarly referred to in the local press as the *Stadttheater*.

FIGURE 12: View of the Hotel Goldener Ring (second building from the left).

FIGURE 13: The "Old Theater" in the Hotel Goldener Ring. View of the Stage (*Zwanzig Jahre* 21).

This "theater-in-a-hotel" represented a not uncommon solution to the need for a place of manifold cultural expression in many provincial centres in the absence of sufficient municipal funds for a new building. The *Hotel Goldener Ring* was later acknowledged to have been "the place for real artistic endeavour and elevating enjoyment." In spite of the "cramped situation and the insufficient equipment," "famous luminaries of the stage and even world-renowned touring companies" found their way to Cottbus. Many a "talented and ambitious person who here entered the stage received exposure for the first time or, if he managed to slip in for a further season, made a name for himself" (*Zwanzig Jahre* 32). The drawback was, of course, that there was a constant flux of companies and directors. This was also the unstable situation in the winter season of 1897–98, when the then well-known actor-director Max Walden, "formerly accredited to the Russian Court," bought advertising space in the local paper, hoping to draw subscribers for the coming season (*Cottbuser Anzeiger*, 4 September 1897). On 23 September 1897, judging from the large announcement in the local paper, he presented his motley company, drawn from theaters all over Germany, to the theater-going public of Cottbus and environs. Young Else Plötz, listed as being "formerly of Berlin's *Central-Theater*," was among the actors. Since the season at the *Central-Theater* had ended somewhat prematurely, on 18 April 1897, and most employees had options of working elsewhere written into their contracts, Else was free to go to Cottbus.

Her experience at the Berlin *Central-Theater* must have gone beyond that of a mere sexually alluring chorus-girl, since she soon found employment as an actress. This was a much better "springboard for a fabled career" than the role of the cheap chorus-girl could provide (Gammel 66). In addition, during the 1896–97 season just ended, the *Central-Theater's* director had specialised in wholesale parodic performances, extraordinarily funny send-ups of operas, operettas, and serious plays—by such authors as Arno Holz, Hermann Sudermann, and Gerhart Hauptmann—then being performed at Berlin theaters of high standing, such as the renowned *Deutsches Theater* (Windelboth 262–64). It would not have been particularly difficult for the young actress to switch over to "serious" versions of productions similar to those she had helped parody once she had found employment for the coming season. Her experience in—and talent for—parody would again show up

Stadt-Theater.

Direction: Max Walden, Kaiserlich Russischer Hofschauspieler a. D.
Winterspielzeit 1897–98.

Personal-Verzeichniss.

Direction: Max Walden (führt die Oberregie).
Bureau-Chef: Ludwig Piorkowski (Directions-stellvertreter).
Regisseure: Ernst Epstein, Walter Rubtisch.
Kapellmeister: Paul Buchwald v. Möllendorff.
Musikdirector: Stabshoboist R. Wilde.
Rendant und I. Kassirer: Julius Voss.
Secretair und Bibliothekar: Willy Tiedt.

Damen:

Clara Böhme, vom Stadttheater in Cöln.
Lucie Boghàty, vom Stadttheater in Hanau.
Anna Collani, vom Stadttheater in Guben.
Charlotte Claar, vom Stadttheater in Frankfurt a. M.
Anny Dewitz, v. Friedrich-Wilhelmstädt. Theater, Berlin.
Gertruda Engel, vom Stadttheater in Lübeck.
Iva Jäger, vom Stadttheater in Königsberg.
Margarethe Kappes, vom Tivoli-Theater in Kiel.
Meta König, vom Schauspielhaus in Potsdam.
Emmy Peters, vom Stadttheater in Breslau.
Elsa Plötz, vom Centraltheater in Berlin.
Erna Reichelt, vom Concordiatheater in Breslau.
Elma Roth, vom Hoftheater in Braunschweig.
Irene Sitardi, vom Stadttheater in Münch.-Gladbach.
Olga Terpitz, vom Stadttheater in Bromberg.

Herren:

Georg Bargbardt, vom Friedrich-Wilhelmstädtischen Theater in Berlin.
Eugen Brahm, vom Stadttheater in Meißen.
Ernst Epstein, vom Friedrich-Wilhelmstädtisch. Theater in Berlin. (Regisseur.)
Willy Kruszynski, vom Fürstl. Theater in Arnstadt.
Richard Leopold, vom Stadttheater in Görlitz.
Edgar Reimerdes, vom Stadttheater in Schweidnitz.
Leopold Rafaëli, vom Stadttheater in Stettin.
Arthur Rotenburg, vom Deutschen Theater in Berlin.
Walter Rubtisch, vom Stadttheater in Rostock. (Regisseur.)
Otto Taube, vom Saison-Theater in Freienwalde.
Ludwig Piorkowsky, vom Residenztheater in Berlin.
Carl Eckert, vom Saison-Theater in Freienwalde.

Technisches Personal:

Theater- u. Maschinenmeister: Louis Wallreuter, vom Theater des Westens in Berlin.
II. Theatermeister: Hans Wallreuter.
Obergarderobier: Reinhold Müller, vom Stadttheater in Görlitz.
Requisiteur: Pilokat.
Souffleuse: Emma Stefany, vom Stadttheater in Meißen.
Friseur: Paul Niedergesäss.

Theater-Orchester wird von der Regimentsmusik gestellt.

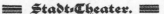

FIGURE 14: Advertisement in the *Cottbus Anzeiger* for Max Walden's company with "Elsa Plötz."

Stadttheater.

Es war für den Theaterfreund ein betrübender Anblick, bei der gestrigen Aufführung des zweiten klassischen Dramas in dieser Saison, des Schiller'schen „Don Carlos" den Zuschauern von kaum 80 Personen besetzt zu sehen. Selbst die Galerie, bei deren Besuchern sich sonst namentlich für Schiller'sche und für einige Shakespeare'sche Dramen eine ausgesprochene Vorliebe kund giebt, war nur äußerst schwach vertreten. Der mangelhafte Besuch, dessen Ursache wir heute nicht weiter nachforschen wollen, wirkte natürlich auch auf die Darsteller etwas niederdrückend ein und benahm ihnen die Lust, das Beste herzugeben, zu dem sie sich sonst vor einem vollen, angeregten Hause aufgeschwungen haben würden.

Auch Frl. Terpitz enttäuschte uns, zur Elisabeth reichte weder die Figur und der äußere Applomb noch die seelische Charakterisirung ganz aus. Gut waren andererseits Frl. Collani als Oberhofmeisterin und Fräulein Plötz als Marquise von Mondekar. — Ueber den Alba des Herrn Jeßner und den Beichtvater des Herrn Brahm wollen wir uns weiter nicht äußern; beiden Rollen fehlte es an der Individualisirung, die sich eben nur aus dem eingehenden Studium nicht nur der Rolle, sondern auch der geschichtlichen Persönlichkeit ergiebt

FIGURE 15: Unsigned review of Schiller's *Don Carlos*, naming "Miss Plötz" (excerpt).

later when she parodied for Greve men she had met (Martens, *F.P. Grove* 94–95) or in her recollections for Djuna Barnes (*Baroness Elsa*, passim).

It appears that Else Hildegard Plötz of Swinemünde (today's Swinoujscie), had changed her given name from "Else" to "Elsa," a slight alteration which nonetheless evokes reference to the well-known figure of "Elsa" from Richard Wagner's opera *Lohengrin*. It is the kind of slight vowel change Greve employed when he decided to call himself Grove (Martens, *F.P. Grove* 236), also re-creating himself.

The weekly advertisements and regular reviews over the next five months of the travelling company's program in the local paper, the *Cottbuser Anzeiger*, quickly reveal the astonishing versatility of the company with regard to the number of new and different plays put on at the theater in the *Hotel Goldener Ring*. There was a good deal of light fare—situation comedies of the day, farces, and folk plays with titles like *Der Sohn der Wildnis* or *Der Millionenbauer*— but there were also classics and serious modern plays: Henrik Ibsen's *Stützen der Gesellschaft*; soon followed by Gotthold Ephraim Lessing's *Minna von Barnhelm*; William Shakespeare's *Romeo und Julia*; an opera, Mozart's *Figaros Hochzeit*; and Gustav Freytag's recent and controversial play, *The Journalists* (*Cottbuser Anzeiger*, September-December 1897). Clearly one of the high points was the staging of Friedrich Schiller's tragedy, *Don Carlos*, on 17 October 1897 and on later dates. This is the only occasion on which the reviewer of the Cottbus paper, otherwise quite critical of some of the actors, takes positive note of one of the youngest members of the cast, "Elsa Plötz": "Miss Collani as the *Oberhofmeisterin* and Miss Plötz as the Marquise de Mondecar, on the other hand, acquitted themselves well."

The role of the Marquise de Mondecar in the tragedy is a small one indeed; she is one of the "three ladies in waiting to the Queen," Elisabeth of Spain. She has few appearances and fewer lines to speak in Act I, Scenes 3–6 before she is banished by the King. Still, her small part requires a good deal of silent acting in important scenes that help set the stage for the ensuing tragic development. Unfortunately, the reviewer says, there were only eighty people in the audience. Clearly, the taste was for more popular kinds of entertainment. The staging of the classics in provincial towns like Cottbus, however, also served an educational purpose and attendance was more or less mandatory for Gymnasium students (who would certainly have paid special attention to one of the youngest and most attractive of the visiting actresses).

There is no further mention of "Elsa Plötz" in the pages of the *Cottbuser Anzeiger*. We have no further printed proof that she played roles in other plays staged by Walden, although this, in all likelihood, must have been the case, since she was a member of the cast assembled for the season. We do not know whether she stayed on as a member of the company until the end of the winter season, in March, or prematurely dissolved her contract to return to Berlin. We are, finally, struck by the coincidence that FPG, whom she presumably did not meet until the summer of 1902, did a similar stint of acting as a student in Bonn in 1898 at the Bonn *Stadttheater*, also figuring in "classic" plays by Gotthold Ephraim Lessing and Friedrich Schiller, although not the same ones, and he certainly never figured in comedies, farces or folk-plays, like Else (Martens, *F.P. Grove* 33–35). Still, their youthful experiences were similar indeed, preparing EFL for her later challenging public role in New York and FPG for his somewhat more traditional later life in the major cities and all of the provinces of Canada.

◆ Orientalism, Else Lasker-Schüler, and the Baroness Else von Freytag-Loringhoven

OF THE BARONESS'S LIFE IN GERMANY, we know what little she chose to acquaint us with in the letters and memoirs written for Djuna Barnes. We also suspect some rather uncertain odds and ends as mediated through Felix Paul Greve's two German novels and through the observations of her contemporaries in Munich and Berlin prior to her departure for the United States. What else do we know of that early period? It has been surmised that Else was more than the sexually desirable creature given a literary identity to fool her lover Felix Paul Greve's creditors, as he presented "her" to his publisher J.C.C. Bruns and to André Gide. She provided him with material to be mined for his writings and he did not hesitate to plunder her memories, or so it seems. Although aware of the long-misused woman's perspective on Else, we must not be overprotective. It may be safely assumed from Felix and Else's long partnership and short marriage that whatever Greve used for his fictions was taken *not without her consent*. If, and to what extent, she may have had a hand in the actual writing of Greve's fictional works we do not know, since she neither asserted herself at the time nor in her memoirs written for Barnes.

Some evidence, however, indicates a small, but not very likely chance that she contributed to Greve's translation work, sharing the incredible textual load under which he staggered. That she herself may have translated Keats's poetry must be doubted in view of the linguistic shortcomings she later demonstrated in New York.[5] We do get a first inkling that in America she was not merely the helpless discarded lover, touchingly inexperienced in the twisty ways of literature, who stumbled onto the New York scene, only to miraculously evolve into that stunning new public persona.

EFL was not "well-born" like the struggling writer, translator, lover and Munich muse of gifted men, Franziska von Reventlow, who, like the Baroness, had also once intended to become a painter (Egbringhoff 105–06). She certainly was not well-connected like the occasional translator Helene Klages, platonically adored by Felix before Else won him over to her (Martens, F.P. Grove 87–95). Finally, she was not as conspicuous as that other contemporary "dame-de-lettre," the wonderful poet, dramatist, and painter Else Lasker-Schüler (1869–1945), then residing in Berlin. The Baroness-to-be, however, shared these women's ironic view of the cerebral men surrounding them. Like these three, Else Greve had learned to forestall utter poverty by attracting well-to-do and artistically minded men (Hjartarson and Spettigue 139f.). This pattern would repeat itself in New York in her attitude toward, and reaction to, such modernist artists as Marcel Duchamp, William Carlos Williams and George Biddle, among others.

In Berlin, she had escaped her all-too-bourgeois marriage to the noted architect August Endell much as Else Lasker-Schüler, that other, and, until recently, much better known Else, had escaped her marriage to the well-to-do physician Dr. Lasker, supporting herself through periods of near squalor before becoming the spouse (1903–1911) of Herwarth Walden, from 1910 the famous editor of the leading Expressionist magazine Der Sturm (Klüsener 65f.). Felix Paul Greve, too, had aimed at becoming the editor of a magazine patterned on the Mercure de France (Ernst and Martens 128). The lives of both Elses appear to parallel each other at a few important points. These I propose to investigate.

While in 1906 and 1907 Felix and Else were "working together" on the translation of the twelve-volume edition of the Arabian Nights, then considered very erotic and exotic, Else Lasker-Schüler was preparing and publishing her third book of poetry which she called *Die Nächte Tino von Bagdads* (The Nights of Tino of Bagdad). Clearly, if Felix and both Elses profited from the strong oriental vogue in Berlin—which had increased since the 1896 Berlin Colonial Exposition with its large-scale reproductions of Cairo and the pyramids in the suburb of Treptow (even the waterworks, still surviving, were built in the shape of a mosque)—then Lasker-Schüler drew on the same vogue that enabled her to take unheard-of liberties in her writing, clothing, and public behaviour. It was, after all, a period when the Near East was on the political agenda of several competing European nations and the Kaiser visited Turkey and Palestine to help enforce German claims (Berman).

There was also a more substantial contemporary European literary trend behind it all, coterminous with the political developments, not to mention the preceding almost three hundred years of German literary orientalism.[6] Before Felix and the two Elses—and contemporaneous with them—books with oriental themes and titles had been published to much public acclaim. Among these was the notable eccentric writer and designer Paul Scheerbart— a friend of Lasker-Schüler's—whose *Tarub, Bagdads berühmte Köchin* (Tarub, The Famous Cook of Bagdhad) was published in 1900 under the imprint of Greve's publisher J.C.C. Bruns (Martens, *Bruns* 72–73), also the publisher of the German translation of Gustave Flaubert's oriental extravaganza *Salammbô* (Martens, *F.P. Grove* 211). Better known to a larger reading audience than Scheerbart was the successful novelist Helene Böhlau. She had married a German gentleman, an engineer working in Turkey, who had assumed a Turkish name. After their divorce, she gleefully continued to appear in public in the appropriate costumes (and continued to sign herself) as "Madame Al-Rashid Bey" (Martens, *Bruns* 54–55). Madame Al-Rashid Bey was the only long-time, bestselling author of the J.C.C. Bruns firm. An eclectic, often biblically-based Orientalism was the order of the day also among other turn-of-the-century artists, from Oscar Wilde to Aubrey Beardsley, in their treatment of the Salome theme. (Greve translated Wilde's *Salomé* and owned a set of Beardsley's drawings).

To be precise: "Orientalism" was increasingly the preferred and pointedly ambivalent mode of public commitment to their heritage on the part of writers and artists of Jewish descent. "Oriental" vaguely denoted both anything Jewish as well as anything from Palestine and the rest of the Arabic

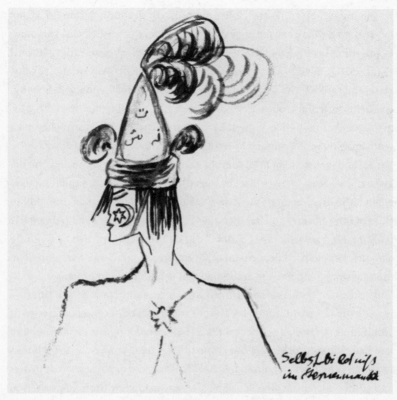

FIGURE 16: Else Lasker-Schüler. Else Lasker-Schüler's drawing of herself as "Prince Yussuf" ("Selbstbildnis im Sternenmantel"). Schiller Nationalmuseum, Deutsches Literaturarchiv, Marbach Germany.

Near East. Else Lasker-Schüler, driven out of Nazi Germany in 1934, settled in Jerusalem. Karl Wolfskehl—Stefan George's most ardent and gifted disciple, and, for a time, a friend of Felix and Else's—was Jewish and proud to be called an "Oriental Dionysos" because of his impressive beard and wide, loosely-hanging clothing (Hoerschelmann 128). Hugo von Hofmannsthal, Else Greve's would-be mentor, likewise loved his oriental designs and clothing. The "orient" in Lasker-Schüler's poems remains, as in Scheerbart's work, an imaginary, a composite place of the imagination, often used, on the one hand, against the then current mood and tone of an increasingly tired aestheticism and, on the other, against the still strong naturalist modes of writing (also practised by Greve in his two novels).

From 1907, Else Lasker-Schüler, then almost destitute, began offsetting her real threadbare existence by assuming an imaginary oriental persona.[7] Using the title employed for her book of poetry, she began calling herself "Tino of Baghdad" (later assuming the name of fictive oriental royalty, "Yussuf, Prince of Thebes") and flamboyantly appeared in public in flowing, colourful "oriental" robes of her own invention, painting her face with half-moons and other devices as well as the Star of David and covering her head with amazing gear designed by herself. Lasker-Schüler, in short, was living her art and incorporating it, becoming herself the work of art she had made. Twelve years later, Greve's Else, by then the Baroness, used a similar method when she turned herself into a work of art called dadaist. She too—in her state of utter poverty and dereliction—tailored her clothes and painted her body, making it speak out (Gammel, "Body Talk"). She turned herself into a risqué, almost parodic, ornament, becoming ornamental, a version of an oriental statement, like the arabesque that is both text and ornament.

If the Baroness was sometimes forced to shun New York's finest— leaping "from patrol wagons with such agility that policemen let her go in admiration" (Naumann, *New York Dada* 169)—in Berlin, Else Lasker-Schüler had had similar problems. Poor "Tino of Baghdad" stole occasional books from her (and Greve's) publisher Axel Juncker's bookstore and the owner had somebody chase after her. She always escaped by timing her theft in such a way that she could jump on the platform of a passing tram, sticking out her tongue at her pursuers (Lasker-Schüler II 524–25).[8] One is reminded of the Baroness's poverty-induced thefts and near-arrests in Greenwich Village.

———

IT BECOMES CLEAR that before the Great War both Elses moved in overlapping circles of the Berlin literati and publishers and followed the same trends. They were subject to similar influences and they had emancipated themselves to follow independent careers as women writers. Orientalism and *Die Frauenfrage*—the issue of women's liberation—were closely allied. The oriental costume, the oriental ornament, and the oriental name made a defiant statement. The bearer begged to differ, and not at all humbly. A woman in oriental costume proclaimed her independence of the ruling, paternally structured, culture. Her allegiance was to an imaginary realm of the imagination, transcending drab everyday reality and the limits imposed on the female sex.[9] It was a way of going to extremes in order to carve out a place for themselves.

The most famous predecessors and older contemporaries of both "misbehaving" Elses were—in addition to Madame Al-Rashid Bey—such famous and politically influential German fighters for the emancipation of women as Helene Lange and Helene Stöcker, then much in the public eye (Peterfy 44–45). Among other European women writers published in the circles in which Felix and Else moved was Marguerite Vallette (1860–1953). She was the wife of Gide's publisher, Alfred Vallette, and wrote under the pen-name Rachilde. Before that, she had been known as "Mlle. Baudelaire." She may have been another model, prolific, eccentric, and self-confident (Martens, *Bruns* 109–11). These women writers were unconventional also in their private lives: they left their parents' houses early; they declined to follow lives laid out for them by others; and they entered into relationships with or married men of their own choice and divorced them when they felt that the independence they praised and had fought for was threatened. All of these were championed by Greve's publisher Bruns. They probably would not have escaped Else's attention.

On her part, Else Lasker-Schüler, poor and acting independently, combined both outlandish elegance and literary activity. She was the outstanding example of the self-made literary woman, holding court in one of Berlin's most famous literary hangouts, the *Café des Westens*. She presented herself in public as a pied-piper of the movement. To sum up: both Lasker-Schüler and "the Greves" had a stake in literary orientalism. They shared publishers (Juncker and Oesterheld). They may have known of each other, after all, for both Elses had worked as illustrators. We still do not know enough of the period 1906–1908 they spent in Berlin to confirm or reject the possibility. Lasker-Schüler's very public example may have helped, directly or indirectly, to tailor EFL as a person and author.

As an author, the Baroness may have profited from the orientalism in setting, mood and reference found in Lasker-Schüler's poems. Indeed, the lines of a 1918 poem by the Baroness, then still explicitly identifying herself

FIGURE 17: Else Lasker-Schüler with flute, 1909–10. Schiller Nationalmuseum,
Deutsches Literaturarchiv, Marbach Germany.

by her less-than-flamboyant German first name—"Else von Freytag von [sic] Loringhoven"—are as conventionally orientalistic as anything by Lasker-Schüler:

Mefk Maru Mustir Daas

The sweet corners of thine mouth   Mustir
So world-old tired   tired to nobility
To more   to shame   to hatred of thineself
So noble souled   so weak a body
Thine body is the prey of mice

And every day the corners of thine tired mouth   Mustir
Grow sweeter helpless   sneer the more despair
And bloody pale-red poison foams from them
At every noble thing   to kill thine soul
Because thine body is the prey of mice
And dies so slowly

So noble is thine tired soul   Mustir
She cannot help to mourn out of thine eyes
Thine eyelids   nostrils   pallor of thine cheek
To mourn upon the curving of thine lip
Upon the crystal of thine pallid ear
To beg forgiveness with flashing smile
Like amber-coloured honey

The sweet corners of thine tired mouth   Mustir
Undo thine sin.   Thine pain is killed in play
Thine body's torture stimulates in play
And silly little bells of perfect tune
Ring in thine throat
Thou art a country devasted   bare   Mustir
Exhausted soil with sandy trembling hills
 No food   no water   and ashamed of it
Thou shiver   and an amber-yellow sun

Goes down the horizon
Thou art desert with mirages which drive the mind insane
To walk   and die   a-starving.

The poem, in its orientalism, not only recalls Lasker-Schüler, but is also as vaguely oriental as Felix Paul Greve's poems in his 1902 volume *Wanderungen* with their *fin-de-siècle* sensibility, undetermined desert settings, and ominous atmosphere (Martens, *F.P. Grove* 72–73). Only the title is mildly anticipatory of the Baroness's later American poems, apparently a somewhat oriental sounding name but also partly homophonically allusive to German words and phrases (*Müsst ihr das?*). Apart from the poem's curious title, fragments of which are repeated throughout the text, there is little of the European Dada poets' *Lautgedichte* (sound poems) of the kind written by Hugo Ball (Döhl 734). In addition, considering the vague oriental references shared with Greve's early poetry, the possibility cannot be discounted that the poem is indeed a look back over her shoulder at her former companion's poems she called "wellcut gems of languagejuggling." In the memoir written for Djuna Barnes, she would indirectly identify her former lover Greve as desert-like when she called him "infertile within himself" (Hjartarson and Spettigue 162, 119). Addressing "Mustir" as a "country devasted bare" in her first poem in *The Little Review*, she also seems to describe the very young F.P. Greve whom she had first met a few months after the publication of his volume of poems with vaguely oriental or African settings. In this context, incidentally, the German hidden in the title of Freytag-Loringhoven's New York "Mustir" poem sounds like a rueful look back: *Müsst ihr das?* (Do you have to?). The somewhat macaronic linguistic method the Baroness employed in the poem just quoted is not far removed from the striking linguistic liberties Lasker-Schüler took in some of her writings, occasionally assuming an "*Ursprache*" (Ur-language) she claimed to have rediscovered and which, she suggested, had been "spoken in the time of King Saul, the Royal Wild Jew." I quote an excerpt:

Elbanaff:
Min salihihi wali kinahu
Rahi hatiman
fi is bahi lahu fassun—

Min hagas assama anadir
Wakan liachad abtal
Latina almu lijádina binassre... (Lasker-Schüler II, 520–21)

This linguistic concoction of pseudo-Latin, pseudo-Arabic, some German and pure fun indeed resembles texts by Ball, Huelsenbeck, Schwitters and other German dadaists of the 1910s and 20s, including Freytag-Loringhoven's own part-English, part-German and occasionally invented language in her later poems, written after 1918.

Just as Else Lasker-Schüler wrote and performed the colourful "Ur-language" of her own making under her assumed names "Tino von Baghdad" and "Prince Yussuf of Thebes," one ought not to be surprised that the Baroness also first submitted the "Mefk Maru Mustir Dass" poem under the oriental-sounding pseudonym "Tara Osrik" (Hjartarson, "Of Greve" 271). "Tara Osrik," indeed, sounds like a name from the deserts of Tartary. Another poem by the Baroness in the "oriental" mode to follow was her "Klink-Hratzvenga (Deathwail): Narin-Tzarissamanili (He is dead!)." Apparently, the oriental colouring was known to her and came easily to her at this early period of her American career. While Else Lasker-Schüler developed her "Ur-language," oriental poems, and colourful personal appearance in Berlin, Felix Paul Greve, having already translated Wilde's play *Salomé*, translated and published André Gide's little play *Saül*, dealing with exactly that "King Saul, the Royal Wild Jew" Lasker-Schüler had in mind when making up her very own pseudo-ancient linguistics. These, then, were some of the experiences she had had and the influences that acted upon Else Greve in Germany, helping her, in New York, to form her public Dada persona as the Baroness, beginning where she had left off in Berlin, with the Oriental mode.

◆ Conclusion

AS A PROMINENT FIGURE in New York Dada and Surrealist circles of painters, poets, photographers, and sculptors, the Baroness Elsa used and further developed the roles and patterns of artistic and public appearance and behaviour she had first adopted in her youth spent as a professional actress in theatrical performances in Berlin and Cottbus. Later, as the companion and wife of Felix Paul Greve, she moved in the circles of writers and artists in Munich and Berlin.

Inferred first appearances as a member of the cast at the Berlin *Central-Theater*, in 1896-97, do not prove, I believe, that young Else had been a kind of *demi-monde*. The Berlin *Central-Theater* was no Montmartre cabaret, luridly lighted, with scantily clad girls available in *chambres separées*. It was, on the contrary, a well known playhouse of solidly bourgeois reputation. Occasional appearances on that stage, surrounded by a large cast of dancers and actors, in the light comedies and farces of the day, would have taught her the function, the value and the techniques of parody and satire as well as the effects of the distortion of the familiar on an audience. She learned, in short, the tricks of the actor's trade. She would also have learned to consciously use and recognise body language. The young and inexperienced girl from the Baltic coast of Pomerania would have used rehearsals and public performances in Berlin and—under the expert direction of Walden—in Cottbus, to acquire self-confidence in the public display of unusual dress and undress. To some degree, the typical dadaist's "power of deceit," mentioned by Hugo Ball, the delight in "any kind of mask," was prefigured for the Baroness in her early acquisition of the skills of the professional actor.

Moreover, had she appeared in a chorus line, for which I have seen no hard evidence, she would by no means have been regarded as a sexually pioneering woman in the forefront of the impending sexual revolution. No Caroline Meeber, she might have been in danger of being abused like many of her young female colleagues of the stage. First exposure to the public as one of many dancing girls, however, might have taught her to be free from stage fright and to develop a degree of ease in the handling of masks and costumes for the stage and, possibly, of a male audience eager to take her out. Whatever the real sexual adventures of young Else Plötz may have been, they would not have been out of the ordinary for a young girl cast out into the world of the capital city and the provincial centers. The bohemian life among young and still not very well-known artists and writers gathering, say, at the Berlin "Wintergarten," *alone* would not have been sufficient to prepare her for the role of the very public heroine of the New York *bohème*, playing the leading role in an artistically rendered version of her life.

When the Baroness, in her memoir, attacked the German dadaist Kurt Schwitters and accused him of a "lack of flourish," she certainly perceived the lack of a crucial actorly quality she herself had mastered from early on. She did not criticise the other artist in terms of aesthetic difference or even difference of method or school. By criticising Schwitters in the terms she did, she identified salient characteristics of her own public performances (shared with Lasker-Schüler), her panache and flamboyance.

It appears that in her *acting* days at the *Central-Theater* in Berlin and the *Stadttheater Goldener Ring* in Cottbus, she had had ample occasion to study at first hand the crucial difference between the techniques of "low" and "high" culture, as exemplified in low comedy, farce and extravaganza on the one hand, and the plays of the modern "classics" of high culture on the other, that were both part of Walden's program. Popular low-comedy theater often profits from the caricature or parody of cultured manners, and it exploits folk characters and folk speech. Folk speech in low comedy flaunts the ungrammatical, indulges in misquotation and gleefully foregrounds "misunderstandings" of "high faluting" speech and manners of polite society. Parody in farce and low comedy subverts the pretensions of high culture. Some of these lessons learned during her acting days in Germany she put to good use in New York.

When we contemplate the Baroness's walking the streets of Greenwich Village, wearing "an inverted coal-scuttle" on her head and "metal tea-balls" as ear-pendants (Reiss 86), we cannot but notice that there is a good deal of able performance in this act containing, on the part of the spectators, hoped for "feats of association." In fact, the New York street now appears to supplant the German stage she knew, the street becoming "a 'scene' or a stage for dramatising the self as a performer" (Poirier 90, 86). Apart from this, in low comedy, the Baroness's curious dress and ornaments, a kind of "disguise," also might be regarded as a theatrical parody of the common housewife's lot *and* as a parody of the urge for costly dress and ornamentation of the conservative, moneyed ladies of society.

Not only Else Greve's and Else Lasker-Schüler's taste for flamboyant public display and role-playing, but also the early Expressionist's linguistic experimentation were essential for preparing Else for the New York Baroness's presentation of experimental language poetry, her version of both Lasker-Schüler's and the other dadaist's creation of one's own "Ur-Language." This language—in Lasker-Schüler, Kurt Schwitters, and the Baroness herself—had to be comically ungrammatical to offend, to provoke, to subvert by doing violence to accepted linguistic standards, that is, the notion of "right speaking" as a mark of traditional high culture and its received notions of poetry and art. To what degree the Baroness's rejection of more traditional modes of poetry and prose—as practised, for instance, by FPG in Germany and Canada—and her resumption of techniques learnt from the German *avant-garde* poetry of Lasker-Schüler, perhaps also profited from the linguistic conventions of German theater's low comedy, farce, and folk-play needs to be investigated further.

Thus the Baroness, as an outstanding artist personality in New York Dada and Surrealism, may primarily be seen as from an early date preparing for, and then sharing in, crucial aspects of the Modernist project. Finally, we can now fix the date and the occasion that set her on the road towards that impressive achievement. Back in Cottbus, while beginning, in September 1897, as one lowly member of Director Walden's acting troupe, she publicly changed her name from sober and girlish "Else" to glamorous "Elsa" of Wagnerian operatic fame. At this point, she began to make over and heighten her everyday self into an evolving extraordinary new ego, a role to be further developed and a life to be chosen. By once again assuming her German stage name "Elsa" in America, she also again highlights not only the inter-action between high and low culture but the progress from an old to a new order in the arts, with the flamboyant performance becoming reality until we, the audience, become unable to tell the *danceuse* from the dance, and the actress from her act.

NOTES

1   This article profits from Paul Hjartarson's discovery of the papers of Else von Freytag-Loringhoven (1986) and his edition, with D.O. Spettigue, of these papers (1992). Also, Cary Nelson's work on the subject was consulted. In addition, I wish to acknowledge Irene Gammel's recent work on this subject (see Works Cited).

2   "The European Art Invasion" is the term Davidson uses in his article in Naumann and Venn's catalogue, *Making Mischief: Dada Invades New York*.

3   Quoted from p. 3–4 of an undated letter to Djuna Barnes, apparently written while Freytag-Loringhoven was still in Berlin, before moving to Paris. I thank the Archives & Manuscript Department of the University of Maryland's McKeldin Library for permission to quote.

4   EFL may, for instance, have been aware that she was providing Barnes with material that the American writer might one day use for her own purposes. Speculations regarding the sources for Felix Volkbein in Barnes's novel *Nightwood*, for instance, were based on Barnes's possible use of the material provided by the Baroness.

5   This is suggested by a reference to a lost manuscript much applauded by the poet and dramatist Hugo von Hofmannsthal who praises a friend of his, a lady translator, who had previously participated in Bruns's Flaubert edition, "Else Greve," in short (Martens *F.P. Grove* 216). Hofmannsthal may have been uninformed of the titular role as translator Greve had caused to be bestowed on Else for legal reasons.

6   Edward Said's (and others') criticism of orientalism, pertinent as it is to the larger question, is not an issue discussed in my paper. A view both more detailed and general, profitable as it may be, is beyond the scope of the present investigation. Regarding German literary orientalism also see my discussion of Friedrich Schlegel and the "arabesque novel" (Martens, *Antinomische Imagination* 128–31).

7   I owe many of the details of Lasker-Schüler's fascinating life and work (as well as a first acquaintance with her drawings) to Sigrid Bauschinger's excellent biography of the poet.

8   Lasker-Schüler's next publisher, Oesterheld, confessed his impecuniousness during their first interview. Oesterheld published Gide's *Saül* in Felix Greve's translation.

9   The "oriental" as a way of escape into the realm of the imaginary also figures prominently elsewhere. Edward Said, for instance, points to Charlotte Bronte's *Jane Eyre* and the heroine's love of the *Arabian Nights* (271).

PART II

FPG
and the Politics of Cultural Mediation

"Il me faut forger une arme de la littérature"

Felix Paul Greve among the Magazines

IN HIS CORRESPONDENCE with André Gide, the German-born author and translator Felix Paul Greve, who later took on a new identity as the Canadian Frederick Philip Grove, succinctly stated that his ultimate goal in life was influence. As his family background, contrary to Gide's, did not allow him to rely on what he considered the most effective means to this end, financial wealth, he had to look for an alternate agency to exert power. This he hoped to find in literature. Writing to Gide in June of 1904, he declares: "L'influence: c'est ça, ce que je souhaite [...]. Je crois l'influence de la vie supérieure à celle de la littérature. [...] La richesse serait une arme admirable. Maintenant il me faut forger une arme de la littérature. Mais le but—c'est la vie" (Ernst and Martens 69–70).[1] Greve became a prolific mediator, translating, among others, Oscar Wilde, H.G. Wells, George Meredith, Gustave Flaubert, and André Gide into German, all the while trying to produce and promote his own works. In this context, periodicals played an important role.

Felix Paul Greve's first publications comprised a review of Stendhal's novel *Lucien Leuwen*, newly released by the French publishing house Éditions de la Revue Blanche, and a commentary on volumes eleven and twelve of Friedrich Nietzsche's complete works. Both appeared in 1901 in the supplement to the Munich *Allgemeine Zeitung*, a renowned daily newspaper that had been founded by Johann Friedrich Cotta at the end of the eighteenth century (Schwarzkopf 1, 16). Greve lived in Munich at that time, pursuing his studies, while attempting, ultimately, to become a writer. That Greve knew the supplement to the *Allgemeine Zeitung* and tried to enter its pages was probably related to the fact that it reprinted the news of the German Archaeological Institute in Rome (Schwarzkopf n.p., 107, 120), where Greve had stayed in early 1901, and that Professor Adolf Furtwängler, Greve's university teacher in archaeology (Martens, *Felix Paul* 116–19), was a regular contributor. With his first review, Felix Paul Greve introduced himself as a connoisseur of French language and literature, especially of its realistic tendencies, which were to become important for his own later writings in Germany and Canada. For the time being, however, Greve renounced these interests and turned to a different, more promising kind of literature to gain him access into the artistic circles of Munich. His second start, so to speak, began with aestheticism, the other end of the range of literary tendencies flowering at the turn of the century, and was prepared for through his commentary on Nietzsche.

In this reorientation Greve might have been influenced by a fellow student of archaeology, Karl Gustav Vollmoeller, who also tried to establish himself as a writer and who, since 1897, had enjoyed close contacts with the poet Stefan George and his circle (Kluncker 33; Martens, *Felix Paul* 48, 77). For George, personal relations were of uppermost importance; as a rule, he only accepted contributions for the circle's magazine, *Blätter für die Kunst*, from artists he or one of his close friends knew in person (Kluncker 29). Thus Greve had to take his time and work his way into the coterie. In August 1902, Greve thought the time ripe to hand in seven poems to be considered for publication in George's *Blätter* (Divay lxi),[2] but his attempt at placing himself in the exclusive magazine proved unsuccessful. Greve, it is true, did fulfill one of the prerequisites of appearing in the *Blätter*, namely the one of not yet being identified with an existing literary group (Kluncker 52). Nonetheless, George was in favour of larger contributions that might reveal the author's artistic specificity, especially in the case of first appearances in the *Blätter*. The material submitted by Greve failed to meet this criterion, as George pointed out in a postcard to Friedrich Gundolf, who since 1900, in close cooperation with George, had been responsible for the *Blätter*'s editorial correspondence (Kluncker 51, 63–64).[3]

But even if Greve's contributions had appeared in the *Blätter für die Kunst*, it seems doubtful that such a publication would have served to gain him wide renown. George's *Blätter* was an atypical magazine insofar as it did not reach out for a receptive public audience that might enjoy its contributions; rather, it addressed itself to poets who worked in a similar vein and would be interested in becoming members of the circle (Kluncker 22, 26, 46).[4] Accordingly, the *Blätter für die Kunst* could not be obtained through the booksellers but had to be subscribed to or consulted in select bookstores in Berlin, Vienna, and Munich where they were on display (Kluncker 62–63).[5] Although from 1898 onwards, the George circle opened itself more to the public, releasing selections from the *Blätter* in a general edition (Kluncker 34), it remained an exclusive group that stood apart from the literary market and that followed its own mechanisms.

Paramount was the intricate relation between literature and the poet's financial situation. Not only did the ideal member of the circle renounce a professional life in order to concentrate on his art, he also avoided publishing in other magazines and reserved his creative energy for the George circle. His contributions to the *Blätter* were not remunerated; on the contrary, he had to pay for the printing costs (Kluncker 53, 60–61). Even if, in the beginning, financial aspects might have been of minor importance to Greve, as he was still receiving a fellowship from Hamburg and could count on the support of his friend Herman F.C. Kilian (Martens, *Felix Paul* 126, 146), they were soon to gain prominence and affect his further career, for he did not enjoy the financial independence of a George.

At any rate, Greve saw his relation to the George circle not as an end in itself, but also as an investment in his future. Close ties to George, he hoped, would impress the publishers and ease his way into print. This can be inferred from his letter of December 1901 to the Hamburg publisher Alfred Janßen, in which he offers the manuscript of his poems *Wanderungen* and points to his exclusive connection.[6] Janßen, however, showed no interest and Greve had to look for an alternative means of publication. With George as his example, he took recourse to a private printing that mirrored the master's products in more than one sense. Just like the *Blätter für die Kunst*, Greve's *Wanderungen* was produced by the Berlin printing house Otto von Holten and could be obtained through the Munich commissioned publishers Jacob Littauer (Kluncker 63).

The George circle's impact on Felix Paul Greve may equally be noticed in another context. Under the influence of the French symbolists, who, at the end of the nineteenth century, rendered international masterpieces into their mother tongue, George and his friends came to value mediation as an important task in their literary careers. Consequently, in George's oeuvre translations amount to approximately the same percentage of publications as his own works; the same holds true for his contributions to the *Blätter für die Kunst* (Kluncker 88). Even if his own prolificacy as a translator forestalled the publication of translations by other members of his circle in the *Blätter* (Kluncker 90), most of them also worked as translators. In this respect, too, Greve lived up to the circle's habits, rendering into German Dante's *Vita Nuova*, Walter Pater's "A Prince of Court Painters" and *Marius the Epicurean*, Robert Browning's "A Blot in the 'Scutcheon" and "In a Balcony" (Divay 219–20; Martens, *Felix Paul* 372; Pacey, *Letters* 520) and starting his translations of the works of Oscar Wilde.[7] However, having failed to have a selection of his poetry printed in the *Blätter für die Kunst*, Greve realized that he had to look for new alliances, if he were to permanently secure a foothold in the literary market.

His attempts at establishing connections and thus furthering his own cause were facilitated by a procedure that Maximilian Harden, editor of *Die Zukunft*, had introduced. Harden invited authors and translators to submit so-called "Selbstanzeigen," that is, short abstracts of their latest works to be published in his magazine under a rubric of their own. From 1902 onward, when he announced his volume of poetry *Wanderungen*, Greve made ample use of this opportunity to draw the attention of readers and publishers to his productions. As Harden allotted enough space for the self-reviews, they were sometimes turned into more extensive discussions. Greve's self-review of his translation of Oscar Wilde's *The Picture of Dorian Gray*, published in 1903, is a case in point. Having been able to interest J.C.C. Bruns publishers in Oscar Wilde's *Intentions*, Greve sought to enlarge his Wilde project and proposed a new German rendition of *Dorian Gray*. Johannes Gaulke's version, which had appeared under the auspices of Max Spohr in Leipzig, was inadequate in Greve's eyes and illustrated nothing more than the necessity of a new translation. For a critical evaluation of Gaulke's text and a defence of his own new translation Greve counted on an article of his entitled "Übersetzungen aus dem Englischen," which was supposed to appear in July 1902 in the supplement to the Munich *Allgemeine Zeitung*. For still unknown reasons, however, the article failed to be published. This was all the more embarrassing to Greve as he referred to this article in the preface to his *Dorian Gray* in order not to repeat himself and to cut his argument short (V). Given this predicament, Greve decided to use the self-review of his *Dorian Gray* in *Die*

Zukunft to explain the state of affairs and supply some of the reasons that he had meant to give in the unpublished article.

Apart from the self-reviews, and as a second opportunity to prove his artistic talent, Greve relied on the publication of excerpts from his works, sometimes accompanied by an explanatory comment. Thus, on 29 November 1902 Greve wrote to J.C.C. Bruns asking whether they would consent to the inclusion of half a chapter of his translation of Wilde's *Dorian Gray* in a magazine. A few days later, Greve specified that he had the *Neue Deutsche Rundschau* in mind (Martens, *Felix Paul* 334–35), a periodical founded in 1890 by Otto Brahm under the title *Freie Bühne für modernes Leben* and connected with the renowned publishing house S. Fischer (Dietzel and Hügel 2: 441–43).[8] Again, Greve's friend Karl Gustav Vollmoeller might have served as the connective link, since he also contributed to the *Neue Deutsche Rundschau*.[9] Although Greve's engagement with this magazine has been known for years, its influence on his career has so far been underestimated. Even if Greve's idea of including a chapter of his translation of Wilde's *Dorian Gray* in the *Neue Deutsche Rundschau* did not materialize for the simple reason that another translator's version was chosen,[10] Greve continued to offer his texts to the editor, Oscar Bie. The latter not only published Greve's translation of James McNeill Whistler's "Ten O' Clock" but also Oscar Wilde's "Lehren und Sprüche für die reifere Jugend," which, from internal evidence, is attributable to Greve.[11] It is a slightly abbreviated, but otherwise identical version of Greve's translation of Wilde's "Phrases and Philosophies for the Use of the Young," of which, in May 1902, 150 copies had been privately printed by J. Gotteswinter, Munich, and sold on commission by J. Littauer Kunsthandlung. As most of the translations in the *Neue Deutsche Rundschau* remained unsigned, it is even possible that Greve translated additional texts for this periodical. One might speculate that another contribution from late 1903 or early 1904 was by Greve. From his correspondence with Rudolf von Poellnitz, it is clear that one of Greve's translations of Wilde's fairy tales had been accepted by this magazine, but at the last instant the text could not be printed because von Poellnitz, in whose Insel Verlag the complete book of fairy tales was to appear, objected to its publication. Greve, who had already dispatched the tale, informed von Poellnitz that he would try to prevent its printing and have the magazine fill the lacuna with something else (Pacey, *Letters* 534–35). The unsigned translation of aphorisms by George Meredith that appeared in the fourth quarter of 1903 is a likely candidate for such a substitution. This probability is enhanced by the fact that in his *Freistatt* article on Meredith, published in September 1904, Greve refers to a few trifles by the British author that he, Greve, had published in translation in magazines.[12]

Although his business relation to the *Neue Deutsche Rundschau* brought Greve into contact with S. Fischer, nothing permanent came of this connection. Only Greve's translation of the correspondence of Robert Browning and Elizabeth Barrett-Barrett appeared under Fischer's auspices in 1905, prepared for by two long excerpts that appeared in the publishing house's own magazine in 1904.[13] As his letters to André Gide reveal, Greve felt offended by S. Fischer, having been treated "comme le premier venu" ("like anybody"), with the result that he considered taking him to court (Ernst and Martens 74, 134). In 1907, Greve still felt the impact of his quarrel with S. Fischer and the *Neue Deutsche Rundschau*, for when editor Oscar Bie wished to include a text by André Gide in his periodical, he ignored Greve's good standing with the French author, contacted Gide directly and proposed Kurt Singer as a possible translator.[14] Discovering Singer's German version of Gide's *Le Retour de l'enfant prodigue* in *Die Neue Rundschau*, Greve, quite understandably, felt frustrated. In his letter of 25 April 1907 he reminded Gide of his promise according to which Greve was to be his only German translator (Ernst and Martens 164). Gide, however, in his dealings with Oscar Bie, had made sure to preserve Greve's interests; he refused to grant *Die Neue Rundschau* exclusive rights so that the text in question would remain in the author's possession allowing Gide to cede the German translation rights again for a book publication.[15] The publishing house Oesterheld, where Greve's translations of Gide's tractates were to appear, nevertheless rejected the insertion of a new German version of *Le Retour de l'enfant prodigue* in the proposed volume precisely because Singer's translation had already appeared in *Die Neue Rundschau*.[16]

This negative experience had been preceded a few years before by an equally distressing occurrence. While working on the translation of André Gide's *Les Nourritures terrestres*, Greve, again, wished to include part of his translation in a magazine and accordingly wrote to Gide:

Pour "hausser" l'intérêt, qui se portera vers vos livres, il me semble habile de publier quelques pages (quelque chose de ciselé) dans un journal. Malheureusement, pour le moment il n'y a pour moi que la "Freistatt."—Toutefois on lit ce journal. Il me semble qu'un auteur comme vous ne perd rien en apparaissant dans un journal secondaire qui néanmoins compte parmi ses collaborateurs quelques écrivains de premier ordre. (Ernst and Martens 78)[17]

The magazine *Freistatt* Greve had in mind was a Munich-based weekly of politics, literature, and art edited by Alexander Freiherr von Bernus and Friedrich Glaser (Dietzel and Hügel 3: 831–32). In 1904, it seems to have been the only magazine that was not afraid to publish the contributions of a man whose name was associated with fraud and jail (Martens, *Felix Paul* 209–21). Gide obviously applauded the procedure but disapproved of the second-rate *Freistatt*, for in his next letter Greve explained:

La revue la plus importante en Allemagne, je crois, c'est *Die Neue Rundschau*. Pour y insérer une partie des *Nourritures*, certainement il serait nécessaire de supprimer le nom du traducteur, parce que moi et M. Bruns, nous avons intenté un procès à M. S. Fischer. Mais si l'on passerait cette traduction d'une partie des Nourritures, ou plutôt cette partie de la traduction des Nourritures par les mains de M. Franz Blei?...Qu'est-ce que vous en dites? (Ernst and Martens 78–79)[18]

Taking up Greve's astonishing proposition, André Gide turned for help to Greve's literary rival, Franz Blei,[19] who then suggested placing the fragment "Menalkas" in Harden's *Zukunft* (Ernst and Martens 80; Theis 11–12). Greve wrote to Gide that in this case one might as well add his name, since Harden was to print a short notice by him on H.G. Wells, which would appear with his signature. Gide, who remained untroubled by Greve's past and was more than content with his translation, agreed to that suggestion (Ernst and Martens 82, 84). He left the decision to Franz Blei, however, and entrusted him to investigate Harden's standpoint in this matter (Theis 14). Ultimately, the translation appeared without Greve's name, which made some people attribute it to Franz Blei. Even worse in Greve's eyes, Maximilian Harden suggested that Greve could consider himself lucky that his translations were taken for Blei's (Theis 41). Greve did not value Blei's translations and even Gide admitted that Greve was the more talented of the two;[20] nevertheless,

Gide tried to convince Greve that he was at fault for blaming Blei alone, as it was Greve who first proposed to omit the translator's name and later wrote that one might add it, if Gide still wanted to.

Greve's rage was all the more extreme as he had had a similar experience with Blei in connection with his first Wilde translation. In July 1902, two months after the publication of Greve's *Lehren und Sprüche für die reifere Jugend*, an excerpt from his translation had anonymously figured in the magazine *Die Insel*. For the clarification of the translator's name, Franz Blei, in whose responsibility fell the compilation of the magazine's final numbers (Salzmann 590; Sarkowski 28), seemed to have relied on the review of Greve's translation that was to appear in the same issue. However, as Blei explained to Gide in December 1905, the review got lost and the Wilde excerpt appeared without any hint as to who its translator was (Theis 41–42). Just as in the case of the "Menalkas" episode three years later, Franz Blei was credited with the translation of the aphorisms,[21] especially since Blei had rendered into German some prose poems by Wilde that had been published in a preceeding number of the same magazine. Greve was reminded of that incident, for in April 1905, one month before the anonymous appearance of his "Menalkas" translation in *Die Zukunft*, Franz Blei had published in the magazine *Freistatt* new aphorisms by Oscar Wilde under the title "Neue Sprüche und Lehren" and around the same time had edited the second edition of his *In Memoriam Oscar Wilde*, which included "Lehren und Sprüche für die reifere Jugend von Oscar Wilde," translated by Franz Blei. As Greve complained to Gide, Blei indeed seemed to have used Greve's earlier efforts as the basis for his own new Wilde publications (Ernst and Martens 147).[22]

Although the rivalry with Blei might have been reason enough for Greve to stop contributing to the *Zukunft* and look for alternatives, a second motive made itself felt: Maximilian Harden was not in favour of André Gide and thus did not support the publication of his texts as wished by Greve.[23] When Greve wanted to promote his translation of Gide's *Saül* by publishing an excerpt in a magazine, he turned to Siegfried Jacobsohn's newly founded *Schaubühne* explaining to Gide that this is an excellent journal for affairs of the theatre (Ernst and Martens 160). The *Schaubühne* with its focus on the renewal of dramatic art[24] differed significantly from the broader *Zukunft*, but still there were close relations between the two. Maximilian Harden supported Jacobsohn in his publishing efforts, taking on the role of mentor

(Pross 72). It comes as no surprise, then, that in September 1905 we find an advertisement for the *Schaubühne* in Harden's *Zukunft*, which might have drawn Greve's attention and directed him to the new magazine. Greve's relation to the *Schaubühne* proved advantageous. Not only could he place two poems and a Gide translation in its pages,[25] he also benefited from Jacobsohn's business connections to Berlin publishing houses. Oesterheld & Co., which edited Jacobsohn's magazine from 1906 to 1908,[26] became the publisher of Greve's new Gide translations, *Ein Liebesversuch und andere Novellen* (1907). When in 1909 the *Schaubühne* changed its alliances to the publishing house Erich Reiss, Greve accompanied the magazine, offering to Reiss his translation of Gide's *Saül* and *La Porte étroite* as well as his rendition of Alexandre Dumas's *Le Comte de Monte-Cristo* (Martens, *Felix Paul* 288). All three of them appeared in 1909.

On closer inspection, Greve's publications in periodicals seem to have conformed to a specific pattern. He started out with reviews and self-reviews, followed by selections from his translated works. In the latter case, Greve's strategy was twofold. He tried to place in magazines excerpts from works for which he had already found a publisher, for example, for his translation of Wilde's *Dorian Gray*, which was to appear with J.C.C. Bruns. He also sought to interest publishing houses in printing full book-length translations of works he had so far only been able to sell in part for inclusion in magazines. Thus Greve drew the attention of Rudolf von Poellnitz to his Whistler translation, which had appeared in the *Neue Deutsche Rundschau*, proposing to release it in book form (Martens, *Felix Paul* 217). Von Poellnitz, however, showed no interest in this offer. From 1904 onward, Greve's contributions to periodicals became more diversified, with his own original works and literary criticism gaining ground. His publications in the magazine *Freistatt* illustrate this development. In June 1904, Greve's poem "Die Hexe" appeared in its pages, succeeded in the next nine months by three installments of poems from the pen of a certain Fanny Essler, a pseudonym probably comprised of Felix Paul Greve and his partner Else Endell.[27] Interspersed among these were Greve's translation of Robert Browning's "Cleon" (July 1904), an unsigned and so far overlooked translation of Algernon Charles Swinburne's "Phaedra" (February 1905), which Greve mentions in a letter of 1904 to Gide (Ernst and Martens 74), as well as an article on George Meredith (September 1904). The importance of the *Freistatt* for Greve's career is not restricted to the fact that it served him as a publishing outlet. In at least one case, it propelled him to new creative work. In September 1904, the *Freistatt* published a two-part article by August Endell on the Bavarian National Museum, in which Endell, the husband of Greve's lover Else, criticized the architecture of the building, the arrangement of the museum's collections, and some of its regulations. It is very likely that here we have the kernel for Greve's unpublished farce "Das Blutbad im bayrischen Nationalmuseum," which he mentioned in a letter to Gide and in his novel *Maurermeister Ihles Haus*.[28]

The strategic necessity of having one's name appear in magazines, if success in literary matters was one's aim, was so obvious to Greve that he planned to found his own periodical, scheduling the appearance of the first number for April 1906. He had a political and literary weekly in mind, "a sort of German 'Mercure de France,'" as he wrote to H.G. Wells (Martens, *Felix Paul* 252), which was to be called "Einundzwanzigstes Jahrhundert." Outlining his plans to Gide in the late summer of 1905, Greve described the literary scope of the journal as international, with contributors coming from all nations and to include the French writer himself. For publicity and propaganda, Greve counted on his novel *Fanny Essler*, which, he was sure, would make a stir, and not only in the artistic circles it depicted (Ernst and Martens 128, 138). Eventually, though, Greve had to abandon his plans of founding his own periodical because he could not secure the funding for such a venture. A few years later, still seeking independence from his publishers, he envisioned the founding of his own publishing house. "Dans deux ans je serai éditeur moi-même,"[29] he wrote to André Gide on 11 December 1908 and the next day he signed his letter to Gide with the words "F.P. Greve futur éditeur" ("F.P. Greve future publisher") (Ernst and Martens 181–82). But neither in Germany nor later in Canada would Greve be able to realize these plans.

Traditionally, literary magazines have served as the major marketplace in the literary system, providing authors with opportunities to establish contacts with critics, editors, and publishing houses that, in the best case, could lead to life-long associations and secure permanent influence. In the case of Greve, however, not everything ran as smoothly as desired. His editors denied him the esteem he longed for and the public, although fond of his translations, did not appreciate his own literary works. Greve's disillusionment is clearly expressed in a letter to Gide of 1907:

> Ça durera encore environ 10 ans, avant d'être débarrassé de mes dettes.
> Et alors? Alors la vie commencera. Le succès? Mais je n'y compte plus.
> Je me suis défait de mes illusions. Le travail, voilà tout. Force de travail
> je gagne, je "fais" vingt mille marks par an. On commence à me lire:
> eh bien, peut-être ça raccourcira un peu la période du travail: peut-
> être, mais je n'y compte plus. Je fais des livres, comme le cordonnier
> fait des bottes. La vie? C'est "Wirken", je ne sais pas le mot français.
> On ne peut pas "wirken" par des livres. On "wirkt" par l'argent. C'est
> ma théorie, du moins. (Ernst and Martens 161, 163)[30]

In 1904, Greve still hoped that even without financial wealth he might be of influence and thus partake in what to him was the epitome of life. Literature seemed a passable weapon in the struggle for prominence and recognition. In 1907, however, Greve regarded literature basically as a means of earning his livelihood and paying off his debts. The literary success that might have resulted in the opportunity to exert power had faded into the distance because the circumstances Greve found himself in allowed only for craftsmanship, not artistry.

In the long run, the negative experiences undergone in Germany taught Greve not to rely exclusively on the production of literature as a means of income after he had established himself in Canada. As he explained to Raymond Knister on 26 April 1929:

> Let us not forget that 'Art for art's sake' is nonsense. It is very hard to
> explain briefly just what I mean. But I may say that I have made it a
> rule to make what money I need by other activities rather than by
> writing. [...] I have recently been attacked in an unfair way: Grove
> himself fights for money, it was said; why else autograph books in
> bookstores; why lecture from coast to coast? Well, exactly; I lecture
> because I can make a few pennies that way without selling my
> writing. (Pacey, *Letters* 267)[31]

And in a postscript he adds: "Balzac and Scott—two great geniuses who scattered their unique talents by writing for money at a feverish rate" (267). This, no doubt, may be taken as a very elucidating comment on his own literary career in Germany, a career that, in the end, did not yield the influence he had hoped for.[32]

NOTES

1 "Influence, this is what I desire. I consider the influence of life superior to that of literature. Wealth would be an admirable weapon. Now I have to forge a weapon from literature. But the final goal is life." All translations are the author's own.

2 Greve wrote to Karl Wolfskehl, an influential member of the George circle, in order to inquire about the time frame for sending manuscripts: "Ich möchte Sie fragen, wann ich wohl an Herrn George Manuscr. schicken muss, wenn ich Aussicht haben will, dass das eine oder andere Verslein von mir in die Bl[ätter] kommt. Mir würde *sehr* viel daran liegen" ("I would like to ask you when I would have to send a manuscript to Mr. George in order to have a chance of seeing one or the other little poem of mine appear in the Bl[ätter]. This would mean *very* much to me") (Divay lxv).

3 George's words were "F.P.G. sandte auch! doch zu wenig um als einführungsbeitrag zu gelten" ("F.P.G. sent something as well! but too little to serve as introductory contribution") (Boehringer and Landmann 120).

4 Thus we may read in the introduction to the first number of the *Blätter*: "wenn wir diese blätter verbreiten so geschieht es um zerstreute noch unbekannte ähnlichgesinnte zu entdecken und anzuwerben" ("when we distribute these pages, it is done to uncover and recruit dispersed and still unknown like-minded people") (Kluncker 26).

5 These were Behr's bookstore in Berlin, Leopold Weiss in Vienna, and Littauer's Kunstsalon in Munich, which, in 1896, had substituted Léon Vanier's bookstore in Paris.

6 "Der Verfasser des mit gleicher Post an Sie abgehenden Manuscriptes, in Hamburg beheimatet, steht dem Münchener Kreise der 'Blätter für die Kunst' nahe" ("The author of the manuscript dispatched to you under the same cover, a resident of Hamburg, is closely associated with the Munich circle 'Blätter für die Kunst'") (Martens, *Felix Paul* 319). Greve equally referred to the George circle when he wrote his first letter to the publishing house J.C.C. Bruns offering a translation of Wilde's *Intentions* (Martens, *Felix Paul* 320–21) and when he introduced himself to Rudolf von Poellnitz, managing director of the Leipzig publishing house Insel (Pacey, *Letters* 516).

7   According to Else von Freytag-Loringhoven, Greve started to translate "more for pleasure than business" (Hjartarson and Spettigue 69); with Oscar Wilde, however, Greve picked an author whose aesthetic was not only close to that of the George circle, but who had currently attracted wide public interest so that his translations fell on fertile ground.

8   In 1904, the magazine changed its title to *Die Neue Rundschau*.

9   Karl Gustav Vollmoeller, "Catherina, Gräfin von Armagnac und ihre beiden Liebhaber," *Neue Deutsche Rundschau* 14 (1903): 273–314; Gabriele d'Annunzio, "Francesca da Rimini," trans. Karl Gustav Vollmoeller, *Neue Deutsche Rundschau* 14 (1903): 1063–1101, 1167–1212.

10 As the *Dorian Gray* excerpt in the *Neue Deutsche Rundschau* differs considerably from Greve's versions, which appeared under the auspices of J.C.C. Bruns, it is unlikely that Greve was the anonymous translator.

11 Volume fourteen of the *Neue Deutsche Rundschau* comes close to a special issue on Wilde as it includes, apart from Greve's Wilde translation and an excerpt from someone else's *Dorian Gray*, Max Meyerfeld's "Erinnerungen an Oscar Wilde" and Oscar Bie's review of Greve's *Fingerzeige*.

12 "Im letzten Frühjahr erschien, abgesehen von ein paar Kleinigkeiten, die der Verfasser dieses Aufsatzes schon früher in Zeitschriften publizierte, zum ersten Mal einer der großen Romane des Engländers George Meredith in deutscher Sprache" ("Last spring, one of the great novels of the Englishman George Meredith appeared for the first time in German, apart from a few trifles which the author of this essay published earlier in magazines") (Greve, "Meredith" 721).

13 Robert Browning and Elizabeth Barrett-Barrett, "Briefwechsel," [trans. Felix Paul Greve,] *Die Neue Rundschau* 15 (1904): 774–804, 949–74. Just like Greve's translation of Wilde aphorisms that appeared in the *Neue Deutsche Rundschau* in 1903, this magazine contribution has so far passed unnoticed. Greve's translation is preceded by an article by Rudolf Kassner, "Robert Browning und Elisabeth Barrett Barrett," 769–74.

14 Greve would have preferred Gide to redirect Bie to him: "S'il [Oscar Bie] a demandé votre [André Gide's] collaboration à vous-même, c'est parce qu'il m'a blessé un jour, et que c'est toujours humiliant de demander quelque chose à quelqu'un, qu'on a blessé. Un jour déjà vous lui avez répondu, que c'était à F.P.G. qu'il faudrait s'adresser. Il ne le fit pas alors. Aujourd'hui il l'aurait fait. Mais cette fois-ci vous lui avez épargné la peine" ("If he [Oscar Bie] asked you [André Gide] for your collaboration, it is because he hurt me one day and because it is always humiliating to request something from somebody one has hurt. One day in the past, you answered him that it was F.P.G. that he would have to turn to. He did not do it then. This time he would have done so, but you have saved him the trouble") (Ernst and Martens 169). See also Gide's letter to Bie, n.d. (Theis 73).

15 "J'ai eu soin d'avance d'écrire à Bie que je me réservais tout droit sur cet ouvrage et qu'il m'appartenait de nouveau sitôt après avoir paru dans sa revue, je pensais à vous en demandant cela, car, raisonnablement ce 'traité' doit rejoindre celui du

Narcisse et *Philoctète*, ainsi qu'un *Ajax* que je prépare en ce moment. Vous serez donc libre de vous ressaisir de l'ouvrage, et si c'est votre intention, je vous enverrai d'ici peu le texte français" ("I had already taken care to write to Bie that I had reserved for myself all rights to this work and that it belonged to me even after having appeared in his magazine; demanding this I was thinking of you because, reasonably, this 'tractate' has to be combined with that of *Narcisse* and *Philoctète* as well as the *Ajax* that I am currently preparing. You will thus be free to regain possession of this work again, and if this is your intention, I will soon send you the French text") (Ernst and Martens 165).

16   "Da, wie Sie uns mitteilen, der 'verlorene Sohn' bereits in der 'Neuen Rundschau' in einer Uebersetzung von Kurt Singer erschienen ist, so möchten wir nicht diesen Traktat mit in unseren Band hineinnehmen" ("Because, as you inform us, the 'verlorene Sohn' has already appeared in the 'Neue Rundschau' in a translation by Kurt Singer, we would rather not include this tractate in our volume") (Ernst and Martens 172–73).

17   "In order to 'raise' the interest in your books, it seems wise, in my eyes, to publish some pages (something artfully fashioned) in a magazine. Unfortunately, for the time being, only the 'Freistatt' is available. —At least this journal is *read*. It seems to me that an author like you loses nothing in appearing in a second-rate journal which, nevertheless, counts among its collaborators some writers of the first order."

18   "The most important magazine in Germany is, I think, *Die Neue Rundschau*. In order to place a part of the *Nourritures* there, it certainly would be necessary to omit the name of the translator because I and Mr. Bruns have taken legal proceedings against Mr. S. Fischer. But if this translation of a part of the Nourritures, or rather this part of the translation of the Nourritures were passed through the hands of Mr. Franz Blei? ... What do you think?"

19   "F.P. Grève [sic] qui traduit aussi mes *Nourritures Terrestres* propose de faire paraître un fragment de celles-ci dans un journal bien choisi ou dans une revue. Dans la crainte que son nom trop suspect ne soit un obstacle à cette publication partielle, il propose de *ne pas signer*; le fragment paraîtrait sans nom de traducteur; mais il faudrait alors que quelque intermédiaire s'occupât de le faire passer; j'ai pensé que peut-être votre obligeance ne s'y refuserait pas, et j'ai dit à F.P. Grève que je vous écrirais à ce sujet. Peut-être la publication de ce fragment, bien choisi, peu de temps avant la représentation de Candaule, pourrait-elle y préparer un peu le public. Mais dans quel journal? dans quelle revue plutôt?—de ceci je vous laisse juge, et attends un mot de vous pour savoir si je dois vous faire parvenir ce fragment de traduction" ("F.P. Grève [sic], who is also translating my *Nourritures Terrestres*, proposes to have a fragment of them appear in a well-chosen journal or magazine. Being afraid that his disreputable name might be an obstacle to this partial publication, he proposes *not to sign* it; the fragment would appear without the translator's name; but then some intermediary would have to ensure that it were passed on; I thought that perhaps your readiness would not be refused and I have told F.P. Grève that I would

write to you in this matter. The publication of this well-chosen fragment shortly before the presentation of Candaule would possibly prepare the public a little. But in which journal? or rather in which magazine?—this I leave to you and I am looking forward to a word from you in order to know whether I should arrange for this fragment of the translation to be sent to you") (Theis 11).

20   See Gide's letters to Paul Claudel and Henri de Régnier (Ernst and Martens 53–54).

21   This even holds true for contemporary critics. Thus Ifkovits draws the conclusion that all anonymous translations of the Insel's third volume, with the exception of Oscar Wilde's "The Ballad of Reading Gaol," were by Franz Blei because he received the payment for them (178). Greve's and Blei's statements in their correspondences, however, contradict this point of view (Ernst and Martens 147; Martens, Felix Paul 324; Theis 39, 41–42). See also Verwey's letter to Wolfskehl, summer 1902 (Spettigue, FPG 73). If Blei did receive the payment for the Wilde excerpt, more negative light is thrown on his dealings with Greve.

22   A comparison of Greve's and Blei's translations indicates that Blei not only adopted Greve's title but heavily relied on Greve's versions of the aphorisms.

23   "Harden ne nous favorisera pas beaucoup; il n'a pas 'le nez', comme on dit ici" ("Harden does not favor us much; he does not have 'the nose,' as one says here") (Ernst and Martens 177).

24   See the programmatic article "Zum Geleit" in the Schaubühne's first number (7 Sept. 1905).

25   "Erster Sturm," "Die Stadt am Strande," and "Saul."

26   During the first year of its existence, the Schaubühne had its own publishing house (Dietzel and Hügel 4: 1068).

27   In October 1904, Greve explained to Gide: "Je ne suis plus une personne, j'en sommes trois: je suis 1.) M. Felix Paul Greve; 2.) Mme Else Greve; 3.) Mme Fanny Essler. La dernière, dont je vous enverrai prochainement les poèmes [...] est un poète déjà assez considéré dans certaines parties de l'Allemagne" ("I am no longer one person, I am three: I am 1.) Mr. Felix Paul Greve; 2.) Mrs. Else Greve; 3.) Mrs. Fanny Essler. The latter, whose poems I will send you shortly [...] is a poet already of considerable repute in certain parts of Germany") (Ernst and Martens 74–75). See also Divay lxvi–lxxvi.

28   The letter to Gide reads: "J'ai écrit une farce satirique, dont personne ne veut à cause du ridicule versé sur le gouvernement bavarois et l'administration des musées et des prisons" ("I have written a satiric farce, which nobody likes because it exposes the Bavarian government and the administration of museums and prisons to ridicule") (Ernst and Martens 74).

29   "In two years I will be a publisher myself."

30   "It will require about 10 more years to be rid of my debts. And then? Then life will begin. Success? But I don't count on it anymore. I have freed myself of my illusions. Work, this is all. Because of work I earn; I 'make' twenty thousand marks per year. People are starting to read me; well then, maybe this will shorten the period of work a bit: maybe, but I don't count on it anymore. I make books as the shoemaker

makes boots. Life? This is 'Wirken' [to be of influence], I do not know the French word. You cannot 'wirken' through books. You 'wirkt' through money. This is my theory, at least."

31   Greve's attempts at finding a permanent source of income, however, proved difficult: "In fact, I have tried very hard, of late, to secure some sort of a position in Toronto which would pay for our daily bread. [...] I applied, for instance, for the position as 'Book-Adviser' at Simpson's—a position which recently became vacant; they asked me to come in for a personal interview; but, the moment they saw I wasn't a young man, they expressed their regret; and I went home. Then I applied for work as a proof-reader with the Ryerson Press; I tried to arrange for a series of lectures on The Technique of the Novel; and everywhere I meet with the same stony hostility. It would be amusing if it were not somewhat disastrous" (Pacey, *Letters* 324). Later Greve tried to work as an independent literary adviser and accepted a job in a canning factory (Pacey, *Letters* 418–19).

32   Interestingly enough, Greve's statement echos what in 1904 critic F.D. expressed in the magazine *Freistatt* with reference to Greve: "Bedauerlich aber ist, daß F. P. Greve, der trotz aller Einwände durch Wilde- und Browningübertragungen einen gewissen literarischen Ruf erlangt hat, sein Können an eine ganze Serie überflüssiger Arbeiten verschleudert" ("It is regrettable, however, that F.P. Greve, who despite all objections has gained a certain literary renown through Wilde and Browning translations, is squandering his talents with a whole series of superfluous projects") (1045).

Of Life and Art

FPG and the Writing of Oscar Wilde into Settlers of the Marsh

"[L]IKE THE FACE OF EUROPE my memory is a palimpsest on which writing has overlaid writing."[1] So Frederick Philip Grove famously described his intellectual formation and simultaneously excused his all too frequent lapses of memory in his autobiography, *In Search of Myself*. Despite the self-justificatory quality of this comment, there is undoubtedly, as with so many of Grove's statements, something of truth here. A tramp, a salesman and a farmer, but also a translator, poet, novelist and essayist, Frederick Philip Grove was intimately familiar with, and formed by, a whole range of writers from the ancients of his adolescent studies in the classics to the moderns of his own contemporary age, many of whom he translated. In this essay, I distinguish the remnants of one layer of writing from the palimpsest of Grove's intellectual bibliography, that of Oscar Wilde, one of the central influences in FPG's writing and life. Although the aesthete Wilde and the taciturn Grove seem at first glance mismatched, the similarities between Wilde and Greve may be quickly enumerated. Both were social outsiders who sought by means of intelligence to attain a place at the centre of the cultural worlds they inhabited; both distinguished themselves in their knowledge of the classics; both were devotees of the cult of art who nonetheless purposefully used art as a vehicle with which to acquire social prestige and financial gain; both adopted poetry and drama in the early stages of their respective careers; both were capable of tremendous artistic output even while burdened with intense emotional strain; both were subjected to social ostracism and legal sanction in the form of prison sentences; and, finally, both were ultimately silenced, driven indebted from their preferred cultural milieus—Wilde to France and an impoverished death in Paris, Greve via faked suicide to the tentative prospects of a new writing career in Canada. Beyond these external biographical similarities, however, is the far more extensive influence Wilde's life and writing exerted on the young German translator and writer. To investigate this influence, I focus on Greve's understanding of Wilde, as derived from his translation of Wilde's volume of essays *Fingerzeige* (*Intentions*)[2] and the critical assessment of Wilde contained in three of his most representative studies of Wilde.[3] In developing the thesis that Greve's reading of Wilde was influential to his later writing, published under the name of Frederick Philip Grove, I offer an interpretation of FPG's first Canadian novel, *Settlers of the Marsh*. On the basis of these texts, I indicate how several of Wilde's ideals provided Greve with key concepts that he later modified and employed in his own writing, while the example of Wilde's life, and Greve's criticism of it, offer an indication of the cultural and aesthetic ideals that led Greve to the aesthetic he adopted in Canada. Although fully aware that the attempt to demonstrate formative influence on the basis of textual criticism is fraught with danger, I believe that attention to Wilde brings us a step closer to seeing the literary contributions of Greve and Grove as a single entity.

That Wilde was of importance to Greve may be briefly demonstrated at several levels. As a model of personal behaviour, for instance, it is now known that in playful moments, Greve occasionally styled himself according to Wilde's model, adopting the mask, so to speak, of an English dandy, even going so far in Gardone, Italy in 1902 as suggesting to a fellow vacationer that he was Wilde.[4] More substantially, Greve chose Wilde's writings as those amongst the first of what would become an astounding range of translated texts, introducing himself into Germany's translation culture as a literary figure to be taken seriously both as a poet and dramatist in his own right *and* as a translator of world literature. Still further, apart from translating Wilde and attempting to use productions of Wilde's dramas as a vehicle to advance his own literary career, Greve devoted several critical studies to Wilde. Indeed, the final critical work to appear under Greve's name in Germany was the article "Oskar Wilde" reprinted in a collection of literary portraits edited by Adalbert Luntowski in 1911. As a writer in Germany, Felix Paul Greve's works were, to a certain extent, contained within Wildean bookends.

Given this verifiable presence of Wilde in Greve's literary life, it seems possible that significant features of the aesthetic Grove developed in his Canadian works may be sought in Wilde's writings and in Greve's critical articles concerning Wilde. Of immediate relevance here is the need to recognise that Greve did not simply adopt Wilde's celebration of the "truth of masks," and that he did not uncritically celebrate Wilde's veneration of the lie and pose as ideals of artistic creation. Nor did the Canadian Grove attempt to out-Wilde Wilde in the "decadent attempt to subordinate the real world to an artistic concept" in his Canadian literature.[5] Although such an approach would certainly have its appeal in explaining Grove's fictionalising of his past, his own adorning of masks in the autobiographical tellings of his life-story, Greve's relation to Wilde was far more nuanced and Wilde's influence far more complex. In point of fact, Greve was almost exclusively critical of the artistic worth of the English "decadents" and of Wilde the artist, going so far in "Oscar Wilde und das Drama" as to suggest that "Von Wilde kann der Dramatiker nur lernen, wenn er ihn als Gescheiterten betrachtet" (8).[6] Still further, Greve linked Wilde's artistic failure, at least in part, to precisely his adoption of masks and poses:

> ...was Wilde schuf, ist selten ersten Ranges und sein Leben blieb Fragment. [...] Wilde war ein Poseur im großen Stil, und als solcher hat er Momente von grandioser Kraft. Wo bei ihm die Pose aushört, ist er ein Mensch von merkwürdiger Schwäche und seltsamen Widersprüchen. Sein Intellekt ist souverän, wo es herrscht, aber das Gebiet seiner Herrschaft ist begrenzt: daher jene Widersprüche. ("Oskar Wilde" 14–15)[7]

Contrary to Greve's ideal, Wilde's adoption of masks and poses, rather than revealing the truth, drew attention away from the work of art—the source of truth—and centred it upon the secondary element of the artist's life (*Randarabesken* 8–9). In a still more critical gesture, Greve recounted Wilde's fatal turning away from life, a tendency that affected more than his public persona, but rather his very ability to produce art:

> Alles, was er im Leben fand, erschien ihm als nachte, brutale Tatsache, die den Sinn, den er nicht fand, nicht hatte. So kam er schließlich

dazu, das Leben nicht mehr sehen zu wollen. Und seine Schaffenskraft ebbt ab. Er fand in sich selber das einzig Interessante. Die Analysis, die er vielleicht von D'Annunzio lernte, zeigte ihm die sinnvollen Fäden, die durch das geheimnisvolle Wirrsal des eigenen Innern führten. Und er lernte das Leben verachten. Nur noch, so weit es in ihm Emotionen auslöste, ging es ihn an. ("Oskar Wilde" 18–19)[8]

It is this same destructive movement from life to emotion charted here by Greve in Wilde that we will follow below in Niels Lindstedt's brush with near total disaster in *Settlers of the Marsh*.

Despite these criticisms, however, Greve was nonetheless intensely interested in Wilde, precisely because Wilde raised in his art, life and criticism the issue central to FPG's aesthetic—the proportioned co-joining of life and fiction in art of lasting value. Greve saw in Wilde the tragedy of a writer who was destroyed because he confused life with dream, the dream he had advanced in *Intentions*. As Greve would express it, Wilde's oeuvre was "...die Hieroglyphenschrift einer großen Tragödie im Leben eines modernen Menschen, eines Menschen, der Künstler sein wollte und es nicht konnte, weil er das Leben mit dem Traum verwechselt" ("Oskar Wilde" 51).[9]

But what did Greve suggest as a related, although alternative, aesthetic, and to what extent may it be read into Grove's writing? Like the Wilde of *Intentions*, Greve was intensely interested in establishing for art a place at the very forefront of human life. For both Wilde and Greve, art was the ultimate expression of human endeavour. Unlike Wilde, however, Greve did not see the work of art as a product of the submission of life to art. In Greve's aesthetic, life was not to be placed subordinate to art. Indeed, using a highly suggestive metaphor, given both Wilde's and Greve's experiences with debts, Greve suggested that life was the primary element in the constellation life/art. According to Greve, Wilde had misunderstood this and suffered accordingly: "Alle Taten machen uns zu Schuldnern, und die Schulden, die wir durchs Handeln auf uns nehmen, müssen wir eines Tages zahlen: das Leben ist der unerbittlichste Gläubiger. Weh dem, der vergisst, seine Taten als Debet ins Hauptbuch des Lebens zu schreiben: seine Schulden wachsen ins Ungeheuerliche an, und am Tage der Abrechnung ist er bankrott. [...] Wilde zahlte die Schulden seines Lebens mit dem Bankrott" (*Randarabesken* 40, 47).[10]

Greve went beyond simply using Wilde as an example of the perilous risks involved in denying life a role in art, however. And in articulating his vision of the relationship between art and life, we see the rudiments of an aesthetic that would be adopted in Canada by Grove. In essence, Greve adopted a Platonic understanding of artistic representation whereby the ultimate object of representation was the "ideal" or essence of life; this was the ultimate "goal" behind the striving of all things to perfection and the motor for life's eternal process of change, the essential condition of life. As Greve put it in "Oscar Wilde und das Drama": "alles Leben ist Streben nach Vollkommenheit" (22–23).[11] For Greve, this Platonic abstraction, this "ideal," was expressed in concrete terms through the individual and the eternal process of change each individual experienced and exemplified. The function of art was to mediate between the "ideal" and the "real," to represent the "eternal" nature of life and the real experience of the individual, but without emphasising one at the expense of the other. The following is Greve's expression of this concept:

Nun haben wir also gewissermaßen zwei Welten gefunden: die Welt der Ziele und die Welt der Individuen [...] Die Welt der Individuen wird mehr und mehr zum Objekt der Wissenschaft, die täglich mehr von ihrem abstrakten Charakter fallen läßt, um ganz konkret zu werden. Die Welt der Ziele steht in großer Ferne rein abstrakt vor unsrem Geiste, als Objekt der reinen Spekulation. Und wo steht nun die Kunst? Sie bildet eine Brücke zwischen beiden; sie ist nicht Spiegel des einen noch des andern; sie gibt nicht Bilder der Wirklichkeit und auch nicht Bilder der Ideen. Und je nach dem Streben der geistigen Welten einer Zeit tritt sie der realen Welt der Individuen näher oder fliegt sie empor zu jener Welt der reinen Begriffe. Wenn sie zwischen beiden den Kunst des Gleichgewichts fand, schuf sie von je ihre ewigsten Werke. ("O.W. und das Drama" 24–25)[12]

Given the ideal expressed here, it is relatively easy to understand why Greve censured Wilde for drawing too much emphasis to his actual life in his fictional writing. According to Greve's aesthetic principles, Wilde was upsetting art's balancing act between "idea" and "individual." At the same time, however, it is equally understandable why Greve was attracted to certain ideas expressed by Wilde. In "The Truth of Masks" for instance, Wilde made a bipartite distinction between "truth" and "facts" that is similar to Greve's "ideas" and "individuals." The following statement by Wilde from "The Truth of Masks," here in reference to Shakespeare, is representative: "Of course the aesthetic value of Shakespeare's plays does not, in the slightest degree, depend on their facts, but on their Truth, and Truth is independent of facts always, inventing or selecting them at pleasure."[13] Greve also saw art's goal as a striving for truth between the eternal abstraction of life and the random facts of actual human experience. Literature was to be verisimilitudinous, but its "truth" was not to be measured according to adherence to random empirical fact, but rather in its ability to represent "pure concepts" in living form. Approximately forty-five years later, as the Canadian author of In Search of Myself, Grove described the functioning of this same set of aesthetic principles in the creation of such characters as Abe Spalding and Niels Lindstedt. In the instance of Abe Spalding, while travelling across the western prairies, Grove once happened upon a man whose very presence bespoke the truth of the pioneer environment he inhabited. In terms of Grove's novel Fruits of the Earth, however, the importance of this figure was not his physical actuality but the larger truth he seemed to embody for Grove:

> ...somehow he bodied forth for me the essence of the pioneering spirit which has settled the vast western plains.... This man, a giant in body, if not in mind and spirit, had furnished the physical features for a vision which had, so far, been incomplete because it had been abstract.
>
> If I had seen the entirely casual occasion—that is all I can call him; he was not the prototype—of this figure again, if I had heard him speak as no doubt he had been used to speak, without relevance to my creation, that mental vision of mine would have been profoundly disturbed. A perfectly irrelevant actuality would have been superimposed upon my conception of a man who, as I saw him, had perhaps never lived; for he lacked that infusion of myself which makes him what he has become. From a type and a symbol, he would have become an individual; he would have been drained of the truth that lived in him; he would have become a mere fact. (ISM 260–61)

The "real" Abe Spalding was not important for Grove as an actual individual but as the specific, living embodiment of an abstraction. It is in the same context and with the same conceptual vocabulary derived from Greve's Platonic aesthetic that we read Grove's statement concerning his mixing of fact and fiction in his autobiographical writings:

> Imaginative literature is not primarily concerned with facts; it is concerned with truth. It sees fact only within the web of life, coloured and made vital by what preceded it, coloured and made significant by what followed. In its highest flights, imaginative literature, which is one and indivisible, places within a single fact the history of the universe from its inception as well as the history of its future to the moment of its final extinction.[14]

This is art finding a balancing point between the universal and the specific, representing in works of art at once the "ideal" and the "fact," the very features from Wilde's example that were of interest to Greve.

With these still crudely outlined generalizations, then, it is possible to trace the trajectory of Greve's response to Wilde's writing into his aesthetic as the Canadian author Grove. But what of the figure of the artist in Greve's understanding of artistic production? Here, too, Wilde is of importance for both Greve and Grove; for, apart from exemplifying the fundamental error of disregarding "life" in art, Wilde furnished Greve with the highly suggestive figure of the "uprooted" artist. Adopting Gide's concept of the *déraciné* or, in Greve's German, the *entwurzelt*, Greve developed his understanding of an essentially existential condition whereby the individual is uprooted from one cultural environment and placed in another.[15] This uprooted individual, no longer at home in either his native or adopted environment, is ultimately fit to be either a criminal or an artist: "Er taugt zum—Verbrecher oder zum Künstler!" (*Randarabesken* 29). As an artist, the *entwurzelt* individual—who in being uprooted has been made radically aware of the relativity of life—becomes the eternal observer, the existential traveller through the journey of life, both at home in and foreign to all environments:

> Aber jener Entwurzelte, [...] der wird ein Schilderer sein: nach zwei
> Seiten wird er blicken; er steht an einer Wendung des Weges, wo er

die Strasse nach Nordosten und nach Nordwesten überschaut: er ist unweigerlich Künstler! Ein Künstler im Keim: weil er die Dinge als unterschieden sieht; er sieht plastisch. Darin liegt die Begnadung, darin auch die Tragik seines Loses. Er zieht zwei Strassen, und zieht sie beide als Fremder und ist doch auf beiden heimisch. Und ist nicht der Künstler immer der Fremde, trägt er nicht stets das Ahasveruszeichen an der Stirn? Alle Künstler sind dekadent, wenn Dekadenz die Folge der Entwurzelung ist: Nur gibt es Grade! Und man könnte sich einen Künstler denken, der vermöge seiner Abstammung—geistiger wie leiblicher—in allen Kulturen und Rassen und Sitten und Religionen der Welt fremd zu Hause wäre: ein Schweifender über der Erde Gewächsen, fremd und zu Hause im Christentum, fremd und zu Hause unter Brahminen am Ganges, fremd und zu Hause beim grossen Erlöser Buddha, fremd und zu Hause im Geist eines Nietzsche wie Augustins—zugleich ein Deutscher, ein Brite, ein Römer, ein Grieche, ein Italiener, Franzose und Schwede und Russe. Ein solcher wäre ganz "entwurzelt" das heisst, er hätte seine Wurzeln überall, er wäre vielwurzlig [...]. (*Randarabesken* 30–31)[16]

As supplement to this Romantic theory of the artist as eternal wanderer, Greve added an important individual feature of his own. Greve suggested that although the artist was uprooted and hence potentially many-rooted, he nonetheless had one root that was stronger than the others, a root from which he drew his life's energy and which, if he remained true to it, would provide him with the stability to produce great works of art. Those artists who did not have one root stronger than the others—in Greve's discussion, a figure like Wilde—such artists were prone to works of art on a smaller scale, decadent art based on paradoxes, aphorisms, and *aperçus* that could not rank with the great works of art, although they revealed the artist himself as interesting (*Randarabesken* 31). For Greve, Wilde was insufficiently rooted in life, and as a result, he sacrificed his abilities to the shallow tastes of the masses in the very process of confusing dream and reality: "Aber die Pose wurde ihm Wirklichkeit, und die Wirklichkeit verblasste daneben, und wo sie nicht blass war, da verwechselte er den Traum und die Dinge, und dafür rächte das Leben sich" (*Randarabesken* 36).[17]

Transferred to the writings of Frederick Philip Grove—recalling in passing that Greve's volume of poetry was entitled *Wanderings*—this understanding of the artist as existential traveller speaks directly to the plot structure and theme of his autobiographical writings, *A Search for America* and *In Search of Myself*. In both works the narrative format is similar: the narrator is uprooted in youth and set out on the road of life as the eternal observer. Although initially uncertain of the telos of his life, successive experiences gradually reveal the direction life has allotted him to take. At home and foreign everywhere, he follows his life's direction to arrive not at a specific place but at an existential calling—that of an artist—a calling that was not to be denied regardless of the material tribulations it entailed. Combined with Greve's aesthetic as I have characterized it, this plot structure could perhaps explain the presence in Grove's autobiography of journeys and locations that seem beyond plausible verification. For Grove, it is not the concrete actuality of these travels which matter, for this is all so much fact, archaeological detail, in Wilde's use of that term. What is important is the "truth" of Grove's life and travels, for he certainly was a traveller who wandered the road of life certain that it was his duty not to squander the viaticum presented to him on life's journey, but to fashion of it a work of art:

> But, unless I was willing, when I came to die, to accept the fact that I had wasted what gifts I had received—the viaticum as I have called it; plus all that had been added to it by my life and by what experience had brought me—I must continue on my path; I must go on striving after my aim.
>
> What was that aim? Briefly, it was to set down, in one comprehensive picture, all that had crystilized out, in my mind, in reaction all I had seen, heard, and felt. That picture I must at least aim at fashioning in a form *which would stand forever*. (ISM 229–30, Grove's italics)

Another dimension of FPG's relatedness to Wilde and Greve's critical response to Wilde may be evinced when the particular mask of autobiography is replaced with that of fiction, here in the instance of *Settlers of the Marsh*. In this novel, Grove's first published in Canada, he develops in fictional form several of the aesthetic and ethical principles articulated in his criticism of Wilde. Like *A Search for America* and *In Search of Myself*, *Settlers of the Marsh* recounts the existential journey of a man struggling to find his way along life's path. In this instance it is the young Swedish immigrant, Niels Lindstedt, who, although initially aware of the correct course in his life and possessed of the will and vision to follow it, is seduced by vaguely articulated sexual urges to follow a false path. Robbed by degrees of his will-power and subsequently punished for deceiving "life" and his vision of an ideal existence, Lindstedt is chastened and redeemed by sorrow and ultimately returned to his (patriarchal) vision of personal, familial and communal well-being. In keeping with the aesthetic ideals outlined, *Settlers of the Marsh*, although verisimilitudinous insofar as it is written with attention to realistic descriptions of pioneer life and natural settings, does not exhibit the realist's concern for depicting the causal importance of socio-historical forces in the lives of characters, who are in turn identified by their connection to a specific time and place. Similarly Grove's novel exhibits but limited naturalist interest in the formative powers of heredity and environment on the development of character. The events played out in the marsh are all but unimpinged upon by historical time and circumstance. The characters interact in an environment untouched—and seemingly untouchable—by forces external to those created in their own isolated, pioneer environment. More than fifteen years pass seamlessly with reference to nothing but the seasons; no cities are named; neither historical events nor personages are alluded to; likewise neither governmental policy nor social or economic developments are allowed incursion into the world of the Big Marsh. In short, although "truthful," Greve's novel is relatively unmoved by depictions of world-historical "facts." Rather, it would seem as if Grove were attempting to narrate something of eternal worth through his representation of a man functioning within the web of a life depicted as simultaneously particular and universal. Hence, Grove's narrative is characterized by attention both to the minutia of pioneer life and the exclusion of events of transitory historical importance. In *Settlers of the Marsh*, Grove dramatized in fictional form the ideals expressed in his criticism of Wilde. In a manner intended to suggest universal themes rather than particular experience, Grove's novel enacts the fortunes of an *entwurzelt* man who, in seeking to establish new roots, is confronted by life with a choice between dream and reality.

Settlers of the Marsh begins with the sole reference to a human settlement, Minor, external to the particular geography of the Big Marsh—a setting itself to be located not on any map of geo-political reality but rather according to the co-ordinates of universal human motivation. The opening paragraphs also introduce Niels Lindstedt as he struggles against the elements in his bid to end the physical journey of immigration from Sweden to the Big Marsh while simultaneously beginning the existential journey entailed in establishing himself and setting down roots in the farming community. Although one journey has ended, another more important one is poised to begin. Lindstedt is identified as an immigrant, a pioneer who by virtue of having left his native Sweden is accorded the advantages of a specific form of life experience. In Greve's account of Wilde, the uprooted individual is presented as one made forcibly aware of the relativity of life, a potential boon for the artist, though fraught also with danger. In *Settlers of the Marsh*, Niels Lindstedt is accorded the same consciousness of life's variability and mysteries and hence is an artist of sorts, although he is possessed of a form of vision appropriate to a pioneer:

> How chance played into life!
> He had emigrated; and the mere fact that he was uprooted and transplanted had given him a second sight, had awakened powers of vision and sympathy in him which were far beyond his education and upbringing.[18]

With this consciousness, this "second sight," Niels is made acutely aware of his limited, transitory position in the greater scheme of existence, as a result of which he is frequently occupied by deliberations on matters of existential import, thoughts in turn recorded in the narrative in the form of interior monologues. As a portion of his psycho-philosophical concerns, Niels is soon possessed of a vision that will guarantee meaning to his life. This vision, described as "eternal," is one of familial security and incorporates spousal love and the presence of children. Essentially, Lindstedt's vision is the civilising one of creating life, family and community. Significantly, the first formulation of this vision is made in the context of a conversation Niels has with his friend and fellow immigrant Lars Nelson, who forcefully expresses the unarticulated feelings Niels has about the liberatory value of work as an independent pioneer. The exercise and expression of one's will through labour in the pioneer creation of life and community out of nothing is identified in Niels's vision as an ideal:

'I'll tell you, I like the work. I'd pay to be allowed to do it. Land I've cleared is more my own than land I've bought.' [...] The last few words had filled them with the exhilaration of a confession of faith. High above, far ahead stood an ideal; towards that ideal they walked.

Suddenly, as they were entering the bush, where the moon light filtered down through the meshes of leafless boughs over head, a vision took hold of Niels: of himself and a woman, sitting of a mid-winter night by the light of a lamp and in front of a fire, with the pitter-patter of children's feet sounding down from above: the eternal vision that has moved the world and that was to direct his fate. He tried to see the face of the woman but it entirely evaded him.... (Settlers 36)

For Niels, the presence of children was in no way merely incidental to his vision, his ideal. Children would be the guarantors of his fixedness as immigrant in a new land: "But if he had children, they would be rooted here....He might become rooted himself, through them...." (Settlers 45). Furthermore, the presence of loved ones is all that humans have as response to the terrible finality of death, as Niels came to realise upon the demise of Sigurdsen, a father-like figure whose death causes him to think of his own dead mother. Children were to offer a kind of existential consolation, without which humans would be left "to shiver in an utter void" (Settlers 102). There is, then, a kind of existential urgency in Niels's desire to start a family, first in surrogate form with Sigurdsen, Bobby and Mrs Lund, and then later with Ellen. In the terms of the aesthetic and ethic established in Greve's Wilde criticism, then, Niels Lindstedt has been established in Settlers of the Marsh as an uprooted pioneer/artist, immigrant/wanderer who, in seeking to realise his dream, is responding to the eternal call of "life" while setting down the "root" that will be the source and proof of his strength and creativity.

In fulfilling the ideal presented to him by life, however, Niels requires a mate, a wife to fulfil his incomplete vision of domestic and communal stability. And here, Settlers of the Marsh reveals further dimensions of FPG's familiarity with Wilde. It is in Niels Lindstedt's choosing of a wife that Grove dramatises the choice Greve saw Wilde presented with—between dream and reality. Upon ultimately choosing Clara Vogel rather than Ellen Amundsen, Lindstedt was punished by life, as was Wilde. It is at this juncture, in Lindstedt's choice between life or dream, as expressed in the figures Ellen and Clara, that Grove's novel exhibits in greater detail Greve's critical assessment of Wilde and his familiarity with Wilde's fiction.

If Ellen represents the potential of life as the female correspondent to Lindstedt's male embodiment of the pioneering spirit and is, as such, the perfect mate and concluding figure in the configuration of Lindstedt's "eternal vision," then Clara Vogel acts as a force inimical to that vision. In the system of binary opposites proposed by Greve in his discussion of Wilde, Clara is dream and decadence opposed to the reality and life of Ellen. This reading of "the gay widow of the settlement" (*Settlers* 30) is supported with reference to the aura of oppressively sweet decay and prettified death that seems ever to surround her. Time and again throughout the novel, Clara Vogel is associated with decay and lassitude via narrative reference to a set of characteristics emblematic of decadence and putrefaction. Repeated reference is made to her "silvery, falsetto laugh" (*Settlers* 51), to "the sweetish scents" (*Settlers* 127) and "enervating aura of scents" (*Settlers* 147) surrounding her, to the "mockery in her eyes" (*Settlers* 52), to the extravagance of her toilette, to the sexually charged ostentation of her dress, to her refusal to work, and to her emotional and physical distance from the pioneer community. And while Niels and the other characters are identified with the pioneer labours of the Big Marsh, Clara is the sole character associated with the nameless local town, which is far removed from the geography and concerns of the rural pioneers. It is in the town where Clara previously worked in the "'art' department of a large store" (*Settlers* 128) and it is in the town, displaced from the land where "he was master" (*Settlers* 89), that Niels deceives his "eternal vision" and succumbs to his desire for Clara.

That Niels's liaison with Clara is a surrender to dream and a form of infidelity to life is made abundantly clear in the scenes before their marriage where Niels is confronted by Clara. In the first lengthy exchange with Clara at Nelson's and Olga's marriage, Niels instinctively feels that association with Clara Vogel could mean nothing but disaster for a man destined by life for other things:

[...] as he went over and sat down by her [Clara's] side, he felt as if he were being entrapped: he felt what was almost a foreboding of disaster. Never in his life had he felt like that; and the memory of this feeling was to come back to him, many years later, when his terrible destiny had overtaken him. Had he obeyed a hardly articulate impulse, he would at once have got up again and gone out. (*Settlers* 51)

In leaving Clara's company shortly thereafter, Niels comes to his senses, feeling "as if he were waking up from a terrible dream" (*Settlers* 53). More explicitly and troubling, moreover, his associations with Clara have a stupefying effect, causing him to resist the essential demands of pioneer life:

But to-night something had happened which he did not understand: he was a leaf borne along the wind, a prey to things beyond his control, a fragment swept away by torrents. [...] A lassitude came over him: a desire to escape life's issues....(*Settlers* 55)

And indeed, even before the disastrous conclusion to Niels's turning away from his ideal of a prosperous pioneer family, the negative, previously intuited effects of marriage to Clara are indicated in Niels's weakened demeanour. The decadence Clara's whole being seems to suggest is felt by Niels in the form of reduced will-power: " [...] the decay in Niels consisted more in a gradual disintegration of will and purpose" (*Settlers* 175).

It is apparent that Grove established in *Settlers of the Marsh* a fictional counterpart to the ethical and aesthetic principles set forth in his criticism of Wilde, whereby an uprooted individual is offered the choice between dream and reality. In choosing dream and decadence, this figure is weakened and ultimately punished by life. In *Settlers of the Marsh*, it is Clara Vogel who embodies the sensual temptations of a dream existence. It is not surprising, then, that representations of her should be traceable back to Greve's interest in Wilde not only at the level of criticism but also in her similarity to an illustrative motif from Wilde's fiction—the corrupted face of decadence.

In *The Picture of Dorian Gray*, Wilde created his famous parable of the terrible honesty and telling power of art. Basil Hallward paints a portrait of his friend Dorian Gray capturing not only the external appearance of Gray but the essence of his being as well. Gray, enamoured of his own beauty and seduced by the example and hedonism of Basil Hallward, sinks into a life of moral turpitude. Rather than his physical body bearing the sign of his soul's corruption, however, it is the face in Gray's portrait that minutely records his descent into decadence. It is the face of the portrait that reveals the putrefaction of Gray's soul. The following is an account of Gray's first discovery of the changes to his face in his portrait:

> As he was turning the handle of the door, his eye fell upon the portrait Basil Hallward had painted of him. He started back as if in surprise. [...] In the dim arrested light that struggled through the cream-coloured silk blinds, the face appeared to him to be a little changed. The expression looked different. One would have said that there was a touch of cruelty in the mouth. [...] The quivering, ardent sunlight showed him the lines of cruelty round the mouth as clearly as if he had been looking into a mirror after he had done some dreadful thing. (*Dorian Gray* 77)

Likewise in *Settlers of the Marsh*, Clara Vogel's face is to be depicted in language and image reminiscent of Wilde's *Dorian Gray* as a means of signalling the depth of her corruption, even behind the mask of transient physical beauty. Clara Vogel is never accorded the philosophical depth and self-awareness of Dorian Gray's hedonism, although she does partake of several features of his life, especially his appearances.

Before marriage to Clara, Niels has but limited occasion to see behind her deceptive mask of gay jollity and half mocking curiosity. For Niels, Clara Vogel, in her unpioneer-like extravagance, is an object of both interest and vaguely intuited fear. It is not until his first meeting with her in town, whereupon he offers to drive her back to the Big Marsh, that Niels has the opportunity to glimpse the essence behind her carefully constructed appearances. Sleeping in the box of his wagon, Clara Vogel's mask slips, allowing Niels to see and describe her with the language of decadence: "Somehow her artificiality was half stripped away; she looked like a relic of ancient temptations...." (*Settlers* 91). After their marriage, however, when Clara has ensconced herself in a boudoir as secluded and devoted to physical luxury as Dorian Gray's chamber, Niels perceives the moral corruption that he is still unable to rationalize. The following lengthy passage describing Niels's observation of his sleeping wife is worthy of extended citation because of the Wildean emphasis it places on sensual richness and moral decay, and the suggestion that the face acts as a kind of mirror to the soul. Similar to Wilde's description in *Dorian Gray*, Niels is startled by the vision that confronts him in the half-light of morning:

> There, as he looked at her in the pale light of a wind-torn dawn, he stood arrested.
>
> From behind the mask which still half concealed her face, another face looked out at him, like a death's-head: the coarse, aged face of a coarse, aged woman, aged before her time: [...] aged, not from work but from...what?
>
> For a moment Niels stared. Something like aversion and disgust came over him. Then carefully, almost fastidiously, he lifted a corner of the satin coverlet, baring the shoulder and part of the breast which were still half hidden under the filmy veil of a lacy nightgown. There, the flesh was still smooth and firm: but the face was the face of decay....(*Settlers* 133)

Accorded this vision of Clara's decadent essence, Niels is fascinated minutes later during breakfast preparations with contemplation of the hidden presence of Clara's true being:

> He scanned her face: he reproached himself for doing so: but there was an irresistible fascination about it. The mask was repaired; but it was an imperfect piece of work, betraying hurry. Since he knew it was there, he could detect the true face under the mask. (*Settlers* 133)

As married life between Clara and Niels progresses, Niels weakens spiritually as a consequence of having allowed himself to be attached to a way of living inimical to the demands of pioneer existence. At the same time, moreover, Clara's moral degradation continues. Niels's attention is repeatedly drawn to the face that is corrupted not by age but, like Dorian Gray, by her betrayal of life. Grove fictionalises Clara's and Niels's descent not only in the narrative representation of such specific events as Niels's distancing of himself from the community and in Clara's refusal to work, but also in the metaphoric depiction of Clara's facial appearance.[19] In using Clara's disfigured face as metonymic representation of her corrupted soul, Grove seems explicitly to have been drawing on Greve's intimate familiarity with Wilde's *The Picture of Dorian Gray*, where the changing features of Gray's face "showed him the real degradation of his life" (*Dorian Gray* 111).

Correspondences between *Settlers of the Marsh* and Wilde's life and fiction go further than *The Picture of Dorian Gray*, however. The coda to Grove's novel, the final chapter "Ellen Again," offers a description of Niels's return to Ellen and the "eternal vision" life has allotted him. In this chapter Niels is shown chastened by life, tempered by sorrow to a fuller understanding of his purpose in life. The summarising message of this chapter seems almost a fictionalisation of the thought expressed in Wilde's *De Profundis*. In this work, Wilde accords suffering a central role in uniting the two features so important to Greve's aesthetic—life and art. For the Wilde of *De Profundis*, suffering offered the purest means of fusing "essential idea" and "accidental existence" into one quintessential expression of life:

> ...but Sorrow is the ultimate type both in Life and Art.
>
> Behind Joy and Laughter there may be a temperament, coarse, hard and callous. But behind Sorrow there is always Sorrow. Pain, unlike Pleasure, wears no mask. Truth in Art is not any correspondence between the *essential idea* and the *accidental existence*; it is not the resemblance of shape to shadow, or of the form mirrored in the crystal to the form itself: it is no Echo coming from a hollow hill, any more than it is the well of silver water in the valley that shows the Moon to the Moon and Narcissus to Narcissus. Truth in Art is the unity of a thing with itself: the outward rendered expressive of the inward: the soul made incarnate: the body instinct with spirit. For this reason there is no truth comparable to Sorrow. (*De Profundis* 920; italics mine)

The terms "essential idea" and "accidental existence" immediately recall Greve's vocabulary from "Oscar Wilde und das Drama" where he proposed that art built bridges between the world of "ideas" and the world of "individuals." And like Wilde, Grove suggests through Niels that the transgressions of life have to be acknowledged with full awareness of individual responsibility and that suffering in human life plays a role of existential primacy. Furthermore, and also analogous to Wilde, *Settlers of the Marsh* seems to indicate that the artistry available to a pioneer—the living out of life's "eternal vision"—is made possible not despite suffering, but because of it. *Settlers of the Marsh* offers the following description of the generative power of suffering and the immediacy of suffering to life. Shortly thereafter, Ellen and Niels take up their now shared dream and begin the artistic project of pioneer life and the establishment of family and community:

> These two have been parted; and parting has opened their eyes. They have suffered; suffering has made them sweet, not made them bitter. Life has involved them in guilt; regret and repentance have led them together; they know that never again must they part. It is not passion that will unite them; what will unite them is love. (*Settlers* 216)

The comedic ending Grove provided *Settlers of the Marsh*, with its symbolic reference to spring and Ellen's desire to emerge from the bush to "wide, open, level, spaces" (*Settlers* 215) is not particularly Wildean. It is, however, for all its inherent conservatism and tentativeness,[20] consistent with the aesthetic FPG indicated in his criticism of Wilde and which he seems resolutely to have attempted to realise in his life and works. In Oscar Wilde, FPG identified an artist failed in the imperative of seeking equilibrium between life and art. FPG's criticism of Wilde's life and art, and the themes and form of such fictions as *Settlers of the Marsh*, suggest that he wished to offer in his art an example of literature that found a balance between "the world of ideas and the world of individuals." That Grove should take up this attempt in his Canadian writing seems at least in part to have resulted from Greve's reading of, and response to, Oscar Wilde.

NOTES

1   Frederick P. Grove, *In Search of Myself* (Toronto: McClelland and Stewart, 1974) 147. All future references to this work will be cited in the text as *ISM*.

2   Greve translated this volume with the help of Herman F.C. Kilian, who contributed
    a translation of "The Critic as Artist." See K. Martens, *Felix Paul Greves Karriere:*
    Frederick Philip Grove in Deutschland (St. Ingbert: Röhrig Universitätsverlag, 1997)
    145–47.

3   The three articles by Greve on Wilde to be referred to throughout this essay are as
    follows: *Randarabesken zu Oscar Wilde* (Minden: J.C.C. Bruns, 1903), hereafter cited as
    Randarabesken. [*Randarabesken* is identical to the "Preface" in *Oscar Wilde: Das Bildnis*
    des Mr. W.H., Lord Arthur Saviles Verbrechen, translated F.P. Greve (Minden: J.C.C.
    Bruns, 1904)]; "Oscar Wilde und das Drama," in *Oscar Wildes Sämtliche Werke in*
    deutscher Sprache, Vol. 7, *Vera oder die Nihilisten* (Wien und Leipzig: Wiener Verlag,
    1908), hereafter cited as "O.W. und das Drama"; and "Oskar Wilde," in *Porträts*, ed.
    Adalbert Luntowski (Berlin: Verlag Neues Leben Wilhelm Borngräber, 1911), here-
    after to be cited as "Oskar Wilde." ["Oskar Wilde" is identical to Greve's earlier
    Oscar Wilde (Berlin: Gose & Tetzlaff, 1903)]. All cited translations are my own.
    [Editorial note: the first article, *Randarabesken zu Oscar Wilde*, is reprinted and trans-
    lated in this volume with the title, "Oscar Wilde: Marginalia in Arabesque."]

4   See K. Martens, *Felix Paul Greves Karriere: Frederick Philip Grove in Deutschland* 169.

5   Walter Pache, "The Dilettante in Exile: Grove at the Centenary of His Birth,"
    Canadian Literature 90 (1981): 190.

6   "A dramatist may learn from Wilde only insofar as he considers him as failed."

7   "...that which Wilde created was rarely of the first order and his life remained a
    fragment. [...] Wilde was a poseur of the highest order, and as such he had
    moments of great strength. Where the pose ends with him, he is a person of odd
    weakness and unusual contradictions. His intellect is sovereign, where it reigns,
    but the breadth of its reign is limited and thus the contradictions."

8   "Everything that he found in life seemed to him naked, brutal fact that lacked the
    sense he did not find in it. Thus he came to the point where he no longer wished to
    see life. And his creative abilities ebbed. The only thing of interest, he found in
    himself. Analysis, which he perhaps learned from D'Annunzio, revealed to him the
    common thread of sense that led through the secretive chaos of one's own inner
    being. And he learned to despise life. He concerned himself with it only insofar as it
    released emotions in him."

9   "...the hieroglyphics of a great tragedy in the life of a modern man, a man who
    wanted to be an artist but could not because he confused life with dream."

10 "Every deed makes of us a debtor, and the debts that we take upon ourselves in the
    course of our actions must one day be repaid. Life is the most relentless creditor.
    Woe to him who forgets to register his acts as debits in the ledger of life; his debts
    grow to monstrous proportions and on the day of reckoning he is bankrupt. [...]
    Wilde paid for the debts of his life with bankruptcy."

11 "Life is a striving for perfection."

12 "Thus to a certain extent we have found two worlds: the world of ideas and the
    world of individuals [...] The world of individuals is becoming ever more the subject
    of scholarship, daily shedding its abstract character to become more concrete. The

world of ideas stands at a great distance, purely abstract before our spirits as an object of pure speculation. And what of art? It builds a bridge between the two; it mirrors neither one nor the other; it provides images neither of reality nor of ideas. And depending upon the spiritual strivings of an age, it approaches closer to the actual world of the individual or flies upward to the world of pure concepts. Where it has found its point of balance between the two, there it has created its most eternal works."

13   Oscar Wilde, *The Complete Works of Oscar Wilde* (New York: Harper & Row, 1989) 1071. All future references to Wilde are drawn from this edition and cited in the text.

14   Frederick Philip Grove, "Author's Note to the Fourth Edition (1939)," *A Search for America* (Toronto: McClelland and Stewart, 1991) 459.

15   Interestingly, Greve's description of the *entwurzelt* is framed in examples highly suggestive of his own experience as a man who in his youth in Europe travelled widely between identities and cultural interests and locations, becoming, as Gide seems to have recognised, an artist of life "fremd und zu Hause" in a variety of contexts. Similarly, it is the formation of the artist in physical and experiential travel that forms the core of Grove's subsequent autobiographical writing. See Klaus Martens, *Felix Paul Greves Karriere* for an account of Greve's European transformations and peregrinations and Grove's *In Search of Myself* and *A Search for America* for descriptions of his North American development.

16   "But the uprooted individual [...] is a portrayer. He looks in two directions simultaneously; he stands at a fork in the path overlooking the way to the north-east and north-west: he is inevitably an artist! A budding artist because he sees the variance of things; his vision is plastic. Therein lies the consolation and the tragedy of his fate. He sees two paths and follows both as a foreigner and is nonetheless at home on both of them. And is not the artist always a foreigner, does he not always carry the mark of Cain on his forehead? All artists are decadent, if decadence is the result of uprooting. And yet there are degrees! And one could well imagine an artist who would be, thanks to his origins—spiritual and physical—both foreign to and at home in all of the cultures, races, customs and religions of the world: a wanderer over the earth, foreign to and at home in Christianity, foreign and at home amongst Brahmins along the Ganges, foreign and at home with the great redeemer Buddha, foreign and at home in the spirit of a Nietzsche and an Augustin—at once a German, a Briton, a Roman, a Greek, an Italian, a Frenchman, a Swede and a Russian. Such an individual would be completely "uprooted," in other words he would have his roots everywhere; he would be many rooted [...]."

17   "But the pose became real to him and reality paled beside it and where it was not pale he mistook dream for reality and for this life took its revenge."

18   Frederick P. Grove, *Settlers of the Marsh* (Toronto: McClelland and Stewart, 1974) 60. Further references to this novel cited in the text as *Settlers*.

19   The extent to which Grove used depictions of Clara's face as a kind of Wildean leitmotif may be seen with reference to pages 88, 91, 133, 151, 152, 157, 163, 169 and 170 in *Settlers*.

20   In this paper I have been concerned with tracing Wilde's presence in Grove's aesthetic, and its realisation in *Settlers of the Marsh*. I have not addressed the artistic or ideological nature of that aesthetic. The vision of pioneer life represented by Niels Lindstedt is certainly conservative, even patriarchal. For a reading more attentive to ideological dimensions of Greve's writing see Irene Gammel, *Sexualising Power in Naturalism: Theodore Dreiser and Frederick Philip Grove* (Calgary: University of Calgary Press, 1994), with reference to *Settlers of the Marsh* and the representations of Ellen and Clara, particularly chapter 12, "The Father's Seduction and the Daughter's Rebellion," 207–31.

"Out of the Wastage of All Other Nations"

"Enemy Aliens" and the "Canadianization" of Felix Paul Greve

MIDWAY THROUGH Felix Paul Greve's first Canadian novel, *Settlers of the Marsh*, the protagonist, Niels Lindstedt, proposes to Ellen Amundsen and is rejected. The rejection devastates Niels. Months later, still seeking to recover his mental and emotion balance, he develops a new plan.

> A new dream arose: a longing to leave and to go to the very margin of civilisation, there to clear a new place; and when it was cleared and people began to settle about it, to move on once more, again to the very edge of pioneerdom, and to start it all over anew... That way his enormous strength would still have a meaning. Woman would have no place in his life. He looked upon himself as belonging to a special race—a race not comprised in any limited nation, but one that cross-sectioned all nations: a race doomed to everlasting extinction and yet recruited out of the wastage of all other nations... (119)

Kristjana Gunnars, in her Afterword to the New Canadian Library edition of *Settlers*, describes this last sentence as "perhaps the strangest statement in the whole book": "The immigrant as 'wastage' from other nations," she declares, "is a low view indeed, and says a great deal about Niels's view of himself and his fellow settlers" (273). In *Scandalous Bodies: Diasporic Literature in English-Canada*, Smaro Kamboureli makes that statement the focus of her detailed and insightful analysis of the novel. I want to take up Kamboureli's analysis of the figure of the immigrant as "wastage" not to call it into question but to recontextualize and refocus it. Whereas Kamboureli analyses what she terms Niels's—and Greve's—"libidinal realism," I intend to focus on the historical circumstances in which Felix Paul Greve settled in Canada and resumed his life as a writer. When Greve settled in Manitoba, Canada's relation with its non-English immigrants in the west was badly strained and would soon be in crisis. In the early years of his teaching and writing life in Canada, Greve saw himself as caught between these non-English immigrants—epitomized in the 1920s by the "non-preferred," central Europeans—and the dominant British society in Canada, removed from both groups and yet mediating between them. This role shaped both FPG's persona as a writer in Canada, and his best-known Canadian texts, *Settlers of the Marsh* and *A Search for America*. Although Greve saw himself as caught between these groups, his early writing was itself mediated, in part, by provincial and federal government policies designed to "Canadianize" its non-English-speaking immigrants. Greve enjoyed considerable success in his role as mediator between the English and the non-English, the "preferred" and the "non-preferred"; indeed, in the late 1920s, FPG himself was taken up as a figure of the "new Canadian," that is, of the "preferred" European immigrant "assimilated" to "British civilization." Greve used his newfound status not only to advance his own career but to argue on behalf of immigrants from the non-preferred nations of central Europe.

With much of Kamboureli's analysis of *Settlers of the Marsh*, I am in agreement. She questions "the value attributed to realism in ethnic literature" and points out that it "relies on a supposed unity between literary representation and social reality" (66). Like Kamboureli, I question that unity. The canonization of *Settlers of the Marsh* suggests, as she argues, that the novel corresponds more to "hegemonic dispositions of the day" than to social reality. The novel employs what Kamboureli terms "the mode of selective realism"; that is, it "refrains from representing those immigrants whose experiences were predicated on the socioeconomic and symbolic values attached to 'wastage'" (51). The immigrants in *Settlers* are almost entirely northern European: what is more, the members of the dominant society, who Greve elsewhere refers to as "Old Canadians," are themselves almost never represented. Of these absences, Kamboureli writes:

So when the narrator puts the sign of 'wastage' under erasure, he produces a story representing the positivism of the dominant society while reflecting the complicity of the author 'outside' the text. The novel's realism, then, attempts to rise above some of the historical specificities of its period. Adopting as he does a selective approach, the narrator tells Niels's story from the point of view of the dominant humanistic ideology. He therefore invokes a spectral history that unwrites the pervasiveness of 'wastage.' From this perspective, the single inscription of 'wastage' in the narrative can only appear to be a reference to a putative reality. (52)

As Kamboureli also points out, because Niels is inarticulate much of the time, he effectively shares the role of protagonist with the narrator: "the more naive [and inarticulate] the novelistic character is, the more sagacious and dazzling the author inside the text can appear to be. Seen in this light," she argues, "Niels occupies a position that often becomes the meeting ground of Grove and the narrator" (46).[1]

For Kamboureli, the reference to the immigrant as wastage in the passage already cited is "the single most important sign invoking the critical consciousness of the author 'outside' the text": "the figure of 'wastage' brings into the novel the social paradigms about ethnicity circulating in Greve's time, paradigms that are not always compatible with Niels's character" (47). Kamboureli's primary referent for these "social paradigms" is J.S. Woodsworth's 1909 study of immigration, *Strangers Within Our Gates*. There is no denying the importance either of Woodsworth himself or of his 1909 study; however, by 1919, when Felix Paul Greve resumed his career as a writer, at least two events had significantly altered the debate over immigration. The first event was the outbreak of World War I. In *In Search of Myself* Greve claims that he arrived in Canada in the 1890s and, thus, that he participated in the first great wave of immigration to western Canada. Between 1891 and 1921 the population of Canada grew by almost four million people, increasing from 4,833,000 to 8,788,000. In the prairie provinces alone, the population grew from 219,000 in 1891 to just under two million in 1921 (Friesen 512). Most of that immigration occurred prior to 1914 and the many of the new immigrants to western Canada were from countries against which, in 1914, Canada went to war. If, as the available evidence suggests, Greve in fact settled in Manitoba in December of 1912, then he experienced not the opening of the west but its closure when Britain declared war on Germany in 1914 and immigrants from countries with whom Britain and its colonies were suddenly at war found themselves designated "enemy aliens," that is, "*unnaturalized* immigrants from countries with which Canada was at war" (Martynowych 323). Those immigrants were gradually stripped of their rights and, in some cases, interned. The impact of the Russian Revolution was no less important. The success of the Bolsheviks in Russia in the fall of 1917 heightened the British colony's fears about its immigrants from central Europe, fears intensified by the events leading up to, and culminating in, the Winnipeg General Strike in 1919. If world war created the category of "enemy alien," the Russian Revolution gave rise to the concept of "socialist revolutionaries." In 1919 fear of "enemy aliens" and "bolsheviks" prompted the dominion government to revise both the Criminal Code and the Immigration Act significantly, to develop, for the first time, a national police force, and to engage in domestic intelligence gathering and counter-subversion activities in Canada. That fear led, in short, to the emergence in Canada of the surveillance state (Kealey). Section 41 of the Immigration Act, passed into law in June 1919, stated that "'any person other than a Canadian citizen [who] advocates...the overthrow by force...of constituted law and authority' could be deported from the country" (Avery 92). In "*Dangerous Foreigners": European Immigrant Workers and Labour Radicalism in Canada, 1896–1932*, Donald Avery writes:

> This sweeping provision reinforced Section 38 of the Act which gave the governor general in council authority 'to prohibit or limit...for a stated period or permanently the landing of immigrants belonging to any nationality or race deemed unsuitable.' It was this section which had been invoked consistently to exclude either U.S. or West Indian Blacks from the country. In 1919 Section 38 was also used to exclude various European immigrants. By Order-in-Council PC 1203, Germans, Austrians, Hungarians, Bulgarians, and Turks were excluded because of their wartime associations; by Order-in-Council PC 1204 Doukhobors, Mennonites, and Hutterites were excluded

because of 'their customs, habits, modes of living and methods of holding property.' (92)

In the years immediately following World War I, as Avery notes, political and cultural acceptability displaced economic considerations as the primary criteria in the formulation of federal policies on immigration (90). Although midway through the decade Canada began once again to accept immigrants from Germany and its wartime allies, the political and cultural acceptability of immigrants remained high on the political agenda and was the subject of considerable debate.

In the early 1920s, then, Canada was preoccupied with the problem of "enemy aliens" and "socialist revolutionaries" in its midst and was intent on reasserting the Anglo-Saxon character of the colony. While the focus was on "enemy aliens" and "Bolsheviks," all non-British immigrants were suspect and fell into the category of "wastage." Following World War I, Canada virtually halted immigration from Asia and, "by determining after 1923 that only citizens of predominantly white Commonwealth countries could be deemed British subjects," the colony "effectively excluded blacks" (McLaren 58). Such people, it was assumed, could not be assimilated into the Anglo-Saxon character of the colony. Those who were not screened out and deported needed to be "assimilated" or "Canadianized." According to the business and intellectual elite, that was the immediate problem. The answer, many argued, was education. In A Study in Canadian Immigration, published by Ryerson Press in 1920, W.G. Smith writes,

What is needed is a new crusade of young Canadians in whom the fires of patriotism burn, who will man the outposts of Canadian nationality. In times of war a half-million of our best were enlisted in a gigantic struggle of destruction. In times of peace can there not be a brigade or two of equally ardent spirits who will engage in the work of construction? The final completion of the immigration task is a great wave of education carried on by patriots who will prepare the highway of the future. (397)

What Smith proposes is, in effect, a cultural war on "new Canadians." Following World War I studies such as J.T.M. Anderson's *The Education of the New-Canadian*, published by J.M. Dent & Sons in 1918, and Smith's *A Study in Canadian Immigration* (1920) displaced Woodsworth's *Strangers Within Our Gates* as touchstones on immigration. In *Our Own Master Race: Eugenics in Canada, 1885–1945* Angus McLaren writes:

> Opposition to immigration in the late nineteenth century had been raised by nativists, nationalists, and labour leaders opposed primarily to the quantity of incoming foreigners; the opposition of the interwar period was increasingly led by professional groups—doctors, social workers, and psychiatrists—employing eugenic arguments to attack the quality of the new arrivals. (66)

Anderson, the author of *The Education of the New-Canadian*, was an inspector of schools in Saskatchewan; Smith, who wrote *A Study in Canadian Immigration*, was an associate professor of psychology at the University of Toronto. Smith's study was in fact commissioned by the Canadian National Committee for Mental Hygiene. As McLaren points out, "The Committee provided anti-immigrationists with added ammunition by asserting that its surveys proved that there was a direct correlation between immigration and insanity, criminality, and unemployment" (59). This is the immigrant as wastage indeed.

It was within this historical context that Felix Paul Greve settled in Canada and resumed his career as a writer. Although Greve immigrated to Canada too late to participate in the pioneering of the west, he arrived in the right place, at the right time to experience the repressive measures taken against immigrant "aliens" and to witness the imposition of the War Measures Act, the suppression of the Winnipeg General Strike, and the emergence of a middle-class Anglo-Canadian nationalism focussed on citizenship and bent upon the "assimilation" of "New Canadians"; what is more, as a foreign teacher working in the immigrant communities of Manitoba, he in fact found himself in the front lines of battle. Greve, who became a naturalized Canadian only in December 1921, identified with those "New Canadians," whose children he and his wife taught, and must have felt himself at risk. As early as the fall of 1915, weeks after the birth of the

Greves' first child, Phyllis May, when anger against "enemy aliens" was mounting in Manitoba and, with that anger, political pressure to abolish the teaching of "enemy alien" languages in public schools, Greve told his wife, Catherine, that "'something might come up' at any time and he might have to 'pick up and leave'" (Makow 116).[2] Greve, it must be remembered, was not only a German national but an "enemy alien" with a criminal record; what is more, although he claimed to be Swedish, he was teaching German and English in one of Manitoba's bilingual German-English public schools and people in the community there "took it for granted that [he] was German" (Stobie, *Frederick* 35). When he began his writing career in Canada in 1919, the colony was tightening its restrictions on immigration and broadening its power to arrest and deport foreigners. Although Greve lived in Manitoba, which in the aftermath of the Winnipeg General Strike was undoubtedly the province of most concern when it came to "enemy aliens" and "socialist revolutionaries"; and although he found himself in the front lines of the battle over the assimilation of immigrants, there is no reference in his Canadian fiction either to the momentous events of the war years or to the retrenchment at war's end. There is also no reference to these events in the published Grove letters though, interestingly, the largest single gap in Desmond Pacey's *The Letters of Frederick Philip Grove* is for the eleven-year period from July 1914 to August 1925.[3] Similarly, there is no reference to any of these events, including the Winnipeg General Strike, in Greve's fictional autobiography, *In Search of Myself*. In short, it is not only in *Settlers of the Marsh* that Greve "produces a story representing the positivism of the dominant society while reflecting the complicity of the author 'outside' the text" (Kamboureli 52): the entire Canadian record is marked by the "selective" approach apparent in *Settlers*. Perhaps not surprisingly, the published criticism on Greve's writing has proved not less selective.

The most detailed and authoritative account of Greve's life in Manitoba is provided by Margaret Stobie in her 1973 monograph on the novelist; it is grounded not only in her study of the extant Greve papers but in the interviews she conducted with residents of the many communities in which Greve and his wife lived between 1913 and 1929, in her examination of school records, and in her perusal of the community newspapers.[4] (Many of the people she interviewed were former pupils of either Greve or his wife.) Although Stobie points out that Greve's first two teaching assignments were in German-English bilingual schools in the Mennonite communities of Haskett and Winkler south of Winnipeg, she makes no mention either of the controversy surrounding the bilingual schools or of the stormy events leading up to their closure in 1916—including the closure of the French schools—and to the suppression of "enemy alien" language instruction in the province. Greve had been granted an interim teaching permit following an interview with Robert Fletcher, Deputy Minister of Education, in Winnipeg. Concerning that interview Stobie writes:

> ...Grove must have been a welcome sight to the deputy minister. Here was a mature man, obviously intelligent, with evident teaching experience, and he spoke both German and English, even though his English had a marked European sound. At the time, Manitoba had an ambitious and idealistic bilingual school system, developing out of the French-English background of the province, but extending to bilingual schools for the settlement of Polish, Ruthenian, Swedish, Austrian, Icelandic, and German newcomers, to try to help them in the transition to their adopted country. Staffing the bilingual schools was a constant problem. (25)

Greve was granted an interim teaching permit in December 1912 and taught at Haskett from January to June 1913. After attending the ten-week normal school for German-English bilingual teachers in the summer of 1913 and writing provincial exams, he was granted professional standing and appointed principal of Winkler Intermediate School in August (Stobie, "Grove's Letters" 67). He thus entered the bilingual school system as it was approaching the limit of its expansion. The ethnic tensions fanned by World War I called Manitoba's bilingual school system into question and eventually led to its abolition.

Opposition to the province's bilingual school system had developed, however, long before the outbreak of war. The bilingual school system had its origin in Section 10 of the Manitoba Public Schools Act (1897). According to Section 10, "Where ten of the pupils in any school speak the French language (or any language other than English) as their native language, the teaching of such pupils shall be in French (or such other language), and English upon the bilingual system" (emphasis added). That provision was one of the terms of the Laurier-Greenway Agreement drafted to resolve the Manitoba School Question. Marilyn Barber offers the following account of the controversy:

> In the 1890s the English-speaking majority, becoming more dominant in the province and encouraged by Ontario, demanded that the existing system of Protestant and Roman Catholic schooling be replaced by a uniform national school system with no special rights for Roman Catholics and with English as the language of instruction. The Roman Catholic minority predominantly French-speaking, led by Archbishop Taché and his successor Archbishop Langevin and supported by Quebec, fought to retain the separate official status of the Roman Catholic schools. The resulting compromise in 1897, known as the Laurier-Greenway Agreement, satisfied neither group. In response to the will of the majority, a uniform nondenominational system was imposed. However, the minority won on the language issue as a bilingual system of education was made mandatory if requested by the parents of ten pupils in a school who spoke French *or any language other than English*. (287; emphasis added)

Immigrants who arrived in western Canada at the turn of the century, particularly those who immigrated under the bloc settlement program, believed they could retain their language, religion and customs: some, like the Mennonites, had made retention of their language, religion and customs a condition of their immigration; others, like the Ukrainians, had that belief reinforced not just by "the reservation of bloc settlement areas for ethnic groups" but by the subsequent development of the bilingual school system, and by the establishment of normal schools for Ukrainian-speaking teachers, as they and other groups exercised their rights under section 10 of the Manitoba School Act (Jaenen 517).[5]

In developing the bilingual school system, however, the ethnic minorities and the provincial government were working at cross purposes. While the ethnic communities regarded bilingual schools as a means of retaining their language, religion and culture, the provincial government and the English majority saw those schools simply "as a transitional stage leading to unilingual English education" (Barber, "Canadianization" 287), that is, as a stage in the assimilation of the immigrants. In the early decades of the twentieth century, government at all levels in Canada was intent on the assimilation of non-English immigrants. They focussed the work of assimilation not on the immigrants themselves but on their children; the primary setting for that work was the public school; and its medium was instruction in English language and culture. The following statement by a Manitoba school inspector, written in 1906, reflects the English-Canadian view:

> The great work of the public school in Canada is the formation and development of a high type of national life. This is particularly true in Western Canada, with its heterogeneous population. Here are to be found people of all countries, from the keen, clever American, with highly developed national ideals, equal to but perhaps somewhat antagonistic to our own, to the ignorant peasantry of central and Eastern Europe and Asia. These incongruous elements have to be assimilated, have to be welded into one harmonious whole if Canada is to attain the position that we, who belong here by right of birth and blood, claim for her. The chief instrument in this process of assimilation is the public school. (Maguire 31)

The most visible sign of English-Canadian values was the British flag which, in 1907, the provincial government decreed must be flown outside all schools, including the bilingual schools in ethnic communities. Bilingual schools were a concern both for ethnic minorities and for the English majority: the ethnic minorities worried that a public school education in English, even an education within the bilingual school program, would irretrievably damage their children's relation to their native language and culture; the English majority feared that the ethnic communities would use the bilingual schools to inculcate in the children their own language and culture. Mennonites who opposed the organization of public schools within their settlements did so because it contravened the guarantees they had been given by the federal government when they immigrated and because it threatened to undermine their community's values. The balance between the conflicting interests of the ethnic communities and the English majority was always precarious; the peace, always uneasy; and the pressure to assimilate, unremitting. Thus, in 1909, the year in which Greve faked his own suicide and crossed the Atlantic, "the Liberal *Manitoba Free Press*...commenced an extraordinary editorial campaign demanding that the provincial government institute unilingual English-language instruction for all Manitoba children" (Friesen 346). Four years later, in the first week of January 1913, when Greve took up his teaching position in the German-English school at Haskett, J.W. Dafoe, the editor of the *Manitoba Free Press*, began a series of fifty-four articles on "The Bilingual Schools of Manitoba" in which he attacked "the critical lack of schools in immigrant districts, the low standards of education, and especially of the teaching of English, in the schools which did exist" (Barber, "Canadianization" 291).[6]

When Greve began teaching in the German-English school in Haskett in January 1913, he found himself in the middle of a struggle over bilingual education. The position he took up in Winkler in the fall of 1913 was not just as teacher but as principal with all the additional responsibilities and social prestige that involved; what is more, Winkler Intermediate School, his first assignment as a teacher with full professional standing, was scheduled to host the Annual Conference of German-English Bilingual Teachers in Southern Manitoba that fall and Greve wanted to make a good impression (Stobie, "Grove's Letters" 69). Here was a recent immigrant seeking to adjust to a new country, a new culture, a new community and a new job. As his letters to I.J. Warkentin indicate, Greve was under considerable stress.[7] To these pressures must be added the additional problem created when on August 4, 1914 Canada entered World War I and German-Canadians were classified as "enemy aliens." Canada's entry into the war came two days after Greve married Catherine Wiens in the Anglican Church in Swift Current and just weeks before he was to commence his second year as principal. Although the full impact of the war was not felt until lists of missing, dead and wounded began to appear in Canadian newspapers, the government of Robert Laird Borden was forced to address the issue of "enemy aliens," particularly of German and Austro-Hungarian army reservists, immediately. After some confusion, "the Militia Department was directed, on 7 August, to arrest all German officers and reservists and to keep their Austrian counterparts under surveillance. Next day, the government assured German nationals that they would not be interfered with provided that they did not try to aid the enemy" (Martynowych 324). "On 15 August," Orest Martynowych writes:

the Borden government announced its comprehensive policy toward enemy aliens: any subject of an enemy country whose departure from Canada might be helpful to the enemy, or anyone engaged in espionage, transmitting information to the enemy, or helping others to escape, would be subject to internment. All, however, who continued to pursue their "ordinary avocations" *and signed a "parole" to report to the police at regular intervals* and to observe the law would remain free. *Parolees who failed to report or who changed their place of residence or work without police approval would be interned* (PC 2150). A proclamation on 2 September reassured enemy aliens that they could continue to hold property and conduct business provided that they did not aid the enemy. Another, next day, commanded them to hand in their firearms, ammunition and explosives to the nearest justice of the peace or police officer (PC 2283). (324; emphasis added)

The War Measures Act, unanimously passed by Parliament on August 18, "enabled the federal cabinet to meet the wartime emergency through orders-in-council" (323). In the opening months of the war, the constraints on "enemy aliens" seemed to change almost daily and the continual stream of orders-in-council cannot have reassured members of any ethnic community. According to Donald Avery, "By [the] end of the war over 80,000 enemy aliens had been registered, though only 8,579 of these were actually interned. This number included: 2,009 Germans, 5,954 Austro-Hungarians, 205 Turks, 99 Bulgarians, and 312 classified as miscellaneous" (66).

Within months of the outbreak of World War I, the German immigrant went from being characterized as "only slightly less desirable than Englishmen" to "absolutely impossible to assimilate as a Canadian citizen" (Thompson 74, 76).[8] As John Herd Thompson notes, "the wartime reaction to the German immigrant" was a "spectacular reversal of judgment" (74). How did German-Canadians respond to these developments? They responded, Thompson suggests, by "informally 'chang[ing]' their nationality":

Frederick Philip Grove, then principal of a Manitoba school, became a Swede, one of the most popular alternative identities. Thousands of others verbally crossed the Baltic to join him or became Norwegian or Dutch, the other possible countries of refuge. The census reports of 1911 and 1921 provide some interesting figures to demonstrate this. In 1911, 18,696 residents of Manitoba, Saskatchewan, and Alberta gave their place of birth as Germany. In 1921, with little in or out migration, the figure had declined to 13,242. The 1911 figure for those born in Sweden, Norway, and Holland is 33,826. In 1921, again with little migration, it is 38,925. The difference between this increase and the German decrease is only 355. Since the statistic refers to *place of birth*, natural increase does not change these figures. Towns with German names responded as well. The most famous Canadian change-over was Berlin, Ontario, which became Kitchener, but Dusseldorf and Carlstadt, Alberta, also were rechristened, as Freedom and Alderson. (76–77)

Greve's claim to Swedish nationality, like his change of name, in fact predates the outbreak of war. Writing to Isaac J. Warkentin—his predecessor as principal at Winkler who was then studying at Leipzig University—on February 10, 1914, six months prior to the war, Greve declares that his father was a Swede, his mother, a "Scotchwoman," and that he "was raised in Germany" (Pacey, *Letters* 11).[9] Even before the Canadian public reversed its opinion regarding Germans, then, Greve felt compelled to conceal his identity. After all, he had faked his own suicide and left behind him in Germany not only his seemingly insurmountable debts but his criminal conviction for fraud; moreover, he had abandoned his first wife, Else Plötz, in the United States. Presumably he entered the German-English bilingual school system in Manitoba with the account of his nationality and upbringing he gave to Warkentin pretty much in place. Presumably, too, as resentment against German-Canadians grew, and as the campaign against the teaching of "enemy alien" languages gained strength, Greve felt compelled to distance himself as far as he could from all things German. Public opinion prompted Andreas Weidenhammer, the Canadian-born inspector for the German-English schools in the district where Greve taught, to change his name to Andrew Willows. As J.J. Healy points out about Weidenhammer's change of name, "The anti-German hysteria of World War I, which changed Berlin to Kitchener, forced a man of German origin, born in Canada, to change his name in his sixties" (89).

In May 1915 the growing "Parliament Building Scandal" forced the resignation of the provincial Conservative government and in the August election the Liberal party, lead by T.C. Norris, gained power. With the new government intent on investigating the bilingual schools, Dafoe renewed his calls in the *Manitoba Free Press* for their abolition. A bill to repeal the bilingual clause of the Public Schools Act was passed in March. In the previous fall Greve and his wife had moved to Virden "whose townspeople," Stobie remarks, "were chiefly from Ontario and the British Isles" (*Frederick* 42). According to Stobie, in the seven years following his two-year tenure in Winkler, Greve

> taught in six different schools, and in one of them for two separate stints. Within one nine-month period he taught in three different schools, a record that he later attributed to the aimless elder son of "The Weatherhead Fortunes." (42)

Greve, however, was not aimless. Stobie attributes the yearly change of schools to Greve's inability to get along with other people but the explanation may not be that simple. During the period in question, that is, from 1915 to 1922, the animosity toward enemy aliens was at its height. While Greve claimed to be Swedish, all foreigners were suspect and he had much to fear: he could not prove his nationality—proof was increasingly a requirement—and he was not a naturalized Canadian. (He did not receive his naturalization papers until December 1921.) Getting along with other people may not have been one of Greve's strengths but relating to others during this period could not have been easy. Is it possible that Greve's departure from Winkler was prompted by his desire to move out of the German-English bilingual school system because of the tensions exacerbated, if not created, by the war, because of the scrutiny the bilingual schools—particularly the German-English schools—were undergoing, and because of his own need to stay out of trouble? Is it entirely coincidental that he moved from the German community of Winkler to a town consisting of people "chiefly from Ontario and the British Isles"? Is it possible, too, that he moved regularly, in part, to lessen the chance that his identity might be challenged? Interestingly, he stopped moving after 1922, when he had received his own naturalization papers and when the resentment against enemy aliens had, in any case, begun to abate.

FIGURE 18: Great War Veterans Association Parade, Winnipeg 4 June 1919. Archives of Manitoba. N12295

FIGURE 19: Great War Veterans Association demonstration at City Hall, Winnipeg 4 June 1919. Archives of Manitoba. N12296

I do not have the space here either to detail all the events relevant to the treatment of "enemy aliens"—and aliens generally—during and immediately following World War I or to relate them to events in Greve's life as a teacher and writer in Manitoba. Four events, however, merit brief comment. The first was the founding of the Great War Veterans' Association in Winnipeg in April 1917. That returning soldiers were a potent force stirring hostility against enemy aliens—indeed, against aliens generally—has never been seriously questioned. This was particularly true in western Canada (figure 18). As Desmond Morton and Glenn Wright note, "The simmering pre-war hostility to immigrants" in western Canada "was given respectability by the war" (71). At its founding convention in Winnipeg, delegates voted "to conscript all aliens, *friendly and hostile*, 'for any service the government deems fit'" (71; emphasis added) and veterans' groups "thereafter regularly petitioned the government to disfranchise 'enemy aliens,' to conscript 'allied aliens' for military service and 'enemy aliens' for labour on soldiers' pay ($1.10 per day) and to suppress all 'enemy alien' newspapers" (Martynowych 421–22). The second event involved the federal government's response to these developments. In September 1917 Borden's Conservative government, which could no longer postpone the need for a federal election, passed the Wartime Elections Act. As Martynowych points out,

> the Wartimes Election act enfranchised all mothers, wives, widows, sisters and daughters of servicemen and disfranchised all Mennonites, Doukhobors, German-speaking immigrants born in Russia, conscientious objectors, and individuals convicted under the Military Service Act or who had applied for exemption. Also disfranchised were immigrants from enemy countries naturalized after 31 March 1902 (unless they had sons, grandsons or brothers on active duty). (423–24)

The purpose of the act was to secure a Conservative victory at the polls or to force the Liberal party into a Union government; nevertheless, Thompson rightly argues, it was passed "because the Borden government had received considerable assurance of its popularity as well as its possible necessity" (80). At the same time, Martynowych notes, the passage of the Wartime Elections Act "appeared to sanction anti-alien prejudice and emboldened nativists and advocates of compuls[ory military service] to press for even more drastic measures, and especially for the conscription of alien labour" (425).

The third event was the Russian Revolution, particularly the Bolshevik seizure of power in October 1917. In the months following that event, Canada's fledging security agencies began hunting for Bolshevik revolutionaries as well as for agents of the German government. In the small prairie towns, the effect was not to shift the focus away from usual enemy aliens but to make all aliens increasingly suspect. In September 1918 a government report linked labour radicalism to Bolshevik conspiracy and "recommended the suppression of radical organizations and foreign-language publications, the extension of search and surveillance operations, and the establishment of a public safety branch to co-ordinate security operations" (Martynowych 436). In the fall of 1918 a flurry of orders-in-council proclaimed a new series of repressive measures directed at "enemy aliens," including bans on "all publications in twelve 'enemy' languages, including Ukrainian, German, Russian and Finnish (PC 2381)," bans on strikes and lockouts (PC 2525) and restrictions on the right of assembly (Martynowych 437). The return of unemployed soldier's at war's end only heightened the tension and led to widespread violence directed against not just "enemy aliens" but "aliens" generally. Many veterans called for the immediate deportation of all enemy aliens and the confiscation of their property. This is the background for the Winnipeg General Strike (figure 19). The fourth event involves the changes made by the federal government to the Immigration Act and to the Naturalization Act in the immediate aftermath of the strike. In the midst of the strike, J.W. Dafoe had argued in the *Free Press* that order could be restored if authorities were "to clear the aliens out of the community and to ship them back to their happy homes in Europe which vomited them forth a decade ago" (Bercuson 127). That sentiment was shared by a great many veterans and the federal government's revision of its immigration and naturalization policy seemed to sanction those views. Changes to the Immigration Act made it possible to deport anyone other than a Canadian citizen for advocating "the overthrow by force...of constituted law and authority"; changes to the Naturalization Act enabled authorities to strip alien radicals of their naturalization and deport them from the country (Avery 92; Martynowych 441). At the same time, the government invoked an extant section of the Immigration Act—section 38, designed "to prohibit or limit...for a stated period or permanently the landing of immigrants belonging to any nationality or race deemed unsuitable"—to prevent Germans, Austrians (including Ukrainians), Hungarians, Bulgarians and Turks from entering Canada because of their "wartime associations" (Avery 92; Martynowych 441). This measure remained in force until 1923.

Are these historical events relevant to an understanding of Greve's Canadian writing? Do they enter into that writing in any form? These events are not only relevant but central to an understanding of Greve's Canadian writing. In support of that argument, I offer three kinds of evidence. No one piece of evidence alone is convincing but the three together are, I believe, persuasive. The first is from Greve's "autobiographical" writing. Although Greve lived more than half of his Canadian years in Ontario and wrote his later novels out of his Ontario experience, in *In Search of Myself* and elsewhere he consistently represents himself as a *prairie writer*, that is, as a Manitoban, and as a *novelist*. In other words, Greve makes his years on the prairie, specifically his years teaching in the small immigrant communities of Manitoba, the crucible of his writing life in Canada. In his autobiographical writing Greve consistently represented himself as a prairie writer and a pioneer and this is how he has been represented by critics. In 1945 Ryerson Press published Desmond Pacey's study *Frederick Philip Grove*, the first monograph on the novelist. At the outset of that study Pacey advanced the representation of the novelist that would remain in force for decades to come. Pacey writes:

> The settlers who pioneered the prairies of Western Canada in the late
> nineteenth and early twentieth centuries were of diverse racial and
> national origins. It is fitting that the writer who recorded in the form
> of fiction the effort and achievement of these people was himself an
> immigrant of mixed racial strains and of extremely cosmopolitan
> background. (1)

Pacey identifies Greve not only as a western Canadian novelist but as an immigrant who participated in the settlement of the west, who, like the western pioneers, was himself of "mixed blood," and who faithfully depicted that era in his fiction. As part of the research for his monograph, Desmond Pacey read a typescript of *In Search of Myself*. If one can trace the biographical details in Pacey's monograph to the autobiography, so, too, can one see behind Pacey's representation of the novelist as an immigrant among the western pioneers Greve's argument in *In Search of Myself* that his life experiences had uniquely fitted him to be a spokesman for the race of pioneers who settled western Canada. Behind the critical representation of Greve as a prairie novelist, in short, lies his own representation of himself as a westerner and as a novelist.

That self-representation can be traced to the 1920s and leads me to the second piece of evidence. I am *not* arguing that Greve resumed his career in Canada to become a spokesman on behalf of European immigrants. I am suggesting, however, that having returned to writing, he seized on immigration and settlement as his subject. In the burst of creativity that came with his return to writing in 1919, Greve in effect worked on several books at once (Makow 120). In addition to the collection of sketches that became *Over Prairie Trails* and led to *The Turn of the Year*, he rapidly planned two other works: one evolved into *Settlers of the Marsh*; the other, into *A Search for America*. In its early stages, *Settlers* was a "Three Book Series entitled LATTER-DAY PIONEERS." As Margaret Stobie points out, an early outline includes a "list of characters in four groups according to their nationality: five English, five Scandinavians, five German (but one is crossed out), and five Slav" (*Frederick* 77). Interestingly, it is this book, his first novel, that Greve reportedly began writing in German (Makow 120). *A Search for America*, in its earliest stages, was variously titled *The Immigrant* or *The Emigrant* and dealt both with the plight of the immigrant and the newcomer's disillusionment with the New World (Stobie, *Frederick* 59–60).

Greve began both books at the height of the colony's panic over its "enemy aliens" and in the midst of tightening restrictions on immigration; by the time they appeared in print, however, circumstances had changed considerably. In the years immediately following World War I, returning soldiers flooded the labour market and, to make matters worse, the colony's economy went into recession; consequently, the demand for immigrant labour was low. By 1925, the year in which *Settlers of the Marsh* was published, the economy had strengthened considerably and the demand for workers was strong. The CPR and the CNR joined forces to persuade the federal government to loosen restrictions on immigration. The result was the Railways Agreement, which effectively gave the two railways a free hand to bring "non-preferred" immigrants into the country. By the time Greve published *A Search for America*, the debate over immigration and the need to assimilate these "non-preferred immigrants" to Anglo-Canadian culture had heated up yet again and forced the Liberal government of Mackenzie King "to have the subject of immigration policy examined by the Select Committee on Agriculture and Colonization" (Avery 110). The books Greve conceived at one moment in the colony's panic over immigrants were taken up in another. It is here that the story gets very interesting and that I must move to my third and final piece of evidence. H.C. Miller, the president of Graphic Press, the Ottawa-based, nationalist publisher, worked hard to convince Greve that *A Search for America* should be released in Canada under Graphic's imprint. Did he do so because he recognized the topicality of Greve's book to the debate over immigration? If he did not, Graham Spry, the National Secretary of the Association of Canadian Clubs, certainly did. Immediately after reading the book, Spry contacted Graphic and began organizing the first of three lecture tours Greve would complete under the auspices of the Association. Greve's first lecture tour in fact coincided with the Select Committee's hearings on immigration policy.

If Greve did not recognize the topicality of *A Search for America* when Spry first approached him with the idea of a lecture tour, he quickly caught on. Although Greve lectured on literary and other topics, he focussed in all three lecture tours on the issues of immigration, assimilation, and nationhood. The position he takes is controversial but, as Enoch Padolsky points out, Greve "shows not only a good grasp of the issues that needed to be addressed but also an awareness of the sensitivities of Canadians on the question" (36). The lecture he gave on his first tour, "Canadians Old and New," in the spring of 1928 was popular and appeared in *Maclean's* before Greve completed the tour. His lecture on assimilation was also published by *Maclean's* and versions of the address on nationhood appeared both in the Association of Canadian Club's journal, *The Canadian Nation*, and in Greve's own collection of essays, *It Needs to be Said*. Greve begins the essay on assimilation with the following statement:

We are worried today over ethnic problems. By certain persons—or shall I call them interests?—a formidable-looking indictment has been drawn up against the immigrant. A great deal has been said about preferred and non-preferred nationalities. I wonder with how much justification. ("Assimilation" 177)

I do not have time here to detail Greve's position on these issues, other than to say that he opposed the concept of preferred and non-preferred nationalities; that he spoke against the concept of assimilation—the foreigners, he argued, had something to give as well as to receive—and that his vision of nationhood was one of cultural pluralism, though it must be remembered that he, like most intellectuals in Canada at the time, ruled out immigration from continents other than Europe and favoured continued restrictions on the immigration of Jewish peoples.

If Greve was critical of the colony's policies on immigration and assimilation, why did Canada's business class and its allies among Canada's middle-class progressives, in effect, give him a platform from which to criticize those policies? The answer, I think, is that Greve's appearance on the platform, regardless of what he said, was itself the message: here was a European immigrant who had been assimilated into Anglo-Canadian culture, who, through his very presence on the platform, demonstrated that foreign immigrants could be transformed into intelligent and loyal citizens of the nation, who could, moreover—in the words of one commentator—rise "from an obscure teaching post to a place of eminence among Canadian authors" (Mount Allison citation 3), who was indeed a distinguished English-Canadian author. On June 7, 1928 R.B. Bennett rose in the House of Commons to declare:

These people [central Europeans] have made excellent settlers; they have kept the law; they have prospered and they are proud of Canada, but it cannot be that we must draw upon them to shape our civilization. We must still maintain that measure of British civilization which will enable us to assimilate these people to British institutions, rather than assimilate our civilization to theirs. That is the point.... We earnestly and sincerely believe that the civilization which we call the British civilization is the standard by which we must measure our own civilization; we desire to assimilate those whom we bring to this country to that civilization, that standard of living, that regard for morality and law and the institutions of the country and to the ordered and regulated development of the country. That is what we desire, rather than by the introduction of vast and overwhelming numbers of people from other countries to assimilate the British immigrants and the few Canadians who are left to some other civilization. (Palmer 119)

Greve, in short, seemed to be living proof that non-English immigrants could successfully be assimilated into British civilization and that the threats seemingly posed by foreign traditions and cultures could be contained.

ACKNOWLEDGEMENT

This essay is part of a larger project on Canadian cultural nationalism in the 1920's. I gratefully acknowledge funding provided by the Social Sciences and Humanities Research Council of Canada and by The University of Alberta.

NOTES

1   This aspect of narration is often seen as a feature of naturalism. On narration in naturalist texts and on Greve's naturalism, see Gammel, *Sexualizing Power in Naturalism: Theodore Dreiser and Frederick Philip Grove* (1994).
2   The tendency of Grove criticism to date has been to interpret such statements as signs of his concealed identity as Greve. I am arguing here for a more complex reading that places Greve's need of concealment within the larger context of Canada's treatment of its "enemy aliens."
3   The subsequent discovery and publication of five letters Greve wrote to his wife between September and November of 1919—see Makow—only serves to underscore the relative paucity of published information regarding this period in FPG's life.
4   The most recent and authoritative account of Greve's life is provided by Klaus Martens in *F.P. Grove in Europe and Canada: Translated Lives* (2001). The primary focus

of Marten's book, however, is on Grove's life in Europe and he does little there to rethink Stobie's account of the Manitoba years.

5   On Ukrainian bloc settlements, see Martynowych 70–75.

6   Barber gives the number of articles as sixty-four. Cf. Donnelly 72 and Martynowych 357.

7   Isaac J. Warkentin (1885–1971) was Greve's predecessor as principal of Winkler Intermediate School. A Mennonite born in Manitoba, he received his BA from Wesley College—now the University of Winnipeg—and served as principal in 1912–13. He resigned that position to study at Leipzig University. He was interned in the Ruhleben Prison Camp shortly after the outbreak of World War I. See Stobie, "Letters From the Mennonite Reserve" and the article by J.J. Healy.

8   This last statement is from the *Winnipeg Tribune*, March 26, 1920 and reflects the post-war concern with the political and cultural acceptability of immigrants rather than with more purely economic measures.

9   For an analysis of the letters see Stobie and Healy. Both authors focus particular attention on the long letter of February 10, 1914 in which Greve makes this statement.

PART III

Translation and **Mediation**

Randarabesken zu Oscar Wilde/
Oscar Wilde: Marginalia in Arabesque

◆ Introductory Note

OSCAR WILDE was a figure of profound importance to the German poet, novelist, playwright, essayist and translator Felix Paul Greve—important as a model of aesthetic orientation for the young writer, probably; as a vehicle for self-introduction into Germany's literary world as a critic, dramatist and translator, certainly; and as personal example of the perils of life as literary *bohémien*, definitely. Greve's ultimately failed, though nonetheless prolific, career as German *Literat* was from beginning to end closely entwined with Oscar Wilde. It was with Wilde that Greve chose, after the publication of his volume of poetry *Wanderungen* and his play *Helena und Damon* in 1902, to introduce himself as an arbiter and mediator of literary taste through his translations of a great contemporary writer. First with his privately-printed translation of Wilde's *Phrases and Philosophies for the Use of the Young* (1902) and his translation of *Intentions* (J.C.C. Bruns, 1902), and then with his critical study of 1903, *Oscar Wilde*, Greve was preparing the German reading public for the arrival of both an ambitious series of Wilde translations *and* further acquaintance with a talented young man of letters, Felix Paul Greve. Unfortunately for Greve, however, fate visited upon him a double set-back in 1903: just as his translations became mired in copyright disputes, so his debut as a young man of letters was hindered by a conviction for fraud. Nonetheless, and despite these hindrances, Greve proceeded out of his early interest in Wilde to translate André Gide and a tremendous range of other authors before his "death" in 1909. Despite his growing interest in other authors, Wilde was not forgotten; and as if to close the circle of his career in Germany, Greve's last critical study to be published in Germany was "Oskar Wilde" in 1911, a reprint of the earlier *Oscar Wilde* of 1903.

Randarabesken zu Oscar Wilde, offered below in translation as "Oscar Wilde: Marginalia in Arabesque," appeared late in 1903 as an independent publication, although it was intended as the foreword to Greve's translations of *The Portrait of Mr. W.H.* and *Lord Arthur Savile's Crime*, in which form it subsequently appeared upon publication of these translations in 1904. Dated October 1903, Bonn, it would seem that Greve wrote this unusual study while serving time in Bonn gaol for his conviction for fraud. Certainly, the embittering, Wildean experience of serving time in prison seems to have coloured Greve's assessment of Wilde. Gone is the more distanced, scholarly tone of Greve's March 1903 study, *Oscar Wilde*, in which criticism of putative aesthetic failings was based on Wilde's psychology. In *Randarabesken*, the twenty-four year-old Greve adopted a rhapsodic, quasi-Nietzschean tone with which to register his sense of aesthetic displeasure and, perhaps more importantly, his personal censure of a man Greve felt had abandoned life and art for dream and pose. In *Randarabesken*, Greve's insights pertain to Wilde, but also reach beyond him seeking a quality of universal validity. For a contemporary audience, *Randarabesken* is certainly of interest not only because of this universalising quality but also because of Greve's suggestive use of extended metaphors of financial ledgers and bankruptcy and for his discussion of the *déraciné*, a category of individual Greve would soon join, as Grove, in the United States and Canada, and which he would describe in his various fictions. Both as a study of Wilde in particular and the dangers to artistic creativity in general, then, *Randarabesken zu Oscar Wilde* provides intriguing insights into Frederick Philip Grove as the man he was—Felix Paul Greve.

1.

Oscar Wilde—ah, kommst du wieder aus deinem Grabe und willst mein
Opfer? Gab ich dir nicht genug, als ich dir Blut und Leben und Arbeit gab?
Bist du wirklich von jenen Seelen, die mit dem einmaligen Opfer nicht
zufrieden sind? Gehörst du zu denen, die wiederkommen—die durch das
Blut eines Kälbleins oder Lammes nicht in ihr Grab zu bannen sind—die
wiederkommen und denen, die ihnen nahe standen, das Blut aus den
Adern saugen, wenn sie im Schlafe liegen? ... bist du ein Vampyr? ... Ah, du
schweigst und blickst mich aus den tiefen Augen an, und dein einst
blühendes, glänzendes Haar ist wirr in die Stirne gestrichen, und dein
geschwungener Mund, der feine mit den wundersamen Linien, lächelt? ...
Was willst du denn? ... Was hebst du die Hände und zeigst sie mir? ... Ah ...
trägst du die Wundenmale, die einst der Grosse trug, den du gelästert und
angebetet hast? Ist das das Rätsel? ... Ah, aber deine Augen! ... Ich traue dir
nicht! ... Und dein Mund—das ist der Mund, der die Kunst des Lügens
pries, und der Gebete zu Satan sandte ... Sage mir, was du willst—denn
deine stummen Zeichen, die Wundenmale deiner Hände genügen mir
nicht! ... Und jetzt gar der Vorwurf in deinem Blick—noch einmal: was
willst du? ... Ja, ja, ich weiss, was du willst. Ich soll es künden, wer du
warst, soll sagen, was du selbst für die Nachwelt nicht zu sagen vermoch-
test ... Und ich versprach es, so sagst du ... ich versprach, dich zu erlösen ...

2.

Genug der Phantasmen! Hinunter in dein Reich, du König des Todes, dass
du nicht hörst, was ich meinen Lesern zuflüstern will! ... Rings um mich ist
nüchterner Tag, und ich sehe im Geist die Köpfe der Leute, die von mir
etwas über einen englischen Dichter zu hören verlangen, und vor mir liegt
ein Brief des Verlegers, der einen Essay über den englischen Dichter will,
um ihn einem Bändchen mit zwei Satiren vorzuheften. Ah, als ich den Brief
erhielt, da sagte ich entschlossen: »Nein!! Nichts mehr von Wilde!« ... Ich
habe ein Verbrechen an ihm begangen, als ich ihn übersetzte, und seitdem
hat er sich mir an die Fersen geheftet und will, ich soll das Verbrechen
sühnen—soll es sühnen, indem ich sein Leben erzähle. Er hat mich nicht

1.

Oscar Wilde—can that be you, returning from the grave once again in search of sacrifice from me?[1] Did I not sacrifice enough in offering up my blood, my life and my work? Are you one of those souls who remain unsatisfied with the offering of a single sacrifice? Are you one of those who keep returning—one who is not to be banished to the grave with the blood of a calf or lamb—who keeps returning to suck the blood from the veins of those dear to them as they lie sleeping? ... Could it be that you are a vampire? ... Ah, you remain silent, gazing at me from your deep eyes, your once full and shining hair matted against your forehead while your delicate, wondrously lined, aquiline mouth laughs? ... What is it you want? ... Why do you lift up your hands to me? ... Ah .... do you bear the signs of suffering that He once bore, He whom you mocked and worshipped? Is that your riddle? ... But those eyes! ... I don't trust you! ... And that mouth— that is the very mouth that extolled the art of lying and addressed prayers to Satan. ... Tell me what it is you want—your wordless gestures and the signs of suffering on your hands are not enough! ... And now that look of reproach—once again, what is it you want? ... Yes, it is true, I know what you want. I am to proclaim to the world who you were, to announce to posterity what you yourself refused to say.... And I promised, as you rightly say, I promised to redeem you.

2.

Enough with phantoms! Descend to your realm, king of death, you needn't hear what I have to whisper to my readers! ... All about me is sober light of day. I see in my mind's eye the heads of the people who demand to hear from me something of an English poet, and in front of me lies a letter from the publisher who requires an essay about an English poet to append to a slim little volume containing two satires. Upon receiving the letter, I resolutely exclaimed: "No!! Nothing more of Wilde!" ... I committed a crime against him in translating him and since then he has pursued me, demanding atonement for my crime; I am to atone for it by recounting his life. He has refused to release me. He even besieged me upon my flight to an altar

losgelassen: er hat mich belagert, wenn es mir gelungen war, irgendwo an einen Altar zu flüchten, der mich vor der Verfolgung zu schützen versprach. Er ist mir übers Meer gefolgt und in die Kammer zu meiner Geliebten. Als ich am Ätna stand und in Gedanken an die Feuerschlünde jubelte, in die ich blicken wollte, da ist er plötzlich neben mich getreten und hat mir gedroht: auch dort oben lasse ich dich nicht los, wenn du mir nicht die Sühne versprichst ... und köstliche Stunden flüsternder Liebe hat er mir vergiftet, indem er einen Pfeil der Satire zwischen die Lippenpaare schoss. Und schliesslich habe ich ihm ein Opfer gebracht: ich habe drei Bücher über ihn geschrieben, und eins davon sogar exzerpiert und die Exzerpte als Essay veröffentlicht; und nun bin ich ihn endlich, endlich los—er ist fort, er lässt mich in Ruhe: seit Wochen, seit Monaten schon: ich träume wieder meine eigenen Träume und bin nicht mehr der Sklave fremden Seins. »Vielleicht hat Gott ihn geholt«—so sagte ich mir—»vielleicht auch der Teufel—und jetzt, wo ich endlich wieder atme und lebe, jetzt soll ich mir freiwillig all die Last wieder auf die Schultern laden? ... ich soll einen Essay über ihn schreiben, damit er mich von neuem fasst und quält? ... « Ah—und ich hatte den Herrn Verleger noch gar im Verdacht, er wolle dies gottverfluchte, so schmale Bändchen mit den zwei Satiren nur etwas schwellen, indem er dem jungen Autor zugleich die Ehre antat, einen Essay aus seiner Feder zu drucken: so konnte er doch ein Opus, das originaliter von ihm stammte, im Druck bestaunen! ... Aber der junge Autor, der gar nicht mehr so drucklüstern war, warf den Brief beinahe entrüstet hin und schrieb aufs Kuvert: »zu beantworten: nein!« ... Aber ach! das war vor zwei Monaten—und inzwischen habe ich gemerkt, dass weder Gott noch der Teufel Wilde geholt hat: er sitzt mir wieder im Blut und stachelt von neuem und ist mit dem schmalen Büchlein des Opfers durchaus nicht zufrieden und will seine Sühne nicht minder energisch als ehedem. Und ich—ich habe mich entschlossen, einen Pakt mit ihm zu schliessen: und von diesem Pakt will ich euch heut' ein Wörtlein sagen ... Ihr wisst, in den alten Märchen—bei Grimm und anderswo—da werden oft mit dem Teufel Pakte geschlossen. Und immer meint der Teufel, er sei der Listige, und lacht sich ins Fäustchen ... und immer ist es nicht wahr: denn das Bäuerlein, das mit ihm paktierte, ist noch etwas listiger und lacht zuletzt. Und ich will heute des Bäuerleins Rolle spielen und statt über Wilde über ein unbeschriebenes Buch reden, das von ihm handelt. Nur darf er nicht

that promised protection from his pursuit. He followed me over the seas and into my lover's chamber. As I stood on Etna and rejoiced in contemplation of the fiery maw into which I wished to peer, he suddenly approached me and threatened me: "Even here I will not release you until you have promised atonement." ... and he poisoned delicious hours of whispering love by shooting an arrow of satire between paired lips. All this, despite the sacrifice I have offered up to him: I have written three books about him, one of which I even selected excerpts from to publish as an essay. Now, however, I am finally free of him, finally free—he's gone, he's been leaving me in peace for weeks now, for months—I am again dreaming my own dreams and am no longer the slave of a foreign being. "Perhaps God summoned him" I said to myself "and then again perhaps the devil—and now that I can finally live and breathe freely, am I again, of my own free will, to burden my shoulders with all this weight? ... am I to write another essay about him, allowing him once again to seize me, to torment me?" At the time, I even suspected the venerable publisher of wanting to pad his curséd little edition of two satires by offering a young author the honour of publishing the product of his pen, thus allowing him to admire in print his own work. An opus! ... But the young author, no longer so impressed by the prospect of seeing himself in print, threw the letter down with something approaching indignation and wrote on the envelope: "To be answered: No!" ... That, however, was two months ago, and in the meantime I have noticed that neither God nor Satan have summoned Wilde. He has taken hold of me, goads me anew and is not at all satisfied with his victim's slender little volume. His demands for atonement are no less urgent than before. And I, what have I done—I have decided to conclude a pact with him; and of this pact, I would like to tell you a little something ... You are no doubt aware that in the fairy tales of old—tales by the brothers Grimm and others—pacts are often concluded with the devil. In these pacts, the devil always thinks that he is the wily one; it is he who secretly laughs up his sleeve ... And yet it never works that way, for the peasant with whom he has struck the pact is just that much wilier and ultimately has the last laugh. Today I intend to play the peasant's role, and instead of speaking about Wilde, I will speak about an unwritten book that deals with

merken, dass dieses Buch nicht geschrieben ist, und deshalb habe ich ihn in die Unterwelt geschickt.

3.

Ich träume von einem Buch über Wilde ... Einem Buch, in dem kein Wort stände, das nicht von ihm handelte oder von ihm eingegeben wäre, und das doch nirgends über ihn zu reden brauchte. Es würde etwas wie eine Biographie, in der aber alles eigentlich Biographische gleichgültig wäre ... Es würde ein Buch voller Abschweifungen, ein Buch ohne Thema, das nur aus »Apropos« bestände ... ein Buch voller Anbetung und voller Widerspruch ... Ein Buch, in dem viel vom Künstler die Rede wäre und wenig von der Kunst ... Ein Buch, in dem alle Töne klängen: vom höchsten Jauchzen verwegenster Lebenslust bis zum gemächlich ironischen Scherzen weltkluger Weisheit—vom Pfeilesschwirren der Paradoxie bis zum schweren Sucherschritt verzweifelter Gewissenspein—vom Herzenstimbre gütiger Erlöserworte bis zum satanischen Lachen mephistophelischer Bosheit—von festen Lauten abwehrender Selbstbehauptung und zähen Eigentrotzes bis zum schmeichelnden Flüstern verschwimmender Hingabe und rührender Liebe—von seltsamen, fremdartig ersonnenen Melodien rhythmisch ruhiger Tage bis zum kurzen Stammeln allen vertrauter Erschütterung—vom weltenfernen Spiel bis zum schauerlich übergewaltigen Ernst ... Und all das wie bunte blühende Blumen auf einer Wiese eingereiht in die Maschen blosser Erzählung, einfach aus einem Leben abgeschriebene Dinge ... Ich wollte nur erzählen und von meinen Erzählungen abschweifen, um wieder zu erzählen ... Und würde man mich nachher fragen: »verbürgst du alles, was du geschrieben hast?« so würde ich vielleicht erstaunt aufblicken und antworten: »aber er hat mir doch alles selber erzählt!« Und sagte man mir: »du hast ihn ja nie gekannt« ... so würde ich entgegnen: »nein, im Leben nicht ... und doch ...«

Ja, ja! es sollte ein wunderschönes Buch werden, das nur von Wilde redete und viel von ihm sagte, und doch würde das ganze vielleicht eine Dichtung sein: ein Abschiedsgedicht an Oscar Wilde ... Ob ich das Buch je schreibe? Ich weiss es nicht; ich weiss nur, dass ich es versucht habe und dass ich fand, ich stehe ihm noch nicht fern genug; ich kann von ihm noch nicht genug als Künstler reden ... Was ich sage, trägt noch den Stempel

him. Wilde, of course, is not to notice that this book is unwritten and thus I have returned him to the underworld.

3.

I dream of a book about Wilde... A book which would contain not a single word which was not in some way about, or inspired by, him, but which nonetheless would never need to address itself directly to him. It would be like a bibliography in which everything actually bibliographical would be irrelevant.... It would be a book full of digressions, a book without a theme, comprised only of "apropos" ... a book full of adoration and contradiction ... a book dealing prominently with an artist and yet but fleetingly with art ... a book which would sound every note—from the highest exultation of a daring will to live to the leisurely, ironic jesting of worldly wisdom—from the whizzing darts of paradox to the burdened, searching step of despairing conscience—from soothing, heartfelt words of redemption to the satanic laughter of mephistophelean evil—from the boisterous sounds of defensive self-assertion and determined self-defiance to the caressing whispers of blind devotion and impassioned love—from the strange, eerie sounding melodies of rhythmically stilled days to the abrupt stammer of shocks familiar to us all—from eccentric playfulness to frighteningly over-powering gravitas .... And all that as if it were a meadow of colourful, blooming flowers arranged in a net of nothing more than narrative, things simply written out of a life. ... I would like nothing more than to write, and from my account to digress, only then to carry on. ... And were someone to ask of me later: "Can you confirm everything you have written?" I would perhaps look up in surprise and answer: "but he told me all of this himself!" And were someone to say: "But you never knew him." ... I would thus respond: "No, in life, never ... and yet ...."

Yes, yes! It would be a wonderful book indeed, one which discussed only Wilde and which had much to say about him. Ultimately, the entire thing might even become a poetic work: a valedictory poem for Oscar Wilde ... Will I ever write this book? I don't know; I know only that I have tried and that I am still too close to him; I am still unable to speak

menschlicher Liebe und menschlichen Hasses—(denn ich hasse ihn
mindestens so sehr, wie ich ihn liebe)—Und der Mensch im Menschen ist
des Künstlers Feind …

4.

Denn das ist das Sonderbare … Man hat es gelesen, in all den Aufsätzen,
die die—meist französischen—Freunde des Dichters nach seinem Tode
über ihn schrieben, man lernt es, sobald man ein wenig an Wilde studiert:
Seine Werke sind nichts, sind nur ein bleicher Abglanz dessen, was er im
Leben war, und trotzdem enthalten sie gerade so viel von seinem Wesen als
Mensch, diesem unheimlich komplizierten Wesen, dass die Lektüre
unfehlbar zum Studium des Menschen oder doch zur Frage nach dem
Menschen führt. Er ist darin wie noch in manchem andern typisch.
Künstlerisch auf gleicher Stufe stehende Werke von einem Flaubert würden
in die Vergessenheit sinken, würden nach zehn Jahren nicht mehr gelesen
werden: Flaubert musste Kunstwerke schaffen, um sich unsterblich zu
machen, Kunstwerke ersten Ranges: … Wilde reisst seine Werke durch sich
mit in die Unsterblichkeit. Seine Werke würden versinken, wären sie nicht
ein Schlüssel zu ihm. Das ist typisch, sagte ich. Denn leben wir nicht in der
seltsamen Zeit, da es der Künstler viele gibt und der Kunstwerke gar so
wenig? … Seht euch doch um. Wer fragt nach Sophokles, wer nach
Böcklin? Wem sagt Velasquez etwas ausser durch seine Kunst? Wer sehnte
sich, in eines Phidias Alltagsleben zu spähen, oder aus dem Munde
Homers anderes zu vernehmen als seine Verse? Hunderte von Gelehrten
haben sich abgemüht, aus spärlichen Nachrichten Lebensbeschreibungen
Shakespeares aufzubauen: Wer zuckt darüber nicht die Achseln? Ich
wenigstens finde nichts Gutes in solchen Versuchen, ausser dass sie mich
lachen machen—und Lachen ist wie das Niesen gesund.—Sie alle, die
grossen Schöpfer von Kunstwerken sind mir nichts—sie sind Brot, alltäg-
liche Menschen, die mich nichts angehen. Sie haben mir nur etwas zu
sagen, sobald sie schaffen—bisweilen sind sie mir gar persönlich unangenehm: Böcklin zum Beispiel, den ich verehre, wie man nur einen Künstler
verehren kann; aber mit ihm leben … in seinem Leben forschen … nein!
alles eher als das! Ich gehe so weit, dass ich sage, der grosse Schaffende ist
bestenfalls im Leben einfach gleichgiltig, unbedeutend: er ist immer unin-

sufficiently of him as an artist ... What I say bears the stamp of human love and human hate—(for I hate him at least as much as I love him)—And the human in an individual is the artist's enemy ...

4.

And it is precisely this which is exceptional here ... It was to be read in all of the articles written by the poet's (usually French) friends after his death; one learns of it immediately upon having studied Wilde even briefly. His works are worthless, merely pale reflections of what he was in life, and nonetheless they retain so much of his being as a person, this unbelievably complex being, that a reading of them infallibly leads to studying the man, or at least to inquiring about him. In this, as in other things, he is entirely typical. Artistically, works of a similar level of quality by a Flaubert would sink into oblivion; they would no longer be read after ten years. To guarantee his immortality, Flaubert had to create true works of art—works of the highest order ... Due to the force of his personality, Wilde's works followed him into immortality. His works would sink out of sight were they not a key to him. This is all quite typical, as I have said. For do we not live in an unusual time, a time in which there is an abundance of artists and few works of art? Simply take a look around you. Who shows any interest in Sophocles, or in Böcklin? What is the source of Velazquez's appeal, if not his art? Who yearns to peer into the daily life of a Phidias or to learn something from the mouth of Homer, other than his verses? Hundreds of learned scholars have toiled to construct an account of Shakespeare's life out of the sparsest of information. Who can do more than shrug his shoulders at this? I at least find nothing valuable in these attempts other than that they make me laugh—and laughing, like sneezing, is healthy. None of them, the greatest creators of works of art, are anything to me—they are bread, everyday people of no concern to me. They have something to say to me only insofar as they create—occasionally they are even repugnant to me personally: Böcklin, for example, whom I esteem as it is only possible to esteem an artist; but to live with him, to conduct research into his life ... never! anything but that! I would go so far as to say that in terms of his life, a great artist is, at best, irrelevant, simply unimportant—he is never of interest. Interesting is his work alone! ... And were I to express it differently:

teressant. Interessant ist sein Werk! ... Und wenn ich es anders sagen soll: der grosse Schaffende ist der versteckte Mensch; er verbirgt sich ganz in sein Inneres: alles, was an ihm interessant ist, bleibt verborgen und versteckt; es kommt nur im Werk zu Tage; es ist das Werk. Alles, was sich bei sonst bedeutenden, aber nicht schaffenden Menschen in der kleinen Münze des Alltags ausgibt, wird hier geizig aufgespart, um es auf einmal hinzuschütten. Ja, ich gehe noch weiter, ich kehre meinen Satz um und sage: Man könnte einen Menschen, der an sich bedeutend ist, zum Schaffen zwingen, indem man ihm die Möglichkeit des freien Lebens und alltäglicher Mitteilung nähme:* in ihm würde sich alles sammeln und stauen, und was er nicht im Leben ausgibt, würde er in Träumen über das Leben ausgeben: und so wäre er ein Schaffender! Ob dieser Schaffende seine Schöpfung auch mitteilt, ist etwas anderes. Ich habe einmal einen Menschen gekannt, der wunderbare Gedichte gedichtet hatte und der sie mir unter dem Druck einer zwingenden Stunde mitteilte, und diese Gedichte haben mein Sein bereichert, und sie wird niemand ausser mir kennen lernen, denn sie sind nicht aufgeschrieben und nicht in Vers und Reim gebracht; und der sie dichtete, starb im Gefängnis.

Ah, der Schaffende lebt nicht ... er träumt das Leben: die Ilias, die Bakchen, Giorgiones Madonna zu Castelfranco, Shakespeares zweiter Richard und manche Gedichte von Goethe sind so vollendeter Traum, um nur ein paar zu nennen. Und dann gibt es Schaffende, die träumen nicht vom Leben, sondern vom Traume über das Leben ... Zu ihnen gehört Walter Pater ... zu ihnen gehört, soweit er ein Schaffender ist, Oscar Wilde.

Aber Wilde! wie anders! Sieht er nicht neben jenen aus wie ein Verschwender? Streut er nicht lachend und mit vollen Händen unter die Menge, was, gehütet und aufgespart und ängstlich vor jedem Blick verborgen, ein Kunstwerk gegeben HÄTTE? ... Und gäbe ich nicht willig all seine Werke hin und noch ein Jahr meines Lebens dazu, wenn er dafür ein paar Nachmittage auf eine Zigarette und eine Tasse Tee zu mir kommen könnte? ... Gebe ich nicht schon ein gut Teil meines Lebens hin, um seinen Wegen nachzuforschen, um von Freunden seine Gespräche zu erfragen, damit mir ein Abglanz seines Lebens lebendig werde? ... Dass ich ihn über-setzte, tut mir jedesmal leid, wenn ich daran denke, dass ich jenes Buch, von dem ich oben sprach, vielleicht nie schreiben werde ... denn was sind seine Werke ohne ihn?

the greatest artist is the hidden person. In his inner being he conceals himself completely. Everything of interest about him remains concealed and hidden; it comes out only in his work—indeed, that is the very work. Everything which is distributed out in the small change of the daily life of otherwise important, though not artistic, people is here greedily hoarded to be poured out all at once. Indeed, I would even go further. I would reverse the order of my sentence to say that one could force a person, who in himself is important, to create by denying him the possibility of undisturbed life and daily communication;[2] everything would gather and collect in him and what he didn't release in life he would release in dreams about life, and thus he would become an artist! Whether such an artist would communicate his creation is something else. I once knew a man who had composed wonderful poems and who communicated them to me under the pressure of trying times and these poems enriched my being, and no one other than I will ever know them, for they were never set to verse and rhyme; and he who wrote them died in prison.

Ah, but of course the artist does not live ... he dreams life: *The Iliad*, *The Bacchae*, Giorgione's Madonna at Castelfranco, Shakespeare's second Richard and selections of Goethe's poems are all such perfect dreams, to name but a few. And then there are those artists who dream not of life, but of the dream about life ... . Walter Pater is such an artist, as is, to the extent that he is an artist at all, Oscar Wilde.

But Wilde! How different he is! Next to those others, does he not seem a wastrel? Does he not dispense, laughing and with open hands, that which could have comprised a work of art, were it protected and saved and nervously guarded from the eyes of others? ... And would I not sacrifice all of his works along with a year of my own life, were he to sit down with me for a few afternoons with a cigarette and a cup of tea? ... Have I not already given up a good portion of my life to learn more of him, to inquire from friends about his conversation so that even a mere reflection of his life would live for me? That I translated him I regret each time I think that the book about which I spoke above will perhaps never be written ... for what are his works without him?

Und Wilde ist darin typisch, sagte ich: denn sind nicht heuzutage von zehn Künstlern immer neun interessanter als ihre Werke? ... Michelangelo schuf Grosses, und durch den Sixtinischen Saal gehen wir alle anbetenden Geistes: aber bei ihm fängt's an: sollte er uns so nahe stehn, weil er im Grunde nicht mehr mit seinem ganzen Blut Schaffender war? ... Wird er uns nicht immer interessanter, je weniger ihm seine Werke glücken? ... und steht er uns nicht am nächsten, wo er am glänzendsten—scheiterte? Immer wieder lese ich in Justis Michelangelo das Kapitel vom Juliusdenkmal. Wie er die Decke malte, danach frage ich wenig: ich geniesse sie selber; aber wie diese vielspältigen, armseligen Trümmer eines riesenhaften Plans, dieses Stückwerk in der Kirche hinter der Via Cavour zustande kam, das interessiert mich ... da interessiert mich der Mensch Michelangelo!

Und bei Wilde sind mir seine Werke nur noch Hilfsmittel, einen Menschen dahinter zu raten.

5.

Man lese Wildes Roman Dorian Gray. Er hat Stellen, die künstlerisch ausgezeichnet sind, er hat Partien, die wie eine grosse Tragödie packen. Trotzdem ist er als Ganzes verfehlt. Aber man gebe ihn einem gescheiten Menschen zu lesen, der sonst von Wilde nichts kennt und weiss. Er möge den Roman nach der Lektüre fortlegen, ihn nicht wiederlesen, ihn endlich ganz vergessen. Meine Frage: kann er ihn vergessen? ... O ja ... den Roman! Aber Wilde nicht. Das ist merkwürdig. Es ist merkwürdig, weil man dabei Wilde durchaus nicht mit Lord Henry Wotton identifiziert. Es bildet sich aus dem Eindruck des Werks die Vorstellung oder Ahnung einer Persönlichkeit, einer sehr merkwürdigen und vielspätigen Persönlichkeit, neben der Lord Henry blass und farblos erscheint. Man kann die gleiche Vorstellung hervorrufen, indem man einem Gespräche Wildes zuhört (bei André Gide zum Beispiel, dessen Notizen über Wilde jetzt auch in einem Buche zugänglich sind: »Prétexte«, Edition du Mercure de France; siehe auch meine Broschüre in den »Modernen Essays« Nr. 29). Sie muss in stärkstem Masse aus dem persönlichen Verkehr entsprungen sein, wo man die Maske sofort als Maske erkannte, und wo eine Geste, eine Bewegung der Hand oder ein Blick die Aussicht in die Hintergründe einer Psyche öffnete. Oft genug sah man auch da noch nicht die Wahrheit hinter der

And in this, Wilde is typical, as I have said. For are not nine out of ten of today's artists more interesting than their work? ... Michelangelo created great works, and we walk through the Sistine Chapel in awe. And yet it all begins with him. Are we really so close to him, because in principal he was no longer an artist at heart? ... Does he not become ever more interesting to us the less his works are successful? ... And is he not dearest to us at the very point where he most gloriously failed? Time and again, I read the chapter on the Julius Memorial in Justi's *Michelangelo*. The way he painted the ceiling—after this I have little to ask; I simply enjoy it for itself. But how this pathetic ruin of a colossal plan came into being, this unfinished work in the church behind the Via Cavour, that is what interests me ... there I am interested in Michelangelo the individual!

With Wilde, however, his works remain for me nothing more than aids for guessing about the person behind them.

5.

Take Wilde's novel *Dorian Gray*. In places it is artistically excellent; it has parts that read like a great tragedy. Nevertheless, as a whole it fails. Yet if one were to give the novel to a sensible person to read, someone who knew nothing from or about Wilde, he would put it down immediately after having read it, never read it again, and eventually forget it completely. But my question is: Could he forget it? Of course, he could. The novel he could forget, but not Wilde. That is odd. It is odd because one would never identify Wilde with Lord Henry Wotton. The work as a whole creates the impression or feeling of a personality, a most unusual and complex personality, beside whom Lord Henry seems pale and colourless. The same impression arises upon hearing one of Wilde's conversations (with André Gide, for example, whose notes about Wilde are now available in book form: *Prétextes*, Edition du Mercure de France; see also my brochure in *Modernen Essays* 29). This impression seems certainly to have arisen during the course of personal interaction, where the mask is immediately recognised as a mask, and where a gesture, the movement of a hand or even a look reveals a glimpse into the background of a psyche. Often enough the

Pose: wahrscheinlich sogar recht selten. Es ist, als blicke man hinter Kulissen und finde wieder Kulissen, und hinter denen wieder: ein Labyrinth voller täuschender Gänge. Aber bisweilen blitzt doch ein plötzlicher Strahl in die letzten und hintersten Kammern der Seele hinein, durch all die bunten, glänzenden Schleier hindurch, mit denen er seiner Seele Heimlichkeiten verhing.

Man denke ihn sich bei seinem Spott über das Evangelium: er lästert! er lästert wirklich! Das heisst: es ist ein Geheimnis dabei, bei diesem Spott ... er spottet, weil er nicht eingestehn will, dass ihm, was er verspottet, im Blute sitzt ...

Ist Wilde heidnisch? O—nein! Es ist merkwürdig, wie sich scharfsichtige Psychologen in diesem Punkte über Leute wie Wilde und Beardsley täuschen können. Anima naturaliter pagana nennt Arthur Symonds Beardsley: es gibt keine grössere Verkehrtheit; damit ist das Wesen des Satanisten im Prinzip verkannt: der Satanist ist Christ! ist nur als Christ verständlich! ... Und Wilde! ... Sein Spott würde im Munde eines Heiden ganz anders geklungen haben, würde schon im Munde eines Nietzsche anders klingen. Das ist überhaupt ein Rätsel: wie kommt es, dass dieselben Worte, in derselben Sprache gedruckt, anders klingen, sobald man sie liest, wenn sie bei Nietzsche stehen, anders, wenn bei Wilde? Aber einerlei—mir scheint, es ist so—vielleicht bilde ich mir's ein. Bei Nietzsche wäre es keine Lästerung, wenn er diesen Hohn auf das Evangelium gösse—bei ihm wäre es Hohn! Oder es nähme den Ton jenes grimmigen Zornes an, mit dem er im Antichristen donnert. Wilde scheint der Freiere! Aber man täusche sich nicht. Nietzsche hat gesagt: am Anfange des Evangeliums stehe der Ehebruch—er sagt es auch anders.

Wilde fragt Gide geheimnisvoll—mit der Bitte, es niemandem weiter zu sagen: »Wissen Sie, warum Christus seine Mutter nicht liebte?«—Und er macht eine kurze Pause, fasst ihn am Arm, tritt zurück, bricht brüsk in Lachen aus:—»Weil sie Jungfrau war!!« ...

Aber es ist verwegenes Spiel! Auch Saul und David und Salomo fielen! Wo lesen wir überhaupt gleichviel vom Abfall von Gott und Göttern wie im »Worte Gottes«? wie im Buch des Volks der fanatischsten Gottesdiener? Fast alle jene Könige unterlagen der ΥΒΡΙΣ. Zu Baal fielen sie ab: sie wurden zu Satanisten ... Warum kennen wir die ὕβριζ nicht mehr? Weil wir

truth behind the pose was not yet to be seen; indeed it was probably seldom seen. It is as if in looking behind one backdrop another was to be seen, and behind it still another—an entire labyrinth of deceptive paths. Occasionally, however, a sudden beam flashes into the furthest, most distant chamber of his soul, through all of the bright, flashy veils with which he had enshrouded his soul.

One is reminded of him as he mocked the Gospel—he blasphemes, he truly blasphemes! And that means, of course, that there is something secretive at play in this mockery ... he mocks because he does not want to admit that what he mocks rests in his blood...

Is Wilde pagan? Certainly not! The extent to which perceptive psychologists can be so mistaken in this point about people like Wilde and Beardsley is amazing. Arthur Symonds calls Beardsley *anima naturaliter pagana*. Nothing could be further from the truth, and in doing so the essential feature of the satanist is unacknowledged—the satanist is a Christian! He is understandable only as a Christian! ... And Wilde! His mockery would have sounded completely different in the mouth of a pagan, would have sounded different even in the mouth of a Nietzsche. That in itself is puzzling. How is it that the same words expressed in the same language sound different upon reading when used by Nietzsche and different again when expressed by Wilde? Whatever the reason, I perceive a difference, although perhaps I am just imagining it. With Nietzsche, it would not have been blasphemous were he to have heaped this derision on the Gospel—it would have been derision! Or it would take the tone of the furious wrath he thundered at the Antichrist. Wilde seems the freer! But here care is in order. Nietzsche said: "At the beginning of the Gospel is adultery"—he said it otherwise, as well.

Wilde asks Gide mysteriously—with the request that he not report it further: "Do you know why Christ didn't love his mother?"—And he pauses a moment, takes Gide by the arm, steps back, and abruptly breaks out into laughter: "Because she was a virgin!!"

Yet this is nothing more than an elaborate game! Saul and David and Salomon also fell! Where is so much to be read about breaking with God and the Gods as in "The Word of God," as in the book of God's most fanatical race of servants? Almost all of the kings succumbed to ΥΒΡΙΣ. They fell to Baal—they became satanists ... Why do we no longer know ὔβριζ?

als Gesamtheit nicht mehr gläubig sind. Nur wer wirklich gefesselt ist, kennt jene Momente der Auflehnung, die das Herz zum ὑβρίζειν treiben. Wo also die ὕβριζ auftritt, wofür ist sie das Zeichen?

Und wie Saul und David und Salomo fand sich auch Wilde zu seinem Gott zurück.

Aber er fällt ab; er spielt: er kann nicht widerstehen; es ist, als müsse, MÜSSE er versuchen, ob ihn der Blitz auch wirklich trifft, wenn er das Verbotene tut. Er m u s s nach dem Apfel greifen, weil er nicht darf. Aber nur der darf nicht, der glaubt—wenn er es auch vielleicht selber nicht weiss.—

Ebenso steht er zu Menschen.

»Sie hören mit den Augen,« sagte er zu Gide, »deshalb will ich Ihnen eine Geschichte erzählen.

»Als Narkissos tot war, waren die Blumen der Felder trostlos und baten den Fluss um Tropfen Wassers, dass sie ihn beweinen könnten.—O! antwortete ihnen der Fluss, wären alle meine Wassertropfen Tränen, ich hätte für mich selber nicht genug, Narkissos zu beweinen: ich habe ihn geliebt.—O! erwiderten die Blumen der Felder, wie hättest du Narkissos nicht lieben sollen? Er war schön.—War er schön ? sagte der Fluss.—Und wer wüsste es besser als du? Jeden Tag spiegelte er, über dein Ufer geneigt, seine Schönheit in deinen Wassern.« ... Wilde machte eine Pause.

—»Wenn ich ihn liebte, erwiderte der Fluss, so war es, weil ich, wenn er sich über meine Wasser neigte, in seinen Augen den Widerschein meiner Wasser sah.« Und dann lachte Wilde ...

»Ich mag Ihre Lippen nicht,« sagte er ein andermal; »sie sind gerade, wie die eines Menschen, der nie gelogen hat. Ich will Sie lügen lehren, damit Ihre Lippen schön werden und gewunden wie die einer griechischen Maske« ...

Und Gide hielt ihn für heidnisch! ... ein Irrtum, ich kann mir nicht helfen! Aber freilich, er hatte etwas von einem heidnischen Gott: die Schönheit Apollos und ein verräterisches Doppelwesen gleich dem des asiatischen Bakchos! ... so schien es vielen.

Because as a collective, we are no longer religious. Only those who are truly bound know that moment of revolt which drives the heart to ὕβρίζειν. What, therefore can ὕβρίζ be a sign of when it appears?

And like Saul and David and Salomon, Wilde also found his way back to his God.

Nonetheless, he lapses, he plays, he cannot resist the temptation; it is as if he were compelled, COMPELLED, even if the lightening bolt were to strike him while attempting the forbidden. He is compelled to grasp for the apple, because it is forbidden him. But only he who believes can be forbidden something—even if he is himself unaware of it.

His relations with people are similar.

"You hear with your eyes" he said to Gide, "and thus I want to tell you a story.

"Upon the death of Narcissus, the flowers of the fields were inconsolable and begged the river for drops of water so that they could grieve for him—O! answered the river, were all of my drops of water tears, I myself wouldn't have enough to grieve for Narcissus, I loved him so.—O! returned the flowers of the field, how would it have been possible for you not to have loved Narcissus? He was so beautiful.—Was he beautiful? said the river.—And who would have known it better than you? Every day, bent over your banks, he saw the reflection of his beauty in your waters." And Wilde paused for a moment.

"My reason for loving him, returned the river, was because as he bent over my waters, I saw the reflection of my waters in his eyes." And upon this Wilde laughed...

"I don't like your lips" he said on another occasion. "They are even, like those of a person who has never lied. I want to teach you to lie, so that your lips will be beautiful, curved like those of a Greek mask" ...

And Gide considered him a pagan! A mistake; I can't help myself. Of course he had something of a pagan God, the beauty of an Apollo and the treacherous dual nature of the Asian Bacchus! ... so it appeared to many.

6.

Ah, ja, ein Bakchos! Er kam aus einem fernen Lande und eroberte sich die Menschen. Und wie Bakchos wollte er ein Löser werden, ein Erlöser! Er wollte den Menschen den Mut zum Leben wiedergeben: zum grossen, freien, vollkommenen Leben: zum Leben, das nichts verdammt, nichts abweist, nichts verschmäht. »Die einzige Möglichkeit, eine Versuchung loszuwerden, ist, dass man ihr nachgibt!« Also gebt ihr nach! Aber ach! der Trugschluss! Willst du denn wirklich das freie Leben? Willst du der Versuchung nachgeben, um sie loszusein, und damit sie nicht in dich hineinfrisst? Ist nicht vielmehr dein Ziel der prickelnde Reiz, den du empfindest, wenn du Verbotenes tust? Betrügst du dich nicht selber, wenn du es anders auslegst? Und zeugen dafür nicht all deine Werke und tausend Worte, der ganze Verlauf deines Lebens selbst? Ah, und noch eins! ... Meinst du im Grunde das wirkliche Leben, die wirkliche Sünde (wem Sünde als dir!!)? Oder ist dein verwegenstes Tun noch ein Traum? ist deine schwerste Sünde nur eine Gedankensünde? ... Ah, wer schreibt das Leben? wer schreibt das Buch, von dem ich träume, um hier noch klar zu machen, was ich meine: die wundersam feinen Fäden blosszulegen, aus denen sich diese Tragödie spinnt. Wie kommt dieser Mensch der scheinbar unwirk-lichen Sünde zu seiner furchtbar wirklichen Sühne? Wo springt es hinüber—wo hört er auf, seine kleinen verwegenen Märchen zu erzählen, und beginnt, sich selber vielleicht unbewusst, die Hand nach der Tat zu heben? wo sind es jene kleinen, verwegenen Märchen, die Folgen haben und Sünde werden und Sühne heischen? Und endlich, wo setzt der Schwindel ein: ich bin dir gleich, du Gott, ich kann alles tun? und meine Taten gelten wie meine Träume, verweilen, wie ein Traum verweht? ... Oder—war sie von je das Wesentliche, die Tat, und das asketische Wort vom Leben des Traums ein Spiel? ... Noch ein Wort sei später am Schluss vergönnt, darüber zu sagen—ein Wort, das vielleicht kaum ausdrücke, was ich ausdrücken möchte: ein Wort vom Schuldbuch des Lebens ... Doch nicht mit Gedanken entwirrt man die Dinge, die unentwirrbar sind—man müsste sein Leben erzählen ...

So kann man nur schattenhafte Ahnungen beschwören.

6.

Ah, yes, a Bacchus! He came from a distant land and conquered the people for himself. And like Bacchus, Wilde wanted to be a saviour, a redeemer! He wanted to return to the people the courage to live, to live a colossal, free, perfect life, a life which condemned nothing, rejected nothing, spurned nothing. "The sole means of ridding oneself of a temptation is to give in to it!" Give in to it then! But mark the fallacy! Do you really desire a free life? Do you want to give in to temptation to free yourself of it and to keep it from consuming you? Isn't the goal much more that exhilarating rush you experience upon doing something forbidden? Are you not deceiving yourself when you present it otherwise? And do not all of your works and your thousands of words, indeed the entire course of your life itself, bear testimony to this? Yes, and one more thing! ... Do you mean in essence real life, the real sin (and for whom a greater sin than for you!!)? Or is your boldest deed still but a dream? Is not your darkest sin but a sin in thought? ... Ah, but who will write of such a life? Who will write the book I dream about to explain what it is I mean, to reveal the wondrously fine thematic threads from which this tragedy was spun. How did this person pass from apparently unreal sins to his terribly real atonement? Where was the crossover made—and where does he cease to tell his bold little fairytales and begin, perhaps unconsciously, to raise his hand to the deed? And lastly, where does the fraud begin: I am equal to you God; I am capable of anything. And my deeds are like my dreams, dispersed, dispersed like a dream. ... Or was that always the most important, the deed itself, and the ascetic word about a life of dreaming a mere game? ... I will allow myself a word about this later in conclusion, a word which will perhaps barely express what I wish to say: a word about the debit ledger of life... And yet it is not with thoughts that one disentangles things which cannot be disentangled—his life will have to be recounted....

Thus only shadowy impressions are to be conjured forth.

Wilde faszinierte, und seine Worte pflegten zu wirken. Die Tiefe seiner Worte festzustellen, gelingt fast nie. Seine Art ist vieldeutig: selbst ob das Absicht oder nicht, errät man selten. Aber vieles lockte er aus den Menschen heraus, und vielen half er über schwere Stunden. Er geniesst dabei: geniesst sich und den anderen; es ist biswilen ein grandioses Versteckenspiel.

Ein Freund kommt in Paris zu ihm. Wilde ist der Vergötterte, der Gott. Er hat den Erfolg, weil er das Genie hat, das persönliche Genie, das alles gewinnt und bezaubert. Er hat sein Genie in sein Leben gelegt, und sich zum König des Lebens gemacht ... eines Schattenlebens, eines Traumlebens, wenn man will, aber jedenfalls des einzigen Lebens, das Wilde anerkennt, und eines Lebens voll Farbe und Glanz und strahlender Glut. Immer als Künstler und unter Künstlern. Und Wilde empfindet sich auch als Künstler. Sein Freund hat über ihn geschrieben, hat mitgeholfen an dem Phantome schaffen, das in der Gesellschaft unter Wildes Namen umläuft. Wildes Freundschaft für ihn ist kaum sehr fest. Aber unbewusst fühlt er, dass er ihm—wenn auch noch so wenig—Dank schuldig ist.

Der Freund ist deprimiert—ein wenig verzweifelt. Sein Vollbringen hielt nicht, was sein Wollen versprach. Er gehört zu jenen aus Zähigkeit und Sentimentalität gemischten Söhnen Englands, denen die Dinge erden-schwer werden. Er kam halbwegs mit dem Ziel zu Wilde, sich aufheitern zu lassen. Wildes Gutmütigkeit bricht durch: Unsinn! Und er hilft ihm Pläne schmieden. Aber des Freundes Verstimmung weicht nicht: »Ja, du, Oscar! du mit deinem Genie! Und dann, wie solltest du keinen Erfolg haben: mit deinem Gesicht! deiner Gestalt! deinen Augen! deinem Haar! Und deine Sicherheit: du forderst, was wir als Geschenk erhoffen. Nach dir sehn sich die Leute auf der Strasse um. Und im Salon stürzt alles auf dich zu. Du bist schön—das ist es. Aber ich« ...

Und Wilde bricht in Lachen aus: ein Lachen, das halb gutmütig klingt und halb vielleicht voll heimlicher Bosheit steckt:

»Aber Nevil!« ruft er. »Was für Unsinn du redest. Ich weiss, dass man sich vor dir fürchtet. Und um deinen Kopf beneide ich dich einfach. Du mit deinem Cäsarenkopf! Ah, kein Augustus oder Cäsar oder Nero

7.

Wilde fascinated and his words were not without effect. It is seldom possible to plumb the depths of his words. His manner is ambiguous and, whether intentionally or not, seldom determinable. And yet he drew much out of other people and he helped many through difficult times. In this he showed passion—passion for himself and for others. It is occasionally a grandiose game of hide-and-seek.

A friend comes to Paris to visit him. Wilde is the adored, the God. He is successful, because he has the genius, the personal genius, of being able to win over, to entrance everyone. He placed his genius in the service of his life and fashioned himself the King of Life ... a shadow life, a life of illusion perhaps, but it was the sole life Wilde acknowledged and it was one full of colour, splendour and radiant ardour. Ever present as an artist, he was ever amongst artists. And Wilde also feels himself an artist. His friend had written about him, had helped in the creation of the phantasm Wilde who circulated in society under the name of Wilde. Wilde's friendship for him is not very strong. And yet he unconsciously feels that he owes him thanks, even if just a little.

The friend is depressed—somewhat in despair. His accomplishments have failed the promise of his desire. He is one of those sons of England in whom tenacity is mixed with sentimentality and for whom things become oppressively weighty. He came to see Wilde with the partial goal of chee-ring himself up. Wilde, with his good-naturedness, breaks through—Nonsense! And he helps him to forge plans. But his friend's disgruntledness refuses to soften: "Of course Oscar, you with your genius! Besides, how could you not be successful with your face, your carriage, your eyes, your hair! And your confidence—you demand what we hope for as a gift. People turn to look at you on the street. And in the salons all attention is directed at you. You are beautiful—that's all there is to be said. But I" ...

And Wilde breaks out in laughter, a laughter that rings out half good-naturedly and perhaps half filled with concealed malice:

"But Neville!" he says. "What nonsense you prattle. I know that you are feared. And your head I simply envy. You with your Caesarean profile! Not, of course, the profile of an Augustus or Caesar or Nero—

selbst—einer von den ganz späten, den eigentlich interessanten, den letzten Heidnischen« ...

Was ist davon wirklich gemeint? was ist aus Gutmütigkeit gesagt und was aus sublimer Bosheit?

Aber den Freund zu trösten, gelang ihm: denn der ging hin und wurde ... eitel. Er fand die vollste Zufriedenheit mit sich selber wieder, und später wurde er ein Philister ...

Ob die Episode passiert ist, wie ich sie schreibe, das kann ich nicht verbürgen: es ist lange her, dass man sie mir erzählt hat. Aber wie ich sie schreibe, gibt sie mir einen Zug zum Bilde Wildes. Und das wollte ich sagen: ich könnte selbst Situationen erfinden, in denen Wilde aufträte. Und ich würde ihn handeln lassen, und sicher sein, dass er so gehandelt hätte, wenn diese Situation eine wirkliche gewesen wäre—wenigstens, dass er so hätte handeln können. Denn ganz sicher kann man bei Leuten wie Wilde nie sein: sie sind verräterisch, sie stecken zu sehr voller Fallen, voller Überraschungen; aber das eine ist sicher: dieser so unendlich viel-spältige Mensch ist immer konkret da; abstrakt ist er kaum zu fassen (die Gründe dafür will ich abstrakt im nächsten Absatz zu geben versuchen). Ich weiss nicht, ob mir klar zu machen gelingt, was ich meine. Die Fäden seiner Psyche sind so fein und laufen so kompliziert durcheinander und hin und her dass man seine Psyche wohl als Gesamtheit, gleichsam mit der Phantasie, zu fassen vermag—dass man sie gleichsam leben kann, aber dass es fast unmöglich ist, sie analytisch klarzulegen. Deshalb ersehne ich jenes Buch, von dem ich sprach, und deshalb sagte ich, es sei möglich, wenn ich sein Leben erzählte, dass es schliesslich eine Dichtung sei. Ich sagte schon oben, die Analyse habe ich versucht—ich habe drei Bücher über ihn geschrieben und Exzerpte aus einem publiziert . . . aber ich fürchte, ich fürchte . . . Nun, jedenfalls ist das gewiss, dass ich selbst in der kleinen Broschüre nicht ohne die Erzählung ausgekommen bin. Ich habe Gespräche erzählen müssen. Und jetzt gehe ich weiter: Um die Gestalt ganz rund herauszubringen, so dass auch der sie sähe, der nicht die Zeit hat, Spinnenfäden entlang zu laufen und auf ersterbende Töne zu lauschen—um das zu tun, sage ich, müsste man zu all dem Material, das man sammeln kann, das ich zum Teil gesammelt habe, neues Material hinzuerfinden, müsste ausfüllen, wo das Leben nur andeutete, müsste Brücken schlagen, wo Lücken stehen, müsste zusammenrücken, was der

one of the late Caesars, the really interesting ones, one of the last pagan Caesars" ...

What is actually meant by this? What was said here good-naturedly and what out of sublime malice?

And yet, he was, nonetheless, able to console his friend, for his friend went forth and became ... vain. He once again became fully satisfied with himself and later developed into a perfect philistine....

Whether this incident ever really took place or not, I cannot confirm with certainty. It has been a long time since I was told this episode. And yet the way I write it gives me an approach to Wilde's image. For this is what I wished to say: I could invent situations in which Wilde appeared. And I would have him act in a way I am sure he would have acted were the situation real—at least the way he could have acted. For with people like Wilde, one can never be sure. They are deceptive, too full of traps, full of surprises. Nonetheless, one thing is certain: this so infinitely complex a person is always concretely present. He is hardly to be grasped abstractly (for reasons which I will attempt to explain, in an abstract manner, in the next paragraph). I am not sure whether I will be able to express what I mean. The threads of his psyche are so fine and so complexly interwoven that one would like to grasp his psyche as a whole, with one's imagination as it were, in order to experience it, but in such a way that it would be impossible to depict it analytically. For this reason I yearn for the book about which I have spoken, and for this reason I said that were I to recount his life, this account could ultimately develop into a poetic work. I have already indicated above that I have attempted to analyse him; I have written three books about him and published excerpts from one of them. Nonetheless I am afraid, I am afraid.... Now it is certain that in this little brochure, even I have not been able to manage without a narrative. I have been forced to recount conversations. And now I will go still further. In order to round off the entire thing in such a way that it will be clear even to those who don't have the time to run after spun-out threads and to listen in on fading tones. To accomplish that, as I say, one would have to add newly invented material to all the material that could be gathered (and that I have partially gathered); one would have to build bridges where his life offered only hints, draw material together where gaps occurred, artistically compose

Zufall trennte, müsste ohne Rücksicht auf die Welt der Dinge dichten—
denn all das, was ich eben sagte, nennen wir ja dichten ... So wüchse aus
der Schilderung eines Lebens die Geschichte einer Seele auf, und sie ist ja
das Interessante für uns: uns interessiert, dass ich es wiederhole, der
Mensch, und das heisst, eine Konkreszenz von Rätseln ...

8.

Seine Werke ... ah ja—geht mir mit seinen Werken! Als ich den Dorian
Gray zum erstenmal gelesen hatte, sagte ich:—»Amüsant! Sehr reizvoll,
sehr geistvoll! aber kaum mehr als amüsant!«—Ich glaubte, ich sei fertig
mit ihm. Ich glaubte nicht, dass er mich weiter beschäftigen werde. Was
ich vermisste, war Grösse. Es ging mir mit all seinen Werken so. Seine
Märchen, die mir jetzt mit das Interessanteste sind, waren mir erst gera-
dezu unangenehm—beinahe widerlich. Ich fand sie sentimental—sie sind
es!—»Ein Engländer!« sagte ich—»wie sollte er nicht sentimental sein! Wo
die Grössten sentimental sind: Meredith! Swinburne!« Aber dann ging mir
das Problem des Menschen auf. Ich entdeckte eines Tages, dass ich nicht
allein war. Ich blickte in rätselhafte Augen: in die Augen eines Menschen,
der in einer Weise »entwurzelt« schien, wie es mir bisher noch nie
begegnet war—und ich sann seit Jahren über das Problem der »déracinés«.

Was heisst denn »déraciné«?—Entwurzelt—wurzellos? Gibt es Bäume
ohne Wurzel? Gibt es solche Menschen? Noch nie hat sich Münchhausen
an seinem eigenen Schöpf aus dem Wasser gezogen: es geht nämlich
nicht, so paradox das heute klingen mag. Und wenn André Gide ruft (in
den »Réponses à M. Barrès«, Prétextes, siehe oben): »déracinons! déracinons les forts!« was heisst das anders als: »enracinons«? ... Ich erkläre
mich deutlicher: wer ist wurzelfest? Doch wohl der, der fest in seiner
Rasse, in der Sitte und dem Glauben seiner Rasse wurzelt. Man kann ihn
einem Baum vergleichen, der im Boden seiner eigentlichen Heimat seine
Wurzeln ausdehnt und strack und grade und stark emporwächst. Bis zu
einem gewissen Punkt stimmt das Gleichnis, von da an hinkt es. Man kann
einen Baum verpflanzen: mitunter schwächt es ihn, mitunter stärkt es ihn,
mitunter verwandelt es ihn. Das hat mit seiner ursprünglichen Kraft gar
nichts zu tun, wie André Gide irrtümlich meint. Es ist das Ergebnis von
Verwandtschaften, Affinitäten—die letzte Folge rein chemischer Prozesse

without regard for the world of reality where coincidence forced separations—for all this, as I have just said, is what we call artistic composition ... And thus from out of the description of a life, the story of a soul would grow, and that is what interests us. For we are, I repeat, interested by people and that entails a concrescence of riddles....

8.

His works ... but please, nothing more about his works. Upon reading *Dorian Gray* for the first time I said to myself: "Amusing! Most charming, very spirited! But hardly more than amusing!" I thought that I was finished with him. I did not believe I would concern myself with him further. What I missed was greatness. I felt the same about all of his works. His fairytales, which I now find amongst the most interesting of his works, struck me at first as unpleasant, almost repugnant. I found them sentimental: "An Englishman!" I thought. "How could he be anything but sentimental. In England even the giants are sentimental: Meredith! Swinburne!" But then the problem of the individual Wilde arose for me. One day I discovered that I was not alone. I looked into enigmatic eyes, into the eyes of a person who appeared in a sense "uprooted," in a way I had never encountered before, and I have pondered the problem of the "déracinés" for years.

But what does "déraciné" mean—uprooted, rootless? Is there such a thing as a tree without roots? Are there people like that? Not even Munchausen pulled himself out of the water by his own hair. It simply doesn't work that way, as paradoxical as that may sound today. And when André Gide calls out (in "Résponses à M. Barrès," *Prétextes*, see above): "déracinons! Déracinons les forts!" what does that mean other than "enracinons?" ... Let me state myself clearly: who is firm in his roots? Undoubtedly he who is firmly rooted in his race, in the customs and beliefs of his race. Such a man can be compared with a tree, which stretches its roots into its native soil to grow straight and direct and strong. This comparison is convincing to a certain extent, but then it loses persuasiveness. For it is possible to transplant a tree. Sometimes transplantation weakens the tree, sometimes it strengthens it, sometimes it transforms it. This has absolutely nothing to do with the tree's original strength, as André Gide mistakenly assumes. It is the result of *verwandtschaften*,

(während die Kraft nach meiner Auffassung etwas Physikalisches ist: man
verzeihe die ganze, etwas weite Abschweifung: man wird sehn, sie ist nur
ein Umweg). Nun gut—mit dem Menschen ist es genau so. Für die
Verwandlung bietet Nordamerika das beste Beispiel: die ausdrucksloseste
deutsche Physiognomie nimmt in wenigen Jahren nach der Auswanderung
den typisch amerikanischen Schnitt an – wenn sie nämlich nicht einfach
verfällt, weil der Organismus zugrunde geht; denn es handelt sich nicht
um eine bloss äusserliche Anähnlichung, sondern um eine langsame
Umbildung des ganzen »Zellenstaates«. Aber das ist Umwurzelung, keine
Entwurzelung: in ein paar Generationen ist die Fremdheit ganz über-
wunden—der ursprüngliche Boden vergessen, abgetan ... Aber nehmen
wir nun in der Familie eines solchen »Umgewurzelten« einen Fall von
Atavismus an!

(Man sieht, es sind genau die naturwissenschaftlichen Probleme der
Variabilität der Arten, wie denn überhaupt die Naturwissenschaft, je weiter
sie fortschreitet, um so mehr zur Bildersprache für den Philosophen wird.)

Nehmen wir an, sage ich, an irgend einer Stelle breche in der
Nachkommenschaft eines also Umgewurzelten der deutsche Instinkt
wieder durch: nehmen wir an, der Instinkt eines norddeutschen Bauern,
der Instinkt des Menschen, der an die Natur gebunden ist ... Wie lebt denn
der Bauer? Mit seiner Scholle verwachsen, abhängig von seinem Boden und
der Befruchtung seines Bodens: er rechnet mit ungeheuren Sicherheiten:
der Frühling kommt, die Zeit der Saat; Wachstum und Ernte; dann
Wintersaat und Ruhe. Die Dinge kehren als Ganzes mit absolutester
Verlässlichkeit zurück, sie kommen von selber wieder ... aus der Ferne, aus
der Stadt gesehen: stabil wie die Küste vom tobenden Meere aus. Die
Sicherheiten nennt er Gott. Des Unsicheren ist verhältnismässig wenig:
dass auch dies ihm günstig sei, darum betet er zu Gott; er selber vermag
kaum etwas dazu zu tun. Auf diese Sicherheiten baut sich seine Sitte, aus
seiner Sitte wächst sein Instinkt.

Dieser Mensch wandert aus—er tut es natürlich nur nach einer vorange-
gangenen »Korruption«—nach Nordamerika; er komme in die Stadt, das
heisst, vom sicheren Land aufs schwanke Meer ... Er sagt, er wird frei! Frei
nämlich vom Boden, vom Wetter, von den Jahreszeiten, von Gott—das
heisst, frei von den Dingen, von relativen Sicherheiten, von allem, was sich
berechnen lässt.—Er tritt in neue Abhängigkeiten: er wird abhängig von

affinities—the final result of purely chemical processes (while according to my understanding, strength is something purely physical: I ask forgiveness for this entire, somewhat obscure digression—it is but a detour, as will become clear). And with humans it is precisely the same. With regard to transformation, North America provides the best example. The most inexpressive German physiognomy takes on a typical American appearance within a few years of emigration, assuming it doesn't simply decay as a result of the decline of the organism; for this is not simply a matter of merely external adaptation, but the long term reformation of an entire "cellular state." But that is transplantation and not an uprooting: in a few generations, the feeling of foreignness is completely overcome, the original soil forgotten, dismissed. ... But now consider a case of atavism in the family of such "transplanted" people! ...

(One sees that it is precisely the scientific problems of the variability of types, as with science in general, the further they advance the more they become a pictorial language for philosophers.)

Let us consider, as I say, the re-emergence of German instinct in the progeny of such a transplanted individual in any given place. Let us consider the instinct of a northern German peasant, the instinct of a person who is bound to nature... And how does such a peasant live? He is integrated into the life of the land, dependant upon his soil and the fertility of his soil. He reckons with unchanging certainties: spring comes, seeding time, growth and harvest, then winter seeding and rest. Things revolve in a circle with absolute dependability; they return of themselves ... seen from a distance, from the perspective of the city, they are as secure as the coast seen from the perspective of a raging sea. These certainties the peasant calls God. Of uncertainties, there are relatively few. And that these should be favourable, he prays to God, for he is hardly in a position to alter things himself. On the basis of these certainties his customs are formed, and from his customs his instincts develop.

Such an individual emigrates to North America, only after a protracted period of "corruption," of course. He arrives in a city, in other words, from the safety of the land he takes to the swelling sea ... I am free! he says. Free from the soil, the weather, from the changing seasons of the year, from God—in other words, free from all of the things which granted him assurance, free from everything, free from his relative certainties. He enters

einer komplizierten Gesamtheit von Menschen, unter ihnen von einem Brotherrn—mit dem Menschen rechnet man nicht mehr wie mit der Sicherheit, dass es im April regnen wird; er wird abhängig von Unsicherheiten: er kann nicht mehr errechnen, er muss erraten. Er tauschte die Herrschaft der Dinge gegen die des Menschen ein. Ihm wachsen neue Instinkte: der Begriff Gott fällt seinem Wesen nach—die Welt wird zur ungeheuer komplizierten Maschine, in der tausend Unberechenbarkeiten berechenbar wirken; das Leben wird zu einem ewigen »wenn ... dann«, es fordert beständige Wachheit von ihm, die Unrast wird Instinkt. So wird er allmählich ein neuer Mensch. In unserem Beispiel komme der Einfluss des fremden Landes hinzu, das heisst: die Verschiedenheit der beiden Lebensbedingungen sei so gross, wie man sie sich nur denken kann (exempli gratia, um alles grob und handgreiflich zu machen). Seine Rasse wandelt sich: er nehme eine Frau aus den Töchtern des Landes; seine Kinder sind amerikanische Städter: eingewurzelt, assimiliert.

Aber die Wissenschaft zeigt uns, dass in diesen Kindern die alte Rasse, die alten Instinkte des Vaters im Keim verborgen weiterleben, nur verdeckt, unterdrückt—mag auch die neue Rasse noch so stabil erscheinen. Und wir alle kennen jene Erscheinungen, deren Kausalität blosszulegen der Wissenschaft noch nicht gelungen ist, die Erscheinungen des Atavismus (uns am häufigsten sichtbar bei Mischung germanischer und jüdischer Rasse). Nun denke man sich ein Kind jener neuen Rasse: als solches mit allen Instinkten des Städters, des Wandermenschen, mit aller Unrast beständigen Kampfes im Leibe, mit dem Bedürfnis fortwährenden Wechsels (das Bedürfnis geboren aus dem Zwang der Jahrhunderte)—und daneben mit jenen alten Instinkten der Ruhe, des stillen Vertrauens auf ewige Sicherheiten, mit jenem Blick des Bauern, der auf die Welt als auf etwas Seiendes blickt: er wird fremd wie ein Kind in der Welt des Kampfes stehen und hülflos seine Hände heben, am Werk des Alltags zu helfen; es wird nicht gehn—aber man stelle ihn hinein in das Bauernleben norddeutschen Flachlands: in ewiger Unrast wird er von einem zum andern greifen; er wird sich verzehren, wenn er warten soll, bis das Korn reift; er wird vor Ungeduld mit dem Fusse stampfen, wenn er sich an die Stunde halten soll, und über den Glauben der Väter wird er mit Sonnenuntergangslächeln staunen. Er ist entwurzelt: das heisst, er hat zwei Wurzeln; widerstreitende

into new dependencies; he becomes dependant upon a complicated collective of humans, among them a taskmaster—people are not to be relied upon with the same certainty that in April it will rain; he becomes dependant upon uncertainties. No longer able to calculate with certainty, he is forced to guess. He has exchanged the sovereignty of things for those of humans. New instincts grow in him; his understanding of God recedes from him. The world becomes a vast, complicated machine which functions predictably according to a thousand unpredictabilities. Life becomes an eternal "all or nothing." Constant vigilance is required of him and restlessness becomes instinctual. And thus he gradually develops into a new and different person. In our example, the influences of the new country would have to be included. The differences between the two sets of living conditions would be as large as one could possibly imagine (*exempli gratia* to be blatantly obvious). His race alters. He takes as a wife a daughter of this new land; his children become Americanised, urban dwellers, fully rooted, assimilated.

Science nonetheless reveals to us, however, that in these children, the former race, the father's former instincts live on hidden in embryonic form, concealed and repressed, regardless as to how stable the race appears. And we are all familiar with the phenomenon of atavism, the causality of which science has not yet been able to reveal (and which is most visible with us in mixtures of the Germanic and Jewish races). Now one imagines a child of this new race with all the instincts of a city dweller, a wanderer, with all of the restlessness of continual struggle in his breast, with the need for continual change (a need born of the compulsion of the century) and along with these he harbours the former instinct for stillness, the peaceful trust in eternal certainties, with the look of a peasant who perceives the world as a living thing. He would be as misplaced as a child in the world of struggle and helplessly raise his hands to help with the work of daily existence. And yet were one to return him to his peasant existence on the flatlands of northern Germany, he would rush from one place to another in eternal unrest; he would consume himself when forced to wait until his harvest were ripe; he would stamp his feet in impatience were he to bide his time and he would laugh the laugh of a dying sun, astonished by the beliefs of his father. He is uprooted, which means that he has

Säfte saugen sie auf, und ihn umspielt jene Vielspältigkeit, ihn beleuchten jene »goldenen Farben, die den Verfall verkünden und verschönen«.

Aber wozu taugt er, wenn er zum einen nicht taugt und zum anderen nicht? ... Soll ich's verraten? ... denn jedermann weiss es ja, nur spricht man's nicht gerne aus ... Er taugt zum—Verbrecher oder zum Künstler!*

9.

Warum ist mir die Luft geruchlos? Weil ich beständig in ihr bin. Der Gegensatz erst lässt uns die Dinge erkennen. Wer nie aus seinem Lande kam und nichts kennt als die Sitten seines Landes, wird schwerlich über sein Land und seine Sitten Urteile fällen; für ihn ist beides etwas Absolutes: verurteilt ist schon in gewissem Sinne »entwurzelt«.

Wird der noch absolut Wurzelsichere sein Land schildern können? Niemand kennt es doch so gut, niemandem sind seine Sitten gleich vertraut! Aber ach, man versuche es doch: er kann sie kaum benennen; denn ihm fehlt ja der Gegensatz, aus dem heraus er sehen und urteilen kann. Er weiss ja nicht, was er von seinen Sitten nennen soll, da er nicht weiss, worin sie sich von anderen unterscheiden. Er kennt die Relativität des Daseins nicht ... Aber jener Entwurzelte, von dem ich oben sprach, der wird ein Schilderer sein: nach zwei Seiten wird er blicken; er steht an einer Wendung des Weges, wo er die Strasse nach Nordosten und nach Nordwesten überschaut: er ist unweigerlich Künstler! Ein Künstler im Keim: weil er die Dinge als unterschieden sieht; er sieht plastisch. Darin liegt die Begnadung, darin auch die Tragik seines Loses. Er zieht zwei Strassen, und zieht sie beide als Fremder und ist doch auf beiden heimisch. Und ist nicht der Künstler immer der Fremde, trägt er nicht stets das Ahasveruszeichen an der Stirn? Alle Künstler sind dekadent, wenn Dekadenz die Folge der Entwurzelung ist: Nur gibt es Grade! Und man könnte sich einen Künstler denken, der vermöge seiner Abstammung—geistiger wie leiblicher—in allen Kulturen und Rassen und Sitten und Religionen der Welt fremd zu Hause wäre: ein Schweifender über der Erde Gewächsen, fremd und zu Hause im Christentum, fremd und zu Hause unter Brahminen am Ganges, fremd und zu Hause beim grossen Erlöser Buddha, fremd und zu Hause im Geist eines Nietzsche wie Augustins—zugleich ein Deutscher, ein Brite, ein Römer, ein Grieche, ein Italiener,

two roots drawing forth conflicting saps and around him ambiguity swirls while he is lit in "the golden hues which announce and beautify decay."

But of what use is he, if he is fit for neither one nor the other? ... Should I reveal it? .... Of course it's obvious to everyone, however unwillingly spoken. He is fit to be either a criminal or an artist.[3]

9.

Why does the air seem odourless to me? Because I am constantly surrounded by it. Only in contrast are things recognisable. And he who has never left his homeland and who knows only the customs of his homeland will find it difficult to pass judgement on his homeland and its customs. For him, both are something absolute: to be judged is, to a certain degree, to be "uprooted."

Can the individual who is absolutely sure of his roots describe his homeland? No one knows it as well as he, no one is as intimate with its customs! But nonetheless, try as he might, he is hardly able even to name them; he lacks the contrast with which to perceive and evaluate them. He knows not which of his customs he should refer to, as he knows not in what way they are to be distinguished from others. He is ignorant of the relativity of being ... But the uprooted individual whom I mentioned above—he is a portrayer. He looks in two directions simultaneously; he stands at a fork in the path overlooking the way to the north-east and north-west; he is inevitably an artist! A budding artist because he sees things as variable; his vision is plastic. Therein lies both the consolation and the tragedy of his fate. He sees two paths and follows both as a foreigner and is nonetheless at home on both of them. And is not the artist always a foreigner, does he not always carry the mark of Cain on his forehead? All artists are decadent, if decadence is the result of uprooting. And yet there are degrees! And one could well imagine an artist who would be, thanks to his origins—spiritual and physical—both foreign to and at home in all of the cultures, races, customs and religions of the world: a wanderer over the earth, foreign to and at home in Christianity, foreign to and at home amongst Brahmins along the Ganges, foreign to and at home with the great redeemer Buddha, foreign to and as much at home in the spirit of a Nietzsche as an Augustin—at once a German, a Briton, a Roman, a

Franzose und Schwede und Russe. Ein solcher wäre ganz »entwurzelt« das heisst, er hätte seine Wurzeln überall, er wäre vielwurzlig (um damit meinen Widerspruch gegen André Gide zu erledigen). Vergessen wir also nicht, wenn wir das Wort »entwurzelt« beibehalten, dass wir uns nur einem Usus fügen und eine Abkürzung gebrauchen, die irre führen kann.

In der Praxis steht es fast immer so, dass von den vielen »Wurzeln« eines Künstlers eine stärker ist als alle anderen: eine gibt ihm Stabilität, gibt ihm die Wirbelsäule sozusagen. Aus ihr saugt er dann seine feste Kraft, den starken Zug, der uns vergessen lässt, dass er im Grunde zu den »Krankheitserscheinungen der Menschheit« gehört. Und wieder gebe ich hier eine These: Je weniger unter den Wurzeln des Gewächses, das wir Künstler nennen, eine vorwiegt, eine an Kraft alle anderen überragt, je mehr sie alle unter sich von gleicher Stärke oder Schwäche sind, und je grösser zugleich ihre Zahl ist: um so weniger wird er an eigentlicher Schaffenskraft besitzen: um so weniger wird er zum grossen Werke neigen; um so mehr wird er seine Gaben in Kleinigkeiten geben—in Paradoxien, in Aphorismen, in Apercus, in kleinen Verschen; um so dekadenter wird er erscheinen, aber ... um so interessanter als Mensch!

Muss ich noch sagen, worin ich die Ursache sehe, dass wir so viele Künstler haben, heute, und so wenig Kunstwerke, wie ich oben behauptete ?

10.

Ah, und Wilde? Haben wir ihn? fassen wir ihn endlich, den Schweifenden mit dem Verräterlachen? Ihn, dem die Wunder des Evangeliums nicht wunderbar genug erschienen, weil er grössere Wunder kannte in seiner Brust? ... Aus tausend Böden sog er sich Nahrung und zog er seine Blüten auf, in allen Zeiten war er geboren und starb er, und Worte vernahm er von Plato nicht minder wie von Baudelaire. Und er trank Blut, Blut Gestorbener—er war ein umgekehrter Vampyr (passez-moi le mot!)! Und er verriet, was er im Innern war, durch äussere Zeichen: er sass am Schreibtisch Carlyles, trug Balzacs Talar und Neros Frisur!* Aber plötzlich wirft er das alles ab, zieht sich mit der vornehm nachlässigen Eleganz des vollendeten Dandy an und geht, eine Sonnenblume in der feinen Hand, durch die Strassen von Paris. Und um seine Lippen spielt ein sphinxenes Lächeln, das Lächeln Toter, die wieder erwacht sind, erwacht zum Leben

Greek, an Italian, a Frenchman, a Swede and a Russian. Such an individual would be completely "uprooted," in other words he would have his roots overall; he would be many rooted (to conclude my contradiction of André Gide). Let us not forget that in retaining the word "uprooted" we are merely bowing to custom and adapting an abbreviation that could be misleading.

In practice, it is almost always the case that of an artist's many "roots," one is stronger than all the others. One root gives him stability, acts as a back-bone, so to speak. Through it, he draws his power, that characteristic of strength that leads us to forget that he is, in principle, "the manifestation of a diseased humanity." And once again I will allow myself a thesis. The less one of the roots of the growth we are here calling an artist predominates, outstrips the others in strength, the more all of the others will be of equal strength—or weakness—while, at the same time, the greater the number of roots, the less he will possess creative power, the less he will tend towards the creation of great works of art, all the more will he devote his gifts to trifles—to paradoxes, to aphorisms, to aperçus, to short verses—all the more decadent will he appear, and, all the more interesting as an individual! Need I still say why I think we have so many artists, today, and so few works of art, as I above suggested?

10.

Yes, and what of Wilde? Do we now have him? Do we now finally grasp him, the roamer with the laughter of a traitor—he for whom the wonders of the Gospel did not seem wonderful enough because he cradled greater wonders in his breast? ... He drew his sustenance from thousands of soils and nourished his blossoms. He was born to and died in all times; he took no fewer words from Plato than from Baudelaire. And he drank blood, the blood of the dead—he was a vampire in reverse (*passez-moi le mot!*)! And he revealed his internal nature by means of external signs: he sat at Carlyle's writing table, wore Balzac's gown, and adopted Nero's hairstyle![4] But suddenly he sheds all of that, clothes himself in the genteel, careless elegance of the perfect dandy and strolls, a sunflower in his delicate hand, through the streets of Paris. On his lips, sphinx-like, laughter plays, the laughter of those dead who have awoken, arisen to contemporary life

des Heut', wo man sich zu seiner Nachbarin niederbeugt und einen Scherz hinflüstert, der schlimmer ist als ein Ehebruch, weil er die Seele vergiftet, statt mit dem Leibe sündigt. Und dann trifft er einen Freund, einen guten Bekannten, und nimmt ihn am Arm, und er erzählt und erzählt, lauter kleine, verwegene Geschichten, die sich, die eine aus der anderen, entwikkeln—er erzählt von allem, denn er weiss alles: er kennt die Ergebnisse ratender Wissenschaft, die aus steinernen Zeichen und Trümmern ein längst vergangenes Leben entziffert; und dieses Leben ist ihm ein Leben: er hat sie gesehen, die geflügelten Drachen, die Saurier und den Leviathan, und hat sie bestaunt und kann sie schildern, und sie sind ihm wirklicher als das letzte Eisenbahnunglück—und er weiss, wie einem indischen Büsser zu Mut ist, der sich gegeisselt hat und gegeisselt, und doch keine Ruhe fand—und von Ramses redet er wie von Pharao oder Napoleon, denn mit ihnen hat er gelebt; er hat Jupiter Ammon verehrt wie die Göttin der Vernunft—und vom Blut des Alkibiades rollt in seinen Adern, und im Schatz des kaiserlichen Haushalts sass er mit Elagabal, und er zählt die Steine auf, die dort durch seine Hände glitten—und mit den Minnesängern ist er durchs Land gezogen, und ihre Verse sind ihm vertraut wie die Verlaines—und Cartesius, Leibniz, Hume und Kant, das sind ihm nicht blosse Namen: er hat an ihrem Tische gesessen und alle Fragen ihrer Philosophie mit ihnen erörtert—und die Krone, die aus dem allen erwuchs, sein eigenes Jahrhundert, er betet es an, er vergöttert es—und von allem erzählt er und spricht davon wie von den alltäglichsten Dingen: denn alles weiss er—es gibt nichts, was ihm verborgen wäre, und über alles redet er bald als Christ, bald als Spötter und bald als Jünger heidnischer Philosophensekten. Und alles ist Pose und alles ist Wahrheit. Alles ist Pose, weil es willkürlich heraufbeschworen wird, und alles ist Wahrheit, weil es doch wirklich in ihm lebt. Und alles ist Pose, weil es nur wirklich im Traum ist, weil es mit dem wirklichen Lebern, mit dem Leben der Dinge im Raume nichts zu tun hat, und alles ist Wahrheit, weil es ihm das ganze Leben ist, weil er ausser dem Traum kein Leben mehr will, und weil er selber an dieses Traumleben als an das wahrhaft wirkliche glaubt. Aber wieder ist alles Pose: so unbegreiflich es scheint, er weiss, dass er spielt, dass er da mehr fremd als zu Hause ist, wo er glauben machen möchte, er sei mehr zu Hause als fremd. Und er verrät sich, verrät sich tausendmal,

where one kneels down to one's neighbour to whisper a joke into her ear that is worse than adultery, because it poisons the soul rather than sinning with the body. And then he meets a friend, an old acquaintance, and takes his arm and talks and talks, recounting nothing but rakish little stories that develop out of each other—he talks of everything, for he knows everything: he is familiar with the results of the science of conjecture which reveals the long concealed life hidden in the stone fragments of ruins. This life is real life to him, he saw it, the winged dragons, dinosaurs and the Leviathan; he looked on in wonder and can describe them for they are more real to him than the most recent railway disaster—and he knows how an Indian penitent feels who has scourged himself and scourged himself and who nonetheless has found no rest—and he talks of Rameses as he does of the Pharaoh and Napoleon, for he lived with them; he worshipped Jupiter Amun like the goddess of Reason—and the blood of Alcibiades flows in his veins and in the treasury of the Imperial household he sat with Elagabalus and counted out the gems that slipped through his fingers—and he roamed throughout the land with the minnesingers and he knows their verse as well as that of Verlaine—and Decartes, Leibniz, Hume and Kant are more than mere names to him, he sat with them at their tables and probed all the questions of their philosophy—and the summation, that which has proceeded from all this, his own century, he worships, he deifies and everything he speaks of, all of the things he describes he speaks of as if they were everyday things, for he knows everything. There is nothing hidden from him and in speaking of these things he talks now like a Christian, now like one who mocks and now like an initiate from a pagan philosophical sect. And all is pose and all is truth. All is a pose because it is randomly conjured forth, and all is real because it does in fact live in him. And all is pose because it becomes real only in his dreams, because it has nothing to do with real life, with the life of things of the surrounding world; and all is truth because it is his life, because he desires no life other than that of a dream and because he himself believes in this dream-life as if it were actual reality. And yet, once again it is all pose: for as incomprehensible as it may appear, he knows that he is playing, that he is more a stranger than one at home precisely at that moment when he wishes to

und in einem klarer als jemals sonst, da nämlich, wo er sein gewohntes Verfahren umkehrt.—

Er ist in der französischen Sprache zu Hause wie deren Meister: was er französisch schrieb, gehört stilistisch zum Feinsten, was die Franzosen haben. Und er sprach die Sprache mit jener Meisterschaft, wie sie selbst dem Eingeborenen nur durch lange Jahre bewusster Übung zuteil wird. Er brauchte gern seltene Worte, die er wie glühende Blumen in seine Rede flocht. Aber er mied den geraden Weg. Er sprach im Gespräch mit leichtem Akzent, wie etwa ein Russe französisch spricht. Und wenn er ein Wort mit Nachdruck sagen wollte, so machte er die Pause und Geste des Ausländers, der nach dem Worte sucht, und das Wort, das dann kam, war eines, wie es selbst der Franzose nur schwer gefunden hätte, ein Wort, das er wie eine Statue hinausstellte aus dem Relief seiner Rede; und er sprach es langsam mit seiner wundervollen, leisen Stimme, indem er es gleichsam im Mund umdrehte und ganz auskostete, und um seine Lippen spielte dann das Lächeln dessen, der sich selbst geniesst und seine eigene Meisterschaft, und er sah die andern an und genoss auch deren Staunen und Bewunderung und Überraschung noch.

Aber die Pose wurde ihm Wirklichkeit, und die Wirklichkeit verblasste daneben, und wo sie nicht blass war, da verwechselte er den Traum und die Dinge, und dafür rächte das Leben sich.

11.

Die Welt auskosten: das Leben ausleben! Das war seine Philosophie. Alle Möglichkeiten des Daseins erschöpfen! Das war es! ... Aber gehört zu den Möglichkeiten des Daseins nicht auch der Mord? Und ist nur dessen Leben vollkommen, der den Kreis der Möglichkeiten ausgelaufen ist—wie kann der ruhn, der nie einen Mord beging? Also begehn wir den Mord! und da zeigt sich's: kann man den Mord im wirklichen Leben begehen, ohne sich zu beschmutzen? Gehört es zum Morde als einer Lebensingredienz, dass eine Strafe darauf steht, dass die Justiz ihn verfolgt, dass er infolgedessen ein Werk der Heimlichkeit ist, und so weiter? ... O nein: aber all das sind Dinge, die der wirkliche Mord unter unseren Formen der Zivilisation unweigerlich mit sich bringt. Wer also wird sich mit all den Dingen beschmutzen, da er doch frei ist, Morde im Traum zu begehen, und alles

suggest that he is more at home than a stranger. And he reveals himself, betrays himself a thousand times—in one thing more clearly than elsewhere—there where he reverses his normal procedure.

Speaking French he is as much at home as the masters of the language: what he writes in French belongs amongst the finest the French have. And he spoke the language with the very mastery attained by natives only after years of conscious practice. He purposefully used unusual words, punctuating his speech with them as if they were blooming flowers. Nonetheless, he avoided the direct route. In conversation he spoke with a light accent, the way a Russian would speak French. And when he wished to use a word with particular expressiveness, he would make a long pause and the gesture of a foreigner searching for a word, and when the word came it would be one which a Frenchman would have had difficulty finding, a word that he placed like a statue out of the relief of his language; and he would pronounce it slowly with his wonderful, light voice, simultaneously rolling it in his mouth while fully savouring its rich flavours, and on his lips played that laughter which enjoys itself and its own mastery, and he would look at the others and revel in their wonder, admiration and surprise.

But the pose became reality for him, and reality paled in comparison with pose, and where it was pale, he mistook dream for reality, and for this, life took its revenge.

11.

To experience life to its fullest, to outlive life, that was his philosophy. To exhaust all of the possibilities of being! That was it! But does not murder also belong amongst the possibilities of being? And is not life perfect only for him who has completed the circle of possibilities—how can he who has never committed a murder find rest? Let us commit a murder then! But there's the crux; is it possible in real life to commit a murder without dirtying oneself? Is not one of the central ingredients of a murder the fact that it is punishable, that it is subject to the law and that as a result it is a work of secrecy, and so on? ... Oh no, but these are things that a real murder inevitably brings with it, given the form of our civilisation. But who would willingly dirty himself with all of these things, if he were free to commit a murder in his imagination, free to enjoy all of the emotions

auszukosten, was ein Mord an Emotionen mit sich bringt, vorausgesetzt, dass man die geheimen geistigen Wege und Brücken zum Mord in seiner Herkunft hat—und so mit allem, nicht nur mit dem Mord. Und fähig dieses Lebens in der Idee ist der »Entwurzelte«, ist der Vielwurzlige, der eben vermöge seiner vielspältigen Abstammung Zugänge zu tausend verschiedenen Leben hat: lebte er wirkliches Leben, er könnte nur einen der Wege gehen, und auch auf ihm würde er ein Fremder bleiben mit der bunten Sehnsucht nach den tausend andern. Aber in seinem Traum geht er sie alle, ist Nero und Dandy zugleich. Und schnell wie einen Gedanken kann er sein Leben ändern: er tut es. Nur wehe! fehlt ihm die Konsequenz: irrt er sich irgendwo und greift in die Wirklichkeit statt in den Traum! Im Dorian Gray ist dieser Teil Wildes in zwei Personen gespalten: theoretisch ersonnen hat diesen Traum vom vollständigen Leben Lord Henry: ausleben soll ihn für ihn sein junger Freund: und weder Lord Henry noch Dorian ahnen, wie sie sich gegenseitig täuschen: der eine, der alles, was für den Traum gemeint war, in Wirklichkeit tut; der andre, der alles, was wirklich geschah, für im Traum getan hält. Und jener geht daran zugrunde. Und Wilde war beides zugleich, Lord Henry und Dorian Gray und noch vieles mehr, und ging doch am gleichen Irrtum zugrunde.

Denn nun komme ich dahin zurück, wo ich oben abbrach. Was Wilde so rätselhaft, so seltsam kompliziert macht, ist, dass in ihm zwei Kämpfe zugleich vor sich gehen: er ist ein Schlachtfeld für zwei Schlachten zugleich. Vier Heere kämpfen gegeneinander in je zwei Paaren; so weit kann man gerade mit der Analysis kommen: man sieht, es ist erbärmlich wenig, was man erreicht, und auch das wenige muss man noch in grotesken Bildern sagen.

Er ist »déraciné«, vielwurzlig, aber zwei Wurzeln halten ihn fester als alles andere: dass ich sie nenne—doch man erschrecke nicht—sie heissen Christentum und das Quiet English Home; es ist, wie ein Fisch an langer Angel hängt: ihm sitzt der Haken in den Kiemen, aber er schwimmt umher, taucht hier in purpurne Höhlen und dort in smaragdene Tiefen, oder er sonnt sich in flacher Wärme über dem gelben Sand; er tut, als wäre er frei; er glaubt vielleicht selber bisweilen an seine Freiheit, und doch ist er gebunden, und irgendwann zieht ihn der Angler an seiner Leine herauf; irgendwann flüchtet sich Wilde zum Glauben zurück und sehnt sich nach

associated with a murder, assuming that one had in one's nature the secret inclinations and predisposition to murder—indeed to everything, not simply to murder. And capable of living the life of the imagination is the "uprooted" individual, the many-rooted one who, thanks to the diversity of his background, has access to a thousand different lives. Were he to live but one real life, he would be able to follow only one life, and in doing so he would remain a stranger to himself, pursued by desire for the thousand other potential lives. But in his imagination, in his dreams, he follows all of them—he is at once, Nero and a dandy. And as quick as a thought, he can change his life; he does it. But woe to him if he lacks the requisite stamina, if he loses his way and proceeds into reality rather than remaining in his dream! In *Dorian Gray*, this part of Wilde is divided into two people: the theoretically conceived Lord Henry has the dream of a complete life, a dream which his young friend is to live out for him. And neither Lord Henry nor Dorian are aware of the extent to which they simultaneously deceive each other: one fulfils in reality all that was meant for a dream, while the other considered all that really transpired the stuff of dreams. And each is destroyed because of this. And Wilde was simultaneously both, Lord Henry and Dorian Gray and much more, and was destroyed by the same error.

With that I now return to the point from which I above broke off. What makes Wilde so mysterious, so unusually complicated is that in him two struggles are being fought out simultaneously: he is a battlefield for two battles at once. Four armies are fighting against each other in two separate pairs, so much can be said at this point from this analysis: as may be seen, pathetically little is to be established and even that little amount must be expressed in grotesque images.

He is "déraciné," many-rooted; nonetheless two roots hold him so much more firmly than all the others that I call them—one need not be surprised—Christianity and the Quiet English Home: his predicament is not unlike that of a fish hooked to a long fishing line. The fish is hooked by the gill but nonetheless swims around; here it dives into crimson caves and there in emerald depths, or it suns itself in warm flat waters above golden sands; it acts as if it were free, perhaps it even occasionally believes in its freedom and yet it is attached and at some point the fisherman reels it in out of the water on his line: at some point Wilde fled back to his belief and

jeder heimischen Sicherheit. Und über dem ganzen Leben vorher liegt jene Hast, jene Inbrunst des Genusses am Schweifen, wie wir nur bei dem sie finden, der sich vor dem Ende fürchtet, der weiss, dass er gefesselt ist, wenn er es auch vielleicht nur unbewusst weiss.

Und daneben jenes zweite: der Kampf des Traumes wider das Leben. Im Reich des Traums war er ja ein König und ein Crösus. Aber schon darin beginnt die Tragödie: er, der im Traum die Schätze Indiens verschwenden konnte, hätte im Leben einsam, zurückgezogen, ein stilles Dasein führen müssen, wenn er nicht einfach pekuniär über seine Verhältnisse leben wollte: das geht, gewiss! wo ward die neunte Symphonie gedichtet! Aber ach. Wilde war doch nicht ganz reveur, wie ich ihn nannte: er brauchte auch äusserlich das Leben im Glanz, und dieses Leben verschlang Geld – und Geld, das er oft nicht hatte. Schwärmern und Idealisten mag es traurig erscheinen, dass im Geld die Tragödie liegen kann, selbst wo es sich um der Erde Grösse handelt; wir, die wir mit härteren Seelen begabt sind und kühlere Augen fürs Leben haben, wir sehen darin beinah das Symbol für alles andere auch. Denn wer in Träumen ein König und Crösus ist, der muss durchs wirkliche Leben in allem ein Bettler gehn: Traum und Leben sind tödliche Gegner, die niemals im Frieden nebeneinander ziehen—und Wilde hat in allem über seine Verhältnisse leben müssen, weil er sich nicht zur resoluten Wahl entschliessen konnte.

Alle Taten machen uns zu Schuldnern, und die Schulden, die wir durchs Handeln auf uns nehmen, müssen wir eines Tages zahlen: das Leben ist der unerbittlichste Gläubiger. Weh dem, der vergisst, seine Taten als Debet ins Hauptbuch des Lebens zu schreiben: seine Schulden wachsen ins Ungeheuerliche an, und am Tage der Abrechnung ist er bankrott. Doppelt wehe dem der gewohnt ist, im Traum mit den grössten Schätzen zu spielen, wenn er sich nicht fürs Leben den einfachen Tatsachensinn des nüchternsten Soll und Haben bewahrt.

Wilde hat noch nach seiner Sühne an seinen Schulden gegen das Leben getragen; weil er versuchte, mit einer Abschlagszahlung noch einmal sich selber zu täuschen, ward ihm der Schluss seines Lebens zur greulichen Farce: die Abschlagszahlung, die ich meine, war jene letzte Reise nach Neapel.

Von dieser Seite aus gesehen wird Wildes Katastrophe zu einem Gewitter der Reinigung: sie wird zum notwendigen Ende, zum erhebenden

yearned for that familiar certainty. His whole life to that point was marked by that haste, that fervency born of a taste for roaming that is only to be found among those who fear the end, who know, even if only unconsciously, that they are hooked.

Alongside this battle is the second one, the struggle of the dream against life. In the realm of the dream he was a king and a Croesus. But here the tragedy begins: he who in a dream could waste the riches of India, in life would have to have lived a lonely, retired and uneventful existence if he were not to live beyond his pecuniary means: this is certainly possible! Where was the ninth symphony composed! But alas, Wilde was not quite entirely a *rêveur* as I called him: externally he also needed a life of luxury and this life demanded money—money he did not always have. For dreamers and idealists it may seem saddening that the tragedy could have its source in money, even when it concerns the greatest of tragedies. But we who are gifted with harder souls and who have a cooler eye for life, we almost see here the symbol for everything else as well. For he who is a king and a Croesus in his dreams must go through real life as a beggar: the dream and life are mortal enemies that will never find peace with one another. And Wilde was forced to live beyond his means in everything because he could not bring himself to a resolute choice.

Every deed makes of us a debtor, and the debts that we take upon ourselves in the course of our actions must one day be repaid. Life is the most relentless creditor. Woe to him who forgets to register his acts as debits in the ledger of life; his debts grow to monstrous proportions and on the day of reckoning he is bankrupt. Double woe to him who is accustomed in dream to play with the greatest treasures when he is unable to preserve himself for life from the common sense of the soberest debits and credits.

Even after his atonement for his debts, Wilde still had to suffer for his debts against life. The conclusion of his life developed into a cruel farce because he attempted with a down-payment to deceive himself again. The down-payment I have in mind was his last journey to Naples.

Seen from this perspective, Wilde's catastrophe serves as the storm that clears the air: it becomes the necessary end, an uplifting conclusion to one

Abschluss einer der furchtbarsten Tragödien, die ich kenne, einer
Tragödie, die mit dem ersten Erfolge Wildes beginnt.

12.

Denn was geschah da? Ich sagte, die Katastrophe wird zum erhebenden
Abschluss: ich meine das wörtlich: denn so schauerlich grotesk das
Satyrspiel der letzten Zeit nach seiner Freilassung in den Ohren gellt, wo
ihn die Kraft so ganz verliess, wo er ein schwankes Rohr für alle Winde
wurde, die zu seinem Ufer kamen—so sehr wurde er vorher zum Helden.

Wilde hatte sich hundertfach an der Gesellschaft versündigt: nicht
durch seinen Hohn, nicht durch die Geisselhiebe, die er ihr ins Gesicht
schlug, und das »Verbrechen«, wegen dessen er verurteilt wurde, ist—
selbst das Gesetz als Massstab genommen—nur eine Kleinigkeit gegen
das, was ich meine—wenn er auch, wie ich glaube, nach dem Buchstaben
des Gesetzes zu Recht verurteilt wurde (denn das englische Gericht, das
ihn verurteilte, sehe ich mit anderen Augen an als—namentlich in
Deutschland, wo man englische Verhältnisse bedauerlich wenig kennt—
üblich ist). Aber Wilde selber wusste, dass diese Katastrophe kommen
musste: er wusste auch, weshalb. Sein Prozess war nur ein Symptom für
eine Gegnerschaft, die viel tiefer lag, als die meisten Beteiligten ahnten. Es
war der Kampf der zivilisierten Menschheit gegen den, der die Basis aller
Zivilisation nicht einmal, nein, hundertmal umgestossen hatte, gegen den,
der die Schulden seiner Taten nicht zahlen wollte, ja, häufig nicht einmal
wusste und merkte, dass er mit ihnen Schulden auf sich genommen hatte;
das geht hinauf vom Allergröbsten, dem rein Pekuniären, bis in die letzten
geistigen Regungen, so weit sie hinaus ins Leben drangen. Er wollte seine
Taten folgenlos—wollte vergessen, dass er sie getan hatte. Er wollte sie
auch nicht tun: nichts scheint mir ernster gemeint, als seine Warnung vor
dem Leben; und doch habe ich ihn in Verdacht (in Verdacht? ... es ist
sicher!), dass er das Leben von oben bis unten kannte; dass er, ohne sich's
einzugestehn, immer und immer wieder fühlen musste, er war zu schwach
für das Leben, und dass er deshalb, statt sich zu verurteilen, das Leben
verurteilte und vor ihm warnte: denn er trug so schwer daran—was sollten
andere noch es nach ihm tun? Und auch vor sich selber flüchtete er dann:
er flüchtete sich in seine Träume, als wolle er gleich dem Vogel Strauss den

of the most terrible tragedies I know, a tragedy that began with Wilde's
first success.

12.

For what happened there? I have said that his catastrophe becomes an
uplifting conclusion. I mean that literally, for however horribly grotesque
the satyr-play of his remaining time after his release rings in one's ears,
when his strength deserted him entirely and he became a frail reed tossed
by every blast of wind that reached his shores—so completely did he
become a hero before this.

Wilde sinned against society a hundred times over, not with his derision, not with the scourging blows with which he struck society in the face;
and even the "crime" for which he was sentenced is—even according to the
law—but a trifling against that which I have in mind—even though, as I
believe, he was justly sentenced according to the letter of the law (I regard
the English law according to which he was sentenced differently than is
usual, especially in Germany, where the situation in England is unfortunately little known). But Wilde himself knew that this catastrophe had to
come; he also knew why. The court proceedings against him were only a
symptom of an animosity that lay much deeper than most of those involved
realised. It was the struggle of civilised humanity against someone who
had not once but a hundred times struck against the basis of all civilisation,
someone who refused to pay the debts of his deeds, indeed, who often did
not even realise that he had taken debts upon himself—that extends from
the crudest, purely pecuniary into the deepest spiritual stirrings which
from thence penetrated into life. He wished to have his deeds without the
consequences, wanted to forget that he was even the author of deeds.
Neither did he want to do them: nothing seems to me more seriously
intended than his warning about life, and I even suspect (suspect? … it is
certain) that he knew life from top to bottom, that he, without ever admitting it, was continually forced to feel that he was too weak for life and thus,
instead of condemning himself, he condemned life and warned of it—for
he made such an effort of it, what were others to do after him? And thus he

Kopf verbergen. Aber niemand glaubt ihm sein »Leben der Betrachtung«, der seine Warnung vor dem Leben gehört hat: nur wer sich im Leben tief beschmutzt hat, sehnt sich so leidenschaftlich nach der Reinheit geistiger Sphären. Aber immer und immer wieder greift er wie blind hinaus in das wirkliche Leben aus seinem Leben des Traums; es ist, wie ich oben sagte, als müsse, müsse er versuchen, ob ihn der Blitz auch wirklich trifft, wenn er das Verbotene tut. Und ihm war alles »Wirkliche« verboten. Ich habe schon in jener mehrmals genannten Broschüre darauf hingedeutet, dass hierin der tiefere Grund lag, warum Wilde sein Schicksal voraussah oder ahnte. Hinter dem Nicht-sehen-wollen, hinter seiner Leugnung des Lebens steht immer das Wissen, dass das Leben, dass die Welt der Dinge stärker ist als er. Es ist, als wollte ein Sklave, der in Träumen ehrgeizig und herrschsüchtig ist, seinen Herrn und die Knute beseitigen, indem er sie leugnet. Genau wie Wilde eben durch seinen Spott auf das Evangelium bewies, dass es vorhanden war, dass es für ihn vorhanden war. Der wirkliche Heide ignoriert es, weil er auch wirklich kaum von ihm weiss.

Und diese Gegnerschaft gegen das Leben, gegen alles, was im Leben stand und also gegen ihn, dieses Bewusstsein fortwährender Sünden an allem, was Zivilisation hiess, schuf in ihm eine Spannung—die gleiche Spannung, aus der heraus Dorian Gray gegen Basil Hallward so bitter wird; auch Wilde war scharf und spitz und bitter geworden: wo früher blühende Blüten standen, stachen jetzt Dornen. Und einen Moment trieb ihn dies Gefühl der Spannung gegen Leben und Gesellschaft zur Flucht. Er liess alles im Stich und fuhr nach Algier. Sein ganzes Auftreten dort—seine Gespräche mit André Gide sind Komödie. Er lässt es auch selber merken. In Algier kämpfte er seinen ersten wirklichen, schweren Kampf, und in diesem Kampfe blieb er Sieger, wurde er Held, fand er den Mut zur ganzen Wahrheit. Er wusste genau, was ihm bevorstand: dem Wesen nach—der Form nach kaum—aber die Form ist relativ gleichgültig: er wusste auf jeden Fall, dass jetzt sein Leben, wie er es bisher geführt hatte, dieses sublime Träumerleben, wo er in tausend Phantomgestalten einherging, während niemand sein wahrstes Angesicht kannte(denn wahr sind sie alle), dieses Leben, in dem er glaubte, unwirkliche Saaten zu streuen, die wirkliche Ernten trugen—das würde zerbrechen: all die Prunkgewänder würden von seinem Leibe fallen, und er in erbarmungsloser Nacktheit dastehn. Und dass er da ging und nicht auswich: das ist sein grösster

fled from himself, he fled into his dreams as if he were an ostrich burying his head in the sand. But no one who heard his warning about life believed his "Life of Observation." Only those who in life are deeply defiled yearn so passionately for the purity of spiritual realms. Nonetheless, again and again he blindly struck out, abandoning his life of the dream for real life. It is, as I said above, as if he had to, simply had to make the attempt, even if the lightening bolt were really to strike him upon attempting the forbidden. For him, everything "real" was forbidden. As I have previously observed in my frequently mentioned brochure, the ultimate reason why Wilde predicted or presumed his fate lies here. Behind his unwillingness to see, behind his denial of life was the knowledge that life, the world of reality, was stronger than he. It is as if a slave, ambitious and domineering in his dreams, were to eliminate his master and the knout by denying them. Just so Wilde, precisely through his mockery of it, proved that the gospel was present, that it was present for him. The real pagan ignores the gospel, because he knows little about it.

And this animosity towards life, towards everything and everyone in it and thus against himself, this conscious, continual sinning against everything civilised created in him a tension—the same tension which would lead to Dorian Gray's bitterness towards Basil Hallward. Wilde also became cutting and pointed and bitter. Nothing more than thorns remained where once fragrant blossoms bloomed. And suddenly, this feeling of tension against life and society drove him to flee. He dropped everything and escaped to Algiers. His entire presence there, his conversations with André Gide, is pure farce. He was not unaware of it himself. In Algiers he fought his first really intense struggle and in this struggle he emerged the victor, a hero and found the courage to acknowledge the truth. He knew exactly what awaited him—in essence but not in form, although the form is relatively unimportant. At any rate, he knew that his life as he had thus far led it, this sublime dream-life wherein he adopted a thousand fantastic forms, while no one knew his true countenance (for they were all true), this life, in which he believed he was sowing seeds which would actually bear fruit, this life he knew would shatter. All his sumptuous robes would fall from his body and he would be left mercilessly naked. That he

Moment—viel grösser als der spätere, wo er noch einmal Gelegenheit hat, auszuweichen und den Schlag zu meiden. Ihm blieb eine Möglichkeit: nicht die, in Frankreich oder auf fremdem Boden sein altes Leben, so gut es eben ging, wiederaufzunehmen und fortzuführen; das war unmöglich und er wusste es. »Es hiesse rückwärts gehen. Ich muss so weit gehen, wie nur möglich ist.« ... Aber die Form, wie er es sagt, ist Komödie: es heisst: »ich halte das Leben nicht mehr aus. Der Zwiespalt in meinem Dasein zerreisst und zerfleischt mich.« ... Aber eine Möglichkeit blieb: zu verschwinden! irgendwo ganz im Dunkeln zu leben! Der Welt das Phantom von sich zu lassen und wie ein Meteor zu verlöschen! Er hat an die Möglichkeit gedacht, daran kann ich nicht zweifeln—aber er hat sie verworfen, und das war gross, weil er seine Eitelkeit der Wahrheit opferte.

Er hatte noch einmal Gelegenheit, auszuweichen, sagte ich: diesmal war es Gelegenheit zur Flucht. Als der Haftbefehl gegen ihn erlassen war, stellte ein Londoner Biedermann die hohe Kaution, die das Gericht verlangte, wenn er bis zum Termin auf freiem Fuss belassen werden sollte. Und als Freunde Wildes mit diesem Biedermann sprachen, sagte er: »Lasst ihn fliehen! ich bin ruiniert, wenn ich die Kaution verliere—aber lasst ihn fliehen, wenn ihr seine Verurteilung fürchtet!« (—Sobald er wollte, gewann Wilde mit einem Blick selbst das Herz des Bourgeois.)—Wilde floh nicht. Es wäre auch nur noch die Flucht vor dem Kerker gewesen, nicht mehr die Rettung seines imaginären Daseins.—Man verstatte eine Anmerkung. Es ist merkwürdig: man hat viel auf das Gericht geschimpft—begreiflicherweise vielleicht in den Kreisen, die der homosexuellen »Bewegung« nahe stehen. Meiner Meinung nach konnte das Gericht gar nicht anders! Die einzige Rettung, die man ihm bieten konnte, war die Gelegenheit zur Flucht. Und die bot ihm selbst das Gericht; ein bezeichnender Zug dafür: als Wilde die Terminzustellung erhalten hatte, wartete man mit der Veröffentlichung, bis abends der letzte Zug nach Paris aus London ausgelaufen war und die Polizei berichtete: Oscar Wilde ist nicht geflohen. Mehr konnte man nicht tun.

nonetheless went forth without attempting to escape, that is his greatest moment, much greater than the later one when he was also confronted with the possibility of escaping and seeking to avoid his fall. One possibility remained to him—not that of returning to his former life and attempting to continue it as well as possible in France or another foreign land: "That would mean retreating, and I must carry on as far as possible." But the form, as he said, is farce. It implied, "I can no longer continue with my life. The rift in my innermost being is tearing me apart." ... But one possibility remained: to disappear, to live somewhere in obscurity, to leave the world a figment of himself and to expire like a meteor! He thought of that possibility, of that I have no doubt—but he cast it aside and that was great, for in doing so he sacrificed his vanity to truth.

He had still another opportunity for escape, as I have said. This time it was the possibility to flee. As the arrest order for him was issued, a man of standing in London put up the bail which the court had demanded before allowing Wilde to remain free until his court date. And as Wilde's friends spoke with this man of standing, he said: "Let him go, I am ruined if he doesn't return the bail—but let him go if he fears his punishment!" (Wilde could win even the heart of the bourgeoisie in a moment if he wanted.) Wilde did not flee. Flight would only have allowed him to save himself from prison, it would not have secured the preservation of his imagination-based existence. If I may be allowed a remark: It is curious that the court which sentenced Wilde has been so thoroughly castigated—understandably, perhaps, in the circles associated with the homosexual "movement." In my opinion, however, the court could not have acted otherwise! The sole alternative that could be offered to him was the possibility of flight. And this was offered by the court itself, as may be evinced by the following characteristic detail: after informing Wilde of the order for his arrest, publication was delayed until evening, after the last train had left London for Paris, and only then were the police informed. Oscar Wilde did not flee. Nothing else could be done.

13.

Wilde zahlte die Schulden seines Lebens mit dem Bankrott.

Sein Auftreten vor Gericht ist zu bedauern. Er versuchte noch einmal, sich die Maske vors Gesicht zu halten, die nicht mehr passte, und man fühlt, wenn man die Verhandlungsberichte liest, an mehreren Stellen, wie er unsicher wird, wie er sich seiner Komödie fast schämt. Und so sehr auch der Schein dagegen spricht, er wusste, dass er verurteilt werden würde. Und er wusste auch, um was es sich handelte, was diese schauerliche Einstimmigkeit, was dieser unerbittliche Hass der ganzen Gesellschaft, von der Aristokratie hinunter bis zum Pöbel, bedeutete: er hat die Verantwortung geleugnet: nicht nur theoretisch, sondern viel schlimmer: praktisch; er ist, um mit Nietzsche zu reden, ein Freitäter gewesen ...

Die Folgen dieses Erwachens, dieses Bankrotts habe ich kurz an anderer Stelle geschildert und ich verweise darauf ... Die Art, wie er dort in dem Küstenstädtchen Le Petit Berneval redet, bestätigt die Richtigkeit meines Exempels.

Schade, dass die Komödie noch einmal begann und zur ironischen Farce wurde! Schade, dass Wilde nach Neapel ging und wiederbeleben wollte, was einmal erstorben war; dass er dem Zufall die Gelegenheit bot, ihn nochmals niederzuschlagen, und diesmal mit der Waffe grotesker Lächerlichkeit: man entzog seinem Freunde den »Wechsel«! Schade auch, dass die Jämmerlichkeit der letzten Pariser Jahre folgen musste, wo er, eine Karikatur auf sich selber, umherging, wo sich die Freunde seiner schämten und im Cafe sich mit dem Rücken zur Strasse setzten, damit man sie nicht in Begleitung dessen erkenne, von dem auf der Strasse und vor den Augen der Menschen angeredet zu werden, sie einst für eine hohe Ehre gehalten, als einen Kitzel ihrer Eitelkeit empfunden hatten ! ... Vielleicht aber ist doch das Leben der grösste Dichter, und wir nur, mit unserer Zersplitterung und Vielspäitigkeit im Leben, suchen im Kunstwerk die Einheit. Folgt doch auch bei den Griechen die Farce der Komödie, und grinst doch bei Shakespeare der Hanswurst zum Rasen der Leidenschaft.

13.

Wilde paid for the debts of his life with bankruptcy.

His appearance before the court is to be regretted. He once again attempted to hold before his face a mask that was no longer appropriate. In reading the court proceedings, one feels in several places how unsure of himself he had become, how ashamed he was of the farce. And despite all appearances to the contrary, he knew that he would be condemned. He also knew what was at stake, what this terrible unanimity of opinion meant, this naked hate from every layer of society, from the aristocracy down to the rabble: he denied all responsibility, not only theoretically but, much worse, practically: to adopt Nietzsche's vocabulary he had been a free agent (*Freitäter*)...

The consequences of this development, this bankruptcy, I have briefly depicted in other places and I draw attention to them now ... The manner in which he spoke at the little sea-side resort of Le Petit Berneval confirms the correctness of my example.

It is a pity that what was begun once more as a comedy developed into an ironic farce! It is a pity that Wilde went to Naples in the attempt to resurrect what had already died, that he offered chance the opportunity to strike him down once again, this time with the weapon of grotesque ridiculousness: "promissory notes" were called in on a friend! It is also a pity that the wretchedness of the last Paris years had to follow, where, a caricature of his former self, he roamed, and where his friends were ashamed of him and sat in cafes with him with their backs to the street so as not to be recognised in his company, to be addressed in the streets before the eyes of others by people who, once, would have considered it an honour but now as a thrill for their vanity! And yet perhaps life is the greatest artist and we, with the fragmentation and ambiguity of our lives, but seek unity in art. Even with the Greeks, farce followed upon comedy, and in Shakespeare the fool grins at the rages of passion.

14.

Die Tragödie endet in Berneval. Es ist die letzte Szene des fünften Aktes.
Wo sind die anderen Szenen und wo die anderen Akte? Kampf und
Niederlage, Kampf und Sieg? Es ist eine Tragödie mit jeder grossen
Erschütterung, voll von allen Tönen, die im Leben moderner Menschen
erklingen: der künstlichste Mensch kommt von den künstlichsten Freuden
zu den wirklichsten Leiden. Keine Sünde, die er nicht kennt; kein Genuss,
von dem er nicht gekostet hätte; kein Verzicht, mit dem er nicht entsagte.
Und alles in Widerspruch und tollem Taumel, Traum und Leben gemischt,
Wahrheit und Pose, dass man sie nicht mehr voneinander kennt: Ein
Dandy, der schliesslich erschüttert vor sich selber steht!

Wo bleiben noch seine Werke? Was gehen sie uns an? Aber bisweilen
gewähren sie einen Blick in diese Psyche—bisweilen, nicht oft. Man lese
die beiden Satiren, die folgen: sie gehören noch mit zum Bezeichnendsten!
Denn wer wollte jedesmal im einzelnen unterscheiden, wo es Wilde ernst
ist und wo er lacht? Sie geben eine Ahnung, eine entfernte, blasse Ahnung
von jener Vielspältigkeit im Blick dieses Sonnenuntergangsmenschen, der
die Dinge von tausend Seiten zugleich sieht. Und deshalb mag dieses Wort
sie begleiten.*

Aber ich höre darum nicht auf, von jenem Buche zu träumen, in dem
lebendig wäre, was ich in den wenigen Worten oben anzudeuten versuchte.
Von jenem Buche, das uns den Menschen gäbe, den Menschen Oscar Wilde
... Könnte ich doch eines Tages erwachen und sehen, mein Traum ist erfüllt
... ein anderer nahm mir die Last von der Seele, und ich kann das
Schauspiel der grossen Tragödie geniessen, statt sie zu schreiben und—
wahrscheinlich!—an meiner Aufgabe zu scheitern!

Bonn, Oktober 1903.
FELIX PAUL GREVE

14.

The tragedy ends in Berneval. It is the last scene of the fifth act. Where are the other scenes and the other acts? Struggle and defeat, struggle and victory? It is a tragedy with all the great emotional blows, full of all the tones that resound through the life of modern man. The most artificial of individuals descends from the most artificial pleasures to the most real suffering. There was not a sin that he did not know, no sensual pleasure that he did not partake of, no renunciation that he didn't refuse. And everything in contradiction and a glorious daze, dream and life mixed, truth and pose, such that neither is to be recognised one from the other. A dandy who ultimately stands broken before himself!

And what of his works? Of what relevance are they to us? Occasionally they allow us a look into this psyche—occasionally, not often. Read the two satires, the following ones; they are still amongst his most characteristic! For who wants on every separate occasion to attempt to discern where Wilde is being serious and where he is laughing? They provide an indication, a distant, faint indication of the multiplicity of the perspective of this doomed man who sees things from a thousand sides simultaneously. And thus may this word accompany them.[5]

Nonetheless, I am not going to cease to dream of that book which would bring to life that which I sought to indicate in the above few words—that book which would give us the individual, the individual Oscar Wilde ... If only I could one day awake and see that my dream had been fulfilled, that another had taken the burden from my soul and I could enjoy the spectacle of the great tragedy, instead of trying to write it and—probably!—failing in my attempt!

Bonn, October 1903.
FELIX PAUL GREVE

1   Ich sage ausdrücklich, dass die Bemerkungen, die ich im Folgenden gebe, die
    Bekanntschaft mit meiner kleinen Broschüre: Oscar Wilde (Moderne Essays, Nr.
    29. Verlag Gose & Tezlaff, Berlin) voraussetzen, und jene Broschüre in ein Paar
    Punkten berichtigen, ja widerrufen soll. [Footnote appended to the title RANDAR-
    ABESKEN ZU OSCAR WILDE on the inside title page.]

2   Darf ich die Gelegenheit ergreifen, auf vortreffliche Gedanken über diesen
    Gegenstand in der Novelle "Timm Krüger" von Thomas Mann hinzuweisen?

3   Ich brauche kaum zu sagen, dass ich hier wie auch im folgenden das Wort Künstler
    ganz allgemein fasse, mit Einschluss, unter anderem, des Philosophen.

4   Ein Hang zum Nachahmen, der sich in seinen Werken zeigt und mehr ist als künst-
    lerische Schwäche.

5   Die Bemerkungen sollen einen Band mit Übertragungen von Oscar Wildes: "The
    Portrait of Mr. W.H." und "Lord Arthur Savile's Crime" einleiten.

NOTES

*   I would like to thank A. Leonard Grove for authorising translation of this work and Klaus Martens for his help and support in this translation and my research on Felix Paul Greve. Translator's note.

1   I wish to emphasize that the comments to be made in the following presume familiarity with my small booklet *Oscar Wilde* (Moderne Essays, Nr. 29, Berlin: Gose & Tetzlaff) and in a few points are intended to correct and even countermand it.

2   Might I take the opportunity to refer to the relevant ideas in this regard found in Thomas Mann's novella *Timm Kröger*?

3   I hardly need to state that here, as in the following, I am using the word artist in its general sense to include, among others, philosophers.

4   A tendency to imitation which appears in his works and which is more than an artistic failing.

5   These comments are to introduce a volume of translations of Oscar Wilde: "The Portrait of Mr. W.H." and "Lord Arthur Savile's Crime."

Works Cited

Anderson, J.T.M. *The Education of the New-Canadian.* Toronto: J.M. Dent & Sons, 1918.

Anderson, Margaret, C. *My Thirty Years' War: The Autobiography, Beginnings and Battles 1930.* 1930. New York: Horizon, 1969.

D'Annunzio, Gabriele. "Francesca da Rimini: Eine Tragödie in Versen." Trans. Karl Gustav Vollmoeller. *Neue Deutsche Rundschau* 14 (1903): 1063–1101, 1167–1212.

Anon. "Zum Geleit." *Die Schaubühne* 1 (7 Sept. 1905): 1.

Avery, Donald. *"Dangerous Foreigners": European Immigrant Workers and Labour Radicalism in Canada, 1896–1932.* Toronto: McClelland and Stewart, 1979.

Barber, Marilyn. Introduction. *Strangers Within Our Gates; Or Coming Canadians.* Toronto: University of Toronto Press, 1972. vii–xxiii.

———. "Canadianization Through the Schools of the Prairie Provinces Before World War I: The Attitudes and Aims of the English-Speaking Majority." *Ethnic Canadians: Culture and Education.* Ed. Martin L. Kovacs. Regina: Canadian Plains Research Centre, 1978. 281–94.

Barnes, Djuna. *Nightwood.* New York: Harcourt, Brace and Co, 1937.

———, ed. "Selections from the Letters of Elsa Baroness von Freytag-Loringhoven." *Transition* 11 (February 1928): 19–30.

Bauschinger, Sigrid. *Else Lasker-Schüler: Ihr Werk und ihre Zeit.* Heidelberg: Lothar Stiehm Verlag, 1980.

Bercuson, David Jay. *Confrontation at Winnipeg: Labour, Industrial Relations, and the General Strike.* Montreal: McGill-Queen's University Press, 1974.

Berman, Nina. *Orientalismus, Kolonialismus und Moderne. Zum Bild des Orients in der deutschsprachigen Kultur um 1900.* Stuttgart: Verlag für Wissenschaft und Forschung, 1997.

Biddle, George. *An American Artist's Story*. Boston: Little, Brown, 1939.

B[ie], O[scar]. "Die Aesthetik der Lüge." Rev. of *Fingerzeige*, by Oscar Wilde, trans. Felix Paul Greve. *Neue Deutsche Rundschau* 14 (1903): 670–72.

Blätter für die Kunst: Auslese für die Jahre 1892/98. Berlin: Bondi, 1899.

Blätter für die Kunst: Auslese für die Jahre 1898/1904. Berlin: Bondi, 1904.

Blätter für die Kunst: Auslese für die Jahre 1904/09. Berlin: Bondi, 1909.

Blodgett, E.D. "Alias Grove: Variations in Disguise." *Configuration: Essays in the Canadian Literatures*. Downsview: EWC Press, 1982. 112–53.

———. Foreword. *F.P. Grove in Europe and Canada: Translated Lives*. By Klaus Martens. Trans. Klaus Martens and Paul Morris. Edmonton: University of Alberta Press, 2001. ix–xv.

Blondel, Nathalie. *Mary Butts: Scenes from the Life, A Biography*. Kingston, N.Y.: McPherson, 1998.

Bochner, Jay, and Justin D. Edwards, eds. *American Modernism Across the Arts*. New York: P. Lang, 1999.

Boehringer, Robert, and Georg Peter Landmann, eds. *Stefan George— Friedrich Gundolf: Briefwechsel*. Munich: Helmut Küpper vormals Georg Bondi, 1962.

Bourdieu, Pierre. *The Field of Cultural Production: Essays on Art and Literature*. Ed. and introd. Randal Johnson. New York: Columbia University Press, 1993.

Brooks, Charles S. *Hints to Pilgrims*. New Haven: Yale University Press, 1921.

Browning, Robert. *Auf einem Balkon—In einer Gondel*. Trans. F.C. Gerden [Felix Paul Greve]. Leipzig: Insel, 1903.

———. "Kleon." Trans. Felix Paul Greve. *Freistatt* 6 (July 1904): 556–59.

Browning, Robert, and Elizabeth Barrett Barrett. *Briefe von Robert Browning und Elizabeth Barrett Barrett*. Trans. Felix Paul Greve. Berlin: S. Fischer, 1905.

———. "Briefwechsel." [Trans. Felix Paul Greve.] *Die Neue Rundschau* 15 (1904): 774–804, 949–74.

Buffet-Picabia, Gabrielle. "Some Memories of Pre-Dada: Picabia and Duchamp." *The Dada Painters and Poets: An Anthology*. Ed. Robert Motherwell. New York: George Wittenborn, 1967. 255–67.

Butler, Judith. "Performative Acts and Gender Constitution: An Essay in Phenomenology and Feminist Theory." *Performing Feminisms: Feminist*

Critical Theory and Theatre. Ed. Sue-Ellen Case. Baltimore and London: Johns Hopkins University Press, 1990. 270–82.

Butts, Mary. "The Master's Last Dancing: A Wild Party in Paris, Inspired by One of Ford Maddox [sic] Ford's." *The New Yorker* 30 March 1998: 110–13.

Cavell, Richard. "Felix Paul Greve, the Eulenburg Scandal, and Frederick Philip Grove." *Essays on Canadian Writing* 62 (1997): 12–45.

————. *McLuhan in Space: A Cultural Geography.* Toronto: University of Toronto Press, 2002.

Cottbuser Anzeiger. Cottbus: n.p., 1897–98.

Davidson, Abraham A. "The European Art Invasion." Naumann and Venn 222–27.

DeVore, Lynn. "The Backgrounds of *Nightwood*: Robin, Felix, and Nora." *Journal of Modern Literature* 10.1 (1983): 71–90.

Dietzel, Thomas, and Hans-Otto Hügel, eds. *Deutsche Literarische Zeitschriften, 1880–1945: Ein Repertorium.* 5 vols. Munich: K. G. Saur, 1988.

Divay, Gabrielle, ed. *Poems by Frederick Philip Grove / Gedichte von Felix Paul Greve und Fanny Essler.* Winnipeg: Wolf Verlag, 1993.

Döhl, Reinhard. "Dadaismus." *Expressionismus als Literatur.* Ed. Wolfgang Rothe. Bern-München: Francke, 1969. 719–39.

Donnelly, Murray. *Dafoe of the Free Press.* Toronto: Macmillan of Canada, 1968.

Dumas, Alexandre. *Der Graf von Monte Christo.* Trans. Felix Paul Greve. Berlin: E. Reiss, 1909.

Duve, Thierry de. "Resonances of Duchamp's Visit to Munich." *Marcel Duchamp: Artist of the Century.* Eds. Rudolf E. Kuenzli and Francis M. Naumann. Cambridge, Mass.: MIT Press, 1996. 41–63.

Egbringhoff, Ulla. *Franziska zu Reventlow.* Reinbek bei Hamburg: Rowohlt, 2000.

Endell, August. "Das Bayerische Nationalmuseum." *Freistatt* 6 (10 Sept. 1904): 738–39.

————. "Das Bayerische Nationalmuseum." *Freistatt* 6 (17 Sept. 1904): 758–60.

————. "Formenschönheit und Dekorative Kunst." *Deutsche Kunst und Dekoration.* Band 2 (1898): 119–25.

————. "Möglichkeit und Ziele einer Neuen Architektur." *Deutsche Kunst und Dekoration*. Band 1 (1897–98): 98–153.

Ernst, Jutta, and Klaus Martens, eds. *"Je vous écris, en hâte et fiévreusement": Felix Paul Greve—André Gide. Korrespondenz und Dokumentation*. St. Ingbert: Röhrig Universitätsverlag, 1999.

Escritt, Stephen. *Art Nouveau*. London: Phaidon, 2000.

Essler, Fanny [Felix Paul Greve and Else Endell]. "Gedichte." *Freistatt* 6 (27 Aug. 1904): 700–701.

————. "Gedichte." *Freistatt* 7 (25 March 1905): 185–86.

————. "Ein Porträt: Drei Sonnette [sic]." *Freistatt* 6 (15 Oct. 1904): 840–41.

F.D. Rev. of *Die Zeitmaschine*, by H.G. Wells, trans. Felix Paul Greve. *Freistatt* 6 (15 Oct. 1904): 1045.

Flanner, Janet. "Elsa von Freytag-Loringhoven [1928]." *Paris Was Yesterday, 1925–1939*. Ed. Irving Drutman. New York: Viking, 1972. 39.

Ford, Ford Madox. *It Was the Nightingale*. Philadelphia & London: J.B. Lippincott, 1933.

Friesen, Gerald. *The Canadian Prairies: A History*. Toronto: University of Toronto Press, 1987.

Freytag-Loringhoven, Baroness Elsa von. "A Dozen Cocktails Please," "Clock, "Literary Five O'Clock," "Orgasmic Toast," "Orgasm," "Subjoyride," unpublished poems. "Matter, Level, Perspective," "Perpetual Motion," unpublished visual poems. Elsa von Freytag-Loringhoven Papers, College Park Libraries, Maryland.

————. "Appalling Heart." *The Little Review* 7.3 (September-December 1920): 47.

————. *Baroness Elsa*. Ed. and introd. Paul I. Hjartarson and Douglas O. Spettigue. Ottawa: Oberon Press, 1992.

————. Letter to Peggy Vail [Guggenheim]. Summer 1927. Typescript prepared by Guggenheim. Elsa von Freytag-Loringhoven Papers, College Park Libraries, Maryland.

————. Letter to Djuna Barnes. "Djuna Sweet—If you would know." c. Spring 1924. Elsa von Freytag-Loringhoven Papers, College Park Libraries, Maryland. Excerpts in Hjartarson and Spettigue, *Baroness Elsa* 201–06.

————. Letter to Djuna Barnes. "Djuna—By a mere accident." c. 1924–25. Excerpts in Hjartarson and Spettigue, *Baroness Elsa* 214–17.

———. Letter to Djuna Barnes. "Dearest Djuna [...] It is marvellous how you love me." c. 1924. Elsa von Freytag-Loringhoven Papers, College Park Libraries, Maryland.

———. Letter to Jane Heap. "Jane Heap, you must have misinterpreted my letter." c. 1923. Golda Meir Archives, University of Wisconsin Library.

———. "Mefk Maru Mustir Daas." *The Little Review* 5.8 (December 1918): 41.

———. "Mineself-Minesoul-and-Mine-Cast-Iron Lover." *The Little Review* 6.5 (September 1919): 3–11.

———. *Oggetto (Object)*. c. 1925–27. Belt with ornaments. Peggy Guggenheim Collection, Venice.

———. "Seelisch-Chemische Betrachtung" [Spiritual-Chemical Reflection]. Elsa von Freytag-Loringhoven Papers, College Park Libraries, Maryland.

Gammel, Irene. *Baroness Elsa: Gender, Dada, and Everyday Modernity: A Cultural Biography*. Cambridge, Mass.: MIT Press, 2002.

———. "The Baroness Elsa and the Politics of Transgressive Body Talk." *American Modernism Across the Arts*. Ed. Jay Bochner and Justin D. Edwards. New York: P. Lang, 1999. 73–96.

———. "Breaking the Bonds of Discretion: Baroness Elsa and the Female Sexual Confession." *TULSA Studies in Women's Literature* 14.1 (Spring 1995): 149–66.

———. "German Extravagance Confronts American Modernism: The Poetics of Baroness Else." Martens, *Pioneering North America* 60–75.

———. "'No Woman Lover': Baroness Elsa's Intimate Biography." *Canadian Review of Comparative Literature* 20.3/4 (Winter 1993): 451–67.

———. "Parading Sexuality: Modernist Life writing and Popular Confession." *Confessional Politics: Women's Sexual Self-Representations in Life Writing and Popular Media*. Ed. Irene Gammel. Carbondale: Southern Illinois University Press, 1999. 47–61.

———. *Sexualizing Power in Naturalism: Theodore Dreiser and Frederick Philip Grove*. Calgary: University of Calgary Press, 1994.

———. "Mirror Looks: The Visual and Performative Diaries of L.M. Montgomery, Baroness Elsa von Freytag-Loringhoven, and Elvira Bach." *Interfaces: Women, Autobiography, Image, Performance*. Ed. Sidonie

Smith and Julia Watson. Ann Arbor: University of Michigan Press, 2002. 289–313.

Geertz, Clifford. *The Interpretation of Cultures: Selected Essays*. New York: Basic Books, 1973.

Giltrow, Janet. "Grove in Search of an Audience." *Canadian Literature* 90 (1981): 92–110.

Gide, André. *Die enge Pforte*. Trans. Felix Paul Greve. Berlin: E. Reiss, 1909.

———. "Die Heimkehr des verlorenen Sohnes." Trans. Kurt Singer. *Die Neue Rundschau* 18 (1907): 596–608.

———. *Der Immoralist*. Trans. Felix Paul Greve. Minden: J.C.C. Bruns Verlag, 1905.

———. *Ein Liebesversuch und andere Novellen*. Trans. Felix Paul Greve. Berlin: Oesterheld, 1907.

———. "Menalkas." [Trans. Felix Paul Greve.] *Die Zukunft* 13.51 (1905): 294–98.

———. *Paludes (Die Sümpfe)*. Trans. Felix Paul Greve. Minden: J.C.C. Bruns Verlag, 1905.

———. "Saul." Trans. Felix Paul Greve. *Die Schaubühne* 3 (8 Aug. 1907): 105–10.

———. *Saül*. Trans. Felix Paul Greve. Berlin: Reiss, 1909.

Goethe, Johann Wolfgang von. *Faust, Part I*. Trans. and introd. Peter Salm. German/English ed. New York: Bantam, 1985.

Greve, Felix Paul. "Die Hexe." *Freistatt* 6 (June 1904): 519.

———. "Die Stadt am Strande." *Die Schaubühne* 3 (6 June 1907): 570.

———. "Erster Sturm." *Die Schaubühne* 3 (7 Feb. 1907): 154.

———. *Fanny Essler*. Stuttgart: Juncker, [1905].

———. "George Meredith." *Freistatt* 6 (3 Sept. 1904): 721–23.

———. "Lucien Leuwen. Ein neues Werk von Stendhal (Henri Beyle)." Rev. of Lucien Leuwen, by Stendhal. *Beilage zur Allgemeinen Zeitung* [Munich] 30 Sept. 1901: 1–2.

———. *Maurermeister Ihles Haus*. Berlin: Karl Schnabel, 1906. *The Master Mason's House*. Frederick Philip Grove. Trans. Paul P. Gublins. Ottawa: Oberon Press, 1976.

———. "Nachgelassene Werke von Friedrich Nietzsche (Band XI u. XII, herausgegeben von Ernst und August Horneffer.)." Rev. of Nietzsche's

Werke, by Friedrich Nietzsche. *Beilage zur Allgemeinen Zeitung* [Munich]
  10 Oct. 1901: 6–7.

———. *Oscar Wilde*. Trans. Barry Asker. Vancouver: William Hoffer, 1984.

———. "Oscar Wilde und das Drama." *Oscar Wildes sämtliche Werke in
  deutscher Sprache*. Volume 7, *Vera oder die Nihilisten*. Wien and Leipzig:
  Wiener Verlag, 1908. 7–102.

———. "Oskar Wilde." *Porträts*. Ed. Adalbert Luntowski. Berlin: Verlag
  Neues Leben — Wilhelm Borngräber, 1911. 12–51.

———. *Randarabesken zu Oscar Wilde*. Minden: J.C.C. Bruns Verlag, [1903].

———. Self-Rev. of *Ausblicke auf die Folgen des technischen und wissenschaftlichen
  Fortschrittes für Leben und Denken des Menschen*, by H.G. Wells, trans. Felix
  Paul Greve. *Die Zukunft* 14.53 (1905): 483.

———. Self-Rev. of *Das Bildnis Dorian Grays*, by Oscar Wilde, trans. Felix
  Paul Greve. *Die Zukunft* 11.44 (1903): 208.

———. Self-Rev. of *Der Immoralist*, by André Gide, trans. Felix Paul Greve.
  Die Zukunft 13.52 (1905): 305–06.

———. Self-Rev. of *Die Zeitmaschine.—Dr. Moreaus Insel.—Die Riesen kommen!*,
  by H.G. Wells, trans. Felix Paul Greve. *Die Zukunft* 13.50 (1905):
  266–67.

———. Self-Rev. of *Fingerzeige*, by Oscar Wilde, trans. Felix Paul Greve and
  Herman F.C. Kilian. *Die Zukunft* 11.41 (1902): 466–67.

———. Self-Rev. of *Wanderungen*, by Felix Paul Greve. *Die Zukunft* 10.39
  (1902): 164–65.

———. *Wanderungen*. Munich: Privately Printed, 1902.

Grove, Frederick Philip. *A Search for America*. c.1927. Toronto: McClelland
  and Stewart, 1991.

———. "Assimilation." Hjartarson, *A Stranger* 177–87.

———. "Canadians Old and New." Hjartarson, *A Stranger* 169–76.

———. *In Search of Myself*. 1946. Toronto: McClelland and Stewart, 1974.

———. *Our Daily Bread*. Toronto: Macmillan, 1928.

———. *Settlers of the Marsh*. 1925. Toronto: McClelland and Stewart, 1974.

Gunnars, Kristjana. Afterword. *Settlers of the Marsh*. NCL Edition. Toronto:
  McClelland and Stewart, 1989.

Healy, J.J. "Grove and the Matter of Germany." Hjartarson, *A Stranger*
  89–105.

Heap, Jane. "Dada." *The Little Review* 8.2 (Spring 1922): 46.

———. "Art and the Law." *The Little Review* 7.3 (September-December 1920): 5–7.

———. "Full of Weapons." *The Little Review* 8.2 (Spring 1922): 33.

Hjartarson, Paul I, ed. *A Stranger to My Time: Essays By and About Frederick Philip Grove*. Edmonton: NeWest Press, 1986.

———. "Staking a Claim: Settler Culture and the Canonization of 'Frederick Philip Grove' as a 'Canadian' Writer." Martens, *Pioneering North America* 19–30.

———. "Of Greve, Grove, and Other Strangers: The Autobiography of the Baroness Elsa von Freytag-Loringhoven." Hjartarson, *A Stranger* 269–84.

———. "The Self, Its Discourse, and the Other: The Autobiographies of Frederick Philip Grove and Baroness Elsa von Freytag-Loringhoven." *Reflections: Autobiography and Canadian Literature*. Ed. K.P. Stich. Ottawa: University of Ottawa Press, 1988. 115–29.

Hjartarson, Paul I., and Douglas O. Spettigue. Introduction. *Baroness Elsa*. By Elsa von Freytag-Loringhoven. Ed. Paul Hjartarson and Douglas O. Spettigue. Ottawa: Oberon Press, 1992. 9–40.

Hoerschelmann, Rolf von. *Leben ohne Alltag*. Berlin: Wedding-Verlag, 1947.

Hughes, Robert. "Days of Antic Weirdness: A Look Back at Dadaism's Brief, Outrageous Assault on the New York Scene." *Time* 149.4 (27 January 1997): 70–72.

Ifkovits, Kurt. "'Guten Tag Herr Dichter der Tapetenfabrik'—Franz Blei und *Die Insel*." *Franz Blei: Mittler der Literaturen*. Ed. Dietrich Harth. Hamburg: Europäische Verlagsantalt, 1997. 172–87.

Jaenen, Cornelius J. "Ruthenian Schools in Western Canada 1897–1919." *Pedagogica Historica* 10.3 (1970): 517–41.

Jones, Amelia. "Eros, That's Life, or the Baroness' Penis." Naumann and Venn 238–47.

———. "'Women' in Dada: Elsa, Rose, and Charlie." Sawelson-Gorse 142–72.

———. "Practicing Space: World War I-Era New York and the Baroness as Spectacular Flâneuse." *Living Display*. Ed. Jim Drobnick and Jennifer Fisher. Chicago: University of Chicago Press. (forthcoming)

Kamboureli, Smaro. *Scandalous Bodies: Diasporic Literature in English-Canada*. Toronto: Oxford UP, 1999.

Kassner, Rudolf. "Robert Browning und Elisabeth Barrett Barrett." *Die Neue Rundschau* 15 (1904): 769–74.

Kealey, Gregory S. "The Surveillance State: The Origins of Domestic Intelligence and Counter Subversion in Canada, 1914–1921." *Intelligence and National Security* 7.3 (1992): 184–89.

Kimmelman, Michael. "Forever Dada: Much Ado Championing the Absurd." *New York Times* (22 November 1996): C1, C4.

Kluncker, Karlhans. *Blätter für die Kunst: Zeitschrift der Dichterschule Stefan Georges*. Frankfurt am Main: Klostermann, 1974.

Klüsener, Erika. *Else Lasker-Schüler in Selbstzeugnissen und Bilddokumenten*. Reinbek bei Hamburg: Rowohlt, 1980.

Korte, Hermann. *Die Dadaisten*. Reinbek bei Hamburg: Rowohlt, 1994.

Krauss, Rosalind E. *Bachelors*. Cambridge, Mass.: MIT Press, 1999.

Kuenzli, Rudolf E. "Baroness Elsa von Freytag-Loringhoven and New York Dada." Sawelson-Gorse 442–75.

———, ed. *New York Dada*. New York: Willis Locker & Owens, 1986.

Lania, Leo [aka Herrmann Lazar]. *Der Tanz ins Dunkel: Anita Berber, Ein biographischer Roman*. Berlin: Schultz, 1929.

Lasker-Schüler, Else. *Gesammelte Werke in drei Bänden*. Ed. Friedhelm Kemp. München: Kösel, 1962.

Leader, Darian. *Freud's Footnotes*. London: Faber and Faber, 2000.

Maguire, T.M. "North Central Inspectoral Division: T.M. Maguire's Report." *Manitoba, Report of the Department of Education*, 1906. 29–32.

Makow, Henry. "Letters From Eden: Grove's Creative Rebirth." Hjartarson, *A Stranger* 107–26.

Mallgrave, Harry Francis, and Eleftherious Ikonomou. "Introduction." *Empathy, Form, and Space: Problems in German Aesthetics, 1873–1893*. Ed. Mallgrave and Ikonomou. Santa Monica: Getty Center, 1994. 1–88.

Martens, Klaus. *Die Antinomische Imagination*. Frankfurt-Bern: Peter Lang, 1986.

———. *Felix Paul Greves Karriere: Frederick Philip Grove in Deutschland*. St. Ingbert: Röhrig Universitätsverlag, 1997.

———, ed. *J.C.C. Bruns' Verlag. Seine Autoren und Übersetzer*. St. Ingbert: Röhrig, 1996.

———, ed. *Pioneering North America: Mediators of European Culture and Literature*. Würzburg: Königshausen & Neumann, 2000.

———. *F.P. Grove in Europe and Canada: Translated Lives.* Trans. Paul Morris in
collaboration with the author. Edmonton: University of Alberta Press,
2001.

Martynowych, Orest T. *Ukrainians in Canada: The Formative Period, 1891–1924.*
Edmonton: Canadian Institute of Ukrainian Studies Press, 1991.

McLaren, Angus. *Our Own Master Race: Eugenics in Canada, 1885–1945.*
Toronto: McClelland and Stewart, 1990.

Meredith, George. "Sentenzen." Trans. anon. [Felix Paul Greve?]. *Neue
Deutsche Rundschau* 14 (1903): 1339.

Meyerfeld, Max. "Erinnerungen an Oscar Wilde." *Neue Deutsche Rundschau* 14
(1903): 400–407.

Monroe, Harriet. "Our Contemporaries: New International Magazines."
Poetry: A Magazine of Verse 19.4 (January 1922): 224–27.

Morgan, Margaret. "A Box, A Pipe, and A Piece of Plumbing." Sawelson-
Gorse 48–78.

Morton, Desmond and Glenn Wright. *Winning the Second Battle: Canadian
Veterans and the Return to Civilian Life 1915–1930.* Toronto: University of
Toronto Press, 1987.

Naumann, Francis M. *New York Dada 1915–23.* New York: Abrams, 1994.

———, ed. *How, When, and Why Modern Art Came to New York: Marius de
Zayas.* Cambridge, Mass.: MIT Press, 1996.

———. "Marcel Duchamp: A Reconciliation of Opposites." *Marcel
Duchamp: Artist of the Century.* Eds. Rudolf Kuenzli and Francis M.
Naumann. Cambridge, Mass.: MIT Press, 1996. 20–40.

———. "New York Dada: Style With a Smile." Nauman and Venn 10–26.

Naumann, Francis M., and Beth Venn, eds. *Making Mischief: Dada Invades
New York.* New York: Whitney Museum of American Art, 1996.

Nause, John, ed. *The Grove Symposium.* Ottawa: University of Ottawa Press,
1974.

Nelson, Cary. *Repression and Recovery: Modern American Poetry and the Politics of
Cultural Memory 1910–1945.* Madison: University of Wisconsin Press,
1989.

Pacey, Desmond. *Frederick Philip Grove.* Toronto: Ryerson, 1945.

———, ed. *The Letters of Frederick Philip Grove.* Toronto: University of Toronto
Press, 1976.

Pache, Walter. "Der Fall Grove — Vorleben und Nachleben des Schriftstellers Felix Paul Greve." *Deutschkanadisches Jahrbuch* 5 (1979): 121–36.

———. "The Dilettante in Exile: Grove at the Centenary of His Birth." *Canadian Literature* 90 (1981): 187–91.

Padolsky, Enoch. "Grove's 'Nationhood' and the European Immigrant." *Journal of Canadian Studies / Revue d'études cannadiennes* 22.1 (1987): 32–50.

Pater, Walter. *Marius der Epikureer.* Trans. Felix Paul Greve. 2 vols. Leipzig: Insel, 1908.

Peterfy, Margit. "Themen der Zeit bei J.C.C. Bruns: Via 'Ethik' in das zwanzigste Jahrhundert." *J.C.C. Bruns' Verlag. Seine Autoren und Übersetzer.* Ed. Klaus Martens. St. Ingbert: Röhrig, 1996. 39–46.

Phelan, Peggy. *Unmarked: The Politics of Performance.* New York: Routledge, 1993.

Podro, Michael. *The Manifold in Perception: Theories of Art from Kant to Hildebrand.* Oxford: Clarendon Press, 1972.

Poirier, Richard. *The Performing Self. Compositions and Decompositions in Languages of Contemporary Life.* New York: Oxford University Press, 1971.

Pound, Ezra. "Canto 95: The Rock Drill Canto." *The Cantos of Ezra Pound.* New York: New Directions, 1971.

Pratt, Mary Louise. *Imperial Eyes: Travel Writing and Transculturation.* New York: Routledge, 1992.

Prenowitz, Eric. Translator's Note. *Archive Fever: A Freudian Impression.* By Jacques Derrida. Trans. Eric Prenowitz. Chicago: University of Chicago Press, 1995. 105–11.

Pross, Harry. *Literatur und Politik: Geschichte und Programme der politisch-literarischen Zeitschriften im deutschen Sprachgebiet seit 1870.* Olten: Walter-Verlag, 1963.

Reilly, Eliza Jane. "Elsa von Freytag-Loringhoven." *Women's Art Journal* 18.1 (Spring/Summer 1997): 26–33.

Reiss, Robert. "'My Baroness': Elsa von Freytag-Loringhoven." *New York Dada.* Ed. Rudolf E. Kuenzli. New York: Willis Locker & Owens, 1986. 81–101.

Rushdie, Salman. "Imaginary Homelands." *Imaginary Homelands: Essays and Criticism, 1981–1991.* London: Granta Books, 1991. 9–21.

Said, Edward. "Islam, Philology and French Culture." *The World, the Text and the Critic*. Cambridge: Harvard University Press, 1983. 268–89.

Salzmann, Karl H. "Die Insel." *Berliner Hefte für geistiges Leben* 4 (1949): 583–94.

Sarkowski, Heinz. *Der Insel Verlag 1899–1999*. Frankfurt am Main: Insel, 1999.

Sawelson-Gorse, Naomi, ed. *Women in Dada: Essays on Sex, Gender, and Identity*. Cambridge, Mass.: MIT Press, 1998.

Die Schaubühne. Advertisement. *Die Zukunft* 13.52 (1905): 461.

Schutte, Jürgen, and Peter Sprengel, eds. *Die Berliner Moderne, 1885–1914*. Stuttgart: Reclam, 1987.

Schwarz, Arturo. *Almanaco Dada*. Milan: Feltrinelli, 1976.

Schwarzkopf, Donata Gabriele. "Die Struktur der Beilage der 'Allgemeinen Zeitung' im Spiegel ihrer Kunstberichterstattung." Diss. Ludwig-Maximilians-Universität Munich, 1951.

Sieburth, Richard. "Dada Pound." *South Atlantic Quarterly* 83 (1984): 1–17.

Smith, W.G. *A Study in Canadian Immigration*. Toronto: Ryerson, 1920.

Spettigue, Douglas O. *FPG: The European Years*. Ottawa: Oberon Press, 1973.

———. *Frederick Philip Grove*. Studies in Canadian Literature. Hugo McPherson, Gary Geddes, gen. ed. Toronto: Copp Clark Publishing Company, 1969.

Stobie, Margaret R. *Frederick Philip Grove*. New York: Twayne Publishers, Inc., 1973.

———. "Grove's Letters From the Mennonite Reserve." *Canadian Literature* 59 (1974): 67–80.

Stevens, Wallace. *Collected Poems*. New York: Knopf, 1954.

Swinburne, Algernon Charles. "Phaedra: Ein Fragment." [Trans. Felix Paul Greve.] *Freistatt* 7 (18 Feb. 1905): 105–07.

Tashjian, Dickran. *Skyscraper Primitives: Dada and the American Avant-Garde, 1910–1925*. Middletown, Conn.: Wesleyan University Press, 1975.

Theis, Raimund, ed. *Franz Blei—André Gide: Briefwechsel (1904–1933)*. Darmstadt: Wissenschaftliche Buchgesellschaft, 1997.

Thompson, John Herd. *The Harvests of War: The Prairie West, 1914–1918*. Toronto: McClelland and Stewart, 1978.

Volke, Werner. *Hugo von Hofmannsthal in Selbstzeugnissen und Bilddokumenten*. Reinbek bei Hamburg: Rowohlts Bildmonographien, 1967.

Vollmoeller, Karl Gustav. "Catherina, Gräfin von Armagnac und ihre beiden Liebhaber." *Neue Deutsche Rundschau* 14 (1903): 273–314.

Whistler, James McNeill. "Ten O'Clock." [Trans. Felix Paul Greve.] *Neue Deutsche Rundschau* 14 (1903): 315–25.

Wilde, Oscar. *Das Bildnis Dorian Grays.* Trans. Felix Paul Greve. Minden: Bruns, [1902].

———. *Dorian Gray.* Trans. Johannes Gaulke. Leipzig: Spohr, [1901].

———. *Dorian Grays Bildnis.* Trans. Felix Paul Greve. 2nd ed. Minden: Bruns, [1903].

———. "Ein Kapitel aus Dorian Grays Bildnis." Trans. anon. *Neue Deutsche Rundschau* 14 (1903): 206–10.

———. *Fingerzeige.* Trans. Felix Paul Greve and Herman F.C. Kilian. Minden: Bruns, [1902].

———. "Gedichte in Prosa." Trans. F[ranz] B[lei]. *Die Insel* 3 (April-May 1902): 119–22.

———. "Lehren und Sprüche." [Trans. Felix Paul Greve.] *Die Insel* 3 (Aug.-Sept. 1902): 206.

———. "Lehren und Sprüche." [Trans. Franz Blei.] *In Memoriam Oscar Wilde.* Ed. Franz Blei. Leipzig: Insel, 1904. 55–77.

———. "Lehren und Sprüche für die reifere Jugend." [Trans. Franz Blei.] *In Memoriam Oscar Wilde.* Ed. Franz Blei. Rev. ed. Leipzig: Insel, 1905. 58–105.

———. *Lehren und Sprüche für die reifere Jugend.* Trans. Felix Paul Greve. Munich: In Commission J. Littauer Kunsthandlung, [1902].

———. "Lehren und Sprüche für die reifere Jugend." [Trans. Felix Paul Greve.] *Neue Deutsche Rundschau* 14 (1903): 101–2.

———. "Neue Sprüche und Lehren." Trans. Franz Blei. *Freistatt* 7 (8 April 1905): 220–22.

———. *Phrases and Philosophies for the Use of the Young.* London: Privately Printed for Presentation, 1894.

———. *The Complete Works of Oscar Wilde.* New York: Harper & Row, 1989.

Williams, David. "Oscar Wilde and a Swede from Nebraska: Masks of Autobiography in *Settlers of the Marsh* and *In Search of Myself.*" *Canada and the Nordic Countries.* Eds. Jorn Carlsen and Bengt Streijffert. Lund: Lund University Press, 1988. 365–76.

Williams, William Carlos. "The Baroness." *The Autobiography of William Carlos Williams*. New York: Random House, 1948. 163–69.

Windelboth, Horst. "Das Central-Theater in Berlin, 1880–1908." Diss. FU Berlin, 1956.

Woodsworth, J.S. *Strangers Within Our Gates Or Coming Canadians*. 1909; rpt. Intro. Marilyn Barber. Toronto: University of Toronto Press, 1972.

Zabel, Barbara. "The Constructed Self: Gender and Portraiture in Machine-Age America." Sawelson-Gorse 22–47.

Zwanzig Jahre Stadttheater 1908–1928. Cottbus: Staedtisches Presse und Verkehrsamt, 1928.

Contributors

RICHARD CAVELL, a past President of the Canadian Comparative Literature Association (CCLA), is the founding Director of the International Canadian Studies Centre at the University of British Columbia. He has recently published *McLuhan in Space: A Cultural Geography* with University of Toronto Press (2002), where he is Joint Editor of the "Cultural Spaces" series.

JUTTA ERNST, Assistant Professor of English and American Studies at the Universität des Saarlandes, Germany, is the author of *Edgar Allan Poe und die Poetik des Arabesken* (1996) and co-editor (with Klaus Martens) of *'Je vous écris, en hâte et fiévreusement': Felix Paul Greve-André Gide. Korrespondenz und Dokumentation* (1999). She has published numerous articles on contemporary American poetry, literary journalism, genre theory, and the translation and mediation of literature. Her current projects include a study on the making of literary modernism. She is a member of the Saarbrücken Centre for Canadian and Anglo-American Cultures (CCAC).

IRENE GAMMEL teaches modern American and Canadian literature and culture at the University of Prince Edward Island. She has published extensively on the Baroness Elsa von Freytag-Loringhoven, Frederick Philip Grove, and L.M. Montgomery. Her publications include *Baroness Elsa: Gender, Dada, and Everyday Modernity: A Cultural Biography* (MIT Press, 2002), *Sexualizing Power in Naturalism: Theodore Dreiser and Frederick Philip Grove* (University of Calgary Press, 1994), and two edited books, *L.M. Montgomery and Canadian Culture* (University of Toronto Press, 1999) and *Confessional Politics: Women's Sexual Self-Representations in Life Writing and Popular Media* (Southern Illinois

University Press, 1999). She served as the president of the Canadian Comparative Literature Association from 1999–2001.

PAUL HJARTARSON, a Professor in the English Department at the University of Alberta, writes and teaches primarily in the areas of Canadian literature and culture. His publications include *A Stranger to My Time: Essays by and About Frederick Philip Grove* (1986) and (with D.O. Spettigue) *Baroness Elsa: The Autobiography of the Baroness Elsa von Freytag Loringhoven* (1992). He is currently completing a book on Canadian cultural nationalism in the 1920s.

TRACY KULBA is a SSHRCC Doctoral Fellow currently finishing her dissertation in the Department of English at the University of Alberta. She is the author of "Citizens, Consumers, Critique-al Subjects: Rethinking the 'Statue Controversy' and Emily Murphy's *The Black Candle* (1922)," *Tessera* (Winter 2001/02) and, as a member of the Concrete Matters Collective, the co-editor of a forthcoming collection of essays on feminist materialist methodologies, *Concrete Matters: Feminist Materialism in Theory and Practice.*

KLAUS MARTENS is a Professor of English and American Studies at Universität des Saarlandes, Germany, and Chair of the Centre for Canadian and Anglo-American Studies (CCAC). He is also a widely published poet and literary translator. His most recent monographs include a tri-lingual edition of the André Gide-Felix Paul Greve correspondence (1997), edited with Jutta Ernst, and his biography of Grove, *F.P. Grove in Europe and Canada: Translated Lives,* published by the University of Alberta Press (2001).

PAUL MORRIS is an Assistant Professor of English and American Studies at the Universität des Saarlandes. His most recent publications have dealt with American and Canadian literature. He is presently completing a book-length study of the role of poetry in Vladimir Nabokov's oeuvre. He is a founding member of the Centre for Canadian and Anglo-American Cultures (CCAC) at the Universität des Saarlandes where he actively promotes the study of Canadian literature and culture.

Index

aestheticism, 55, 70
  art for art's sake, 79
  dandy, the, 86, 166, 167, 172,
    173, 184, 185
  and posing, 134, 148, 149, 168,
    169, 170, 171, 184, 185
Anderson, J.T.M., 112
Anderson, Margaret, 19, 22, 23
anti-Semitism, 24 n.11
Archipenko, Alexander, 25
  Seated Woman, 27
Arensberg, Walter and Louise, 5
Armory Show, 3, 41
Arp, Hans, 38, 42
atavism, 160, 161, 162, 163
Avery, Donald, 110–11, 118, 123–24,
  126

Ball, Hugo, 42–43, 60–62
Barber, Marilyn, 115–16, 117, 129 n.6
Barnes, Djuna, 9, 20, 21, 24, 43, 44,
  45, 46, 51, 52, 53, 60, 64, 65
Beardsley, Aubrey, 54, 148, 149
Benjamin, Walter, 15
Bennett, R.B., 127
Berber, Anita, 22
Bercuson, David Jay, 123
Berman, Nina, 54
Bernstein, Theresa, 18

Elsa von Freytag-Loringhoven, 17
Biddle, George, 16, 18, 53
Bie, Oscar, 73, 74
Blätter für die Kunst, 70–72, 80
Blei, Franz, 75–76, 82 n.18, 83 n.21
Blodgett, E.D., xxiii, 24 n.5
Blondel, Nathalie, 21
body, the, xxxi
  empathic theories of, xxxi–xxxii,
    29–34
  costuming of, xxxii, 8, 16, 20, 22,
    54–57, 62, 63
  as art, 11, 28, 44
Böhlau, Helene, 54
Boix, Richard, 25–26, 38
Bordon, Robert Laird, 117–18, 122
Bourdieu, Pierre, xxviii
Brahm, Otto, 73
Brooks, Charles S., 6
Browning, Robert, 72, 74, 77, 81, 84
  A Blot in the 'Scutcheon, 72
  "Cleon," 77
  In a Balcony, 72
Bruns, J.C.C., 52, 54, 57, 72, 73, 75,
  77, 78, 80 n.6, 82 n.18
Buffet-Picabia, Gabrielle, 5
Butler, Judith, 15
Butts, Mary, xxxii, 21
  "The Master's Last Dancing," 21

Café Voltaire, 42

Cahun, Claude, 22

The Canadian Nation, 126

Cavell, Richard, xxx–xxxii, xxxiv n.3, 9

Central Theater, Berlin, 46, 49, 62, 63

Certeau, Michel de, 15

contact zone, the, xix–xi, xxiv, xxv, xxxiii–xxxiv, xxxiv n.1

Covert, Jean, 5

Crotti, Jean and Yvonne, 5

Dada, 6, 10, 42–43
    and consumer culture, 8
    and domestic objects, 10, 16, 20, 36
    and embodiment, xxxi–xxxii, 28, 35, 36 (*see also* body, the)
    and gender, 11, 15–16, 18, 28 (*see also* gender performance)
    and language, 43, 44, 61, 63–64
    New York Dada, xxxii, 5, 6, 11, 25, 37, 38 n.4, 42
    New York Dada, scholarly field, xv, xxxii, 5, 25, 28
    and mechanical imagery, 10–11, 15, 35–36
    as performative, xxxi, xxxii, 7, 11, 15, 16, 19, 20
    and sexuality, 7–8, 16, 18, 19, 28, 46
    simultaneous poem (*poème simultan*), 43
    sound poems (*Klanggedichte*), 43, 60
    Zurich, 38 n.4, 42, 43

Dafoe, J.W., 117, 120, 123

Davidson, Abraham A., 41, 64 n.2

decadence, xxvii, 22, 87, 92, 98–99, 104 n.16, 165, 167

Demuth, Charles, 5

déraciné, 91, 134, 158, 159, 172, 173 (*see also* Entwurzelt)

DeVore, Lynn, 45

Divay, Gabrielle, 70, 72, 80 n.2

Droste, Sebastian, 22

Duchamp, Marcel, xxxii, 5, 7, 9, 11, 14, 18–19, 25, 34, 38, 41, 46, 53
    Bicycle Wheel, 11
    Bride Stripped Bare By her Bachelors, Even, 35
    Fountain, 6
    Large Glass, 11
    Nude Descending a Staircase, 41
    ready-mades, 9, 11
    Rrose Sélavy, 18–19

Dumas, Alexandre, 77
    Le Comte de Monte-Cristo, 77

Duve, Thierry de, 9

Egbringhoff, Ulla, 53

Endell, August, 8, 28–29, 31–32, 35, 46, 47, 53, 78
    aesthetics of, 31–32
    architecture and interior design of, 31–33

Endell, Else, xxxiv n.3, 77 (*see also* Freytag-Loringhoven, Baroness Elsa von)

entwurzelt, xxvii, 91–92, 94, 104 n.15, 158, 160, 162, 164, 166, 172

Ernst, Jutta, xxii, xxviii–ix

Escritt, Stephen, 31

Fiedler, Conrad, 32
Fischer, S., 73, 74, 75
flânerie, 15
Flanner, Janet, 21
Flaubert, Gustave, 54, 65 n.5, 69,
    142, 143
    Salammbô, 54
Ford, Ford Maddox, 21, 24 n.10
Freistatt, 74–78, 82 n.17, 84 n.32
Freytag-Loringhoven, Baron
    Leopold, 4, 38 n.4
Freytag-Loringhoven, Baroness Elsa
    von (*see also* Greve, Else *and*
    Plötz, Else)
    and acting, 45–52, 63–64
    and androgyny, 7, 16, 18, 20, 22
    "Appalling Heart," 14–15
    and artistic collaboration with
        Greve, 28, 34–35, 45, 52, 53,
        65 n.5, 77, 83 n.27
    autobiography of, 5, 8, 14, 45
    "Cast-Iron Lover," 14, 23
    Cathedral, 13
    and cross-dressing, 18–19
    as dominatrix, 14
    Earring Object, 13
    Enduring Ornament, 12–13
    God, 6, 34, 35
    Limbswish, 12, 13–14
    "Literary Five O'Clock," 6
    and marriage to August Endell,
        46, 47, 53
    and marriage to Felix Paul Greve,
        xxii, 52
    and marriage to Baron Leopold
        von Freytag-Loringhoven, 4
    "Matter, Level, Perspective," 14
    "Mefk Maru Mustir Daas," 10, 24
        n.6, 59–60, 61

    "Mineself—Minesoul—and—
        Cast—Iron Lover," 6
    and modeling, 16, 36
    and mother, 9–10, 24 n.5
    "Orgasm," 6
    "Orgasmic Toast," 6
    performance art of, xxvi,
        xxx–xxxiii, 3, 7–8, 10, 11, 13,
        15–16, 18–23, 24 n.9, n.10,
        32, 35–36, 42, 63, 64
    "Perpetual Motion," 13, 14
    Portrait of Marcel Duchamp (assem-
        blage), 4, 28
    and pseudonyms, use of, 61, 77
    "Spiritual-Chemical Reflection,"
        23 n.1
    "Subjoyride," 6
    as translator, 53, 65 n.5
Friesen, Gerald, 109, 117
Furtwängler, Adolf, 70

Gammel, Irene, xxx, xxxii–xxxiii,
    35, 38 n.1, 39 n.11, 46, 49,
    105 n.20
Gaulke, Johannes, 72
Geertz, Clifford, xxxv n.4
gender performance, xxxii, 7, 9, 11,
    15–16, 18, 22
    and cross-dressing, 9, 18–19
George, Stefan, xxix, 55, 70–72, 80
Gide, André, xxix, 52, 57, 61, 69,
    74–79, 81, 83, 91, 104 n.15,
    133, 146, 147, 148, 149, 150,
    151, 158, 159, 166, 167, 178,
    179
    Les Nourritures terrestes, 74–75
    La Porte étroite, 77
    Le Retour de l'enfant prodigue, 74
    Saül, 61, 76, 77

Gleizes, Albert, 5

Goethe, Johann Wolfgang von, 10, 47, 144, 145
    Faust, 10

Graphic Press, 126

Greve, Else, xxxiv n.3, 53, 55, 61, 63, 65 n.5, 83 n.27 (*see also* Freytag-Loringhoven, Baroness Elsa von *and* Plötz, Else)

Greve, Felix Paul (Grove, Frederick Philip)
    and *Arabian Nights*, translation of, 53
    and artistic collaboration with Else, 28, 34–35, 45, 52, 53, 77, 83 n.27
    "Assimilation," 127
    "Canadians Old and New," 126
    "Die Hexe," 77
    as educator, 112, 114, 117
    and *entwurzelt*, xxvii, 91–92, 94, 104 n.15, 158, 162, 164, 166, 172
    Fanny Essler, 34–35, 45, 46, 47, 77, 78
    and Flaubert, Gustav, 54, 65 n.5, 69, 142, 143
    Fruits of the Earth, 90–91
    "George Meredith," 77
    and Gide, André, xxix, 52, 61, 69, 74–79, 81 n.14, 83 n.27, 91, 104 n.15, 133, 146, 147, 148, 149, 150, 151, 158, 159, 166, 167, 178, 179
    Helena und Damon, 133
    In Search of Myself, xxvii, 85, 90, 93, 94, 104 n.15, 109, 113, 124, 125
    It Needs to be Said, 126

    lecture tours, 79, 84 n.31, 126
    The Letters of Frederick Philip Grove, 72, 73, 79, 80 n.6, 84 n.31, 113
    and marriage to Else Endell, xxii, 52
    Maurermeister Ihles Haus, 9, 45, 78
    and Meredith, George, 69, 73–74, 77, 81 n.12, 158, 159
    Oskar Wilde, 35, 87–88, 103 n.3, 134
    "Oscar Wilde und das Drama," 87, 89, 101, 134
    Our Daily Bread, 24 n.5
    and Pater, Walter, 72, 144, 145
    and pseudonyms, use of, 77
    Randarabesken zu Oscar Wilde, xx, xxii–xxiii, xxvii, xxxv n.6, 87–88, 91–92, 103 n.3, 133–34, 136–87
    A Search for America, xxvii, 93, 94, 104 n.15, 108, 125, 126
    Settlers of the Marsh, xxvii, xxx, 24 n.5, 85–105, 107–08, 113, 124–25, 127
    and Stendhal (Henri Beyle), 69
    "suicide" of, 86, 116–17, 119
    and Swinburne, Algernon Charles, 77, 158, 159
    as translator, xxvii, xxix, 69, 72–77, 80–84, 85–86, 133–34, 137, 145
    Wanderungen, 60, 71, 72, 93, 133
    and Wells, H.G., 69, 75, 78
    and Whistler, James McNeill, 73, 77
    and Wilde, Oscar, xx, xxii–xxv, xxvii, xxix, xxv n.6, 35, 54, 61, 69, 72–73, 76–77, 81, 83, 84, 85–105, 133–34, 136–87

Grove, Frederick Philip (*see* Greve, Felix Paul
Guggenheim, Peggy, 3, 12
Gundolf, Friedrich, 70
Gunnars, Kristjana, 107

Harden, Maximilian, 72, 75–76, 83 n.23
Hardt, Ernst, 46
Hauptmann, Gerhart, 47, 49
Healy, J.J., 119
Heap, Jane, xxxii, 9, 19–20, 22, 23
Hildebrand, Adolf von, 32
Hjartarson, Paul Ivar, xxix–xxx, 5, 23 n.2, 28, 36, 41, 42, 61
Hoerschelmann, Rulf von, 55
Hofmannsthal, Hugo von, 55, 65 n.5
Holz, Arno, 49
Huelsenbeck, Richard, 42, 61

Ibsen, Henrik, 47, 51
immigration (*see also* mediation, as migration)
    the Baroness as immigrant, xx, 4, 38 n.4, 42
    and education, 111–17
        Manitoba Public Schools Act, 114, 115, 120
    FPG as immigrant, xx, 42, 112, 113
    Immigration Act, the, xxx, 110, 123–24
    Naturalization Act, the, xxx, 123
    Niels Lindstedt as immigrant, 94, 95, 96
    and Orders in Council, xxx, 110, 118, 123

and Russian Revolution, xxix, 110, 123
and War Measures Act, the, 112, 118
and Wartime Elections Act, the, 122
as wastage, 107–12
Die Insel, 76
Insel Verlag, 73

Jacobsohn, Siegfried, 76–77
Jaenen, Cornelius J., 115
Janssen, Alfred, 71
Jones, Amelia, 7, 11, 15, 19, 35, 36
Joyce, James, 19, 23
Jugend, 31
Jugendstil movement (Art Nouveau), xxx, 28, 31, 47
Juncker, Axel, 56, 57

Kamboureli, Smaro, 107–09, 113
Kealy, Gregory S., 110
Keats, John, 53
Kelman, Mark, 12
Kilian, Herman F.C., 71, 103 n.2
Klages, Helene, 53
Kluncker, Karlhans, 70–72
Knister, Raymond, 79
Krauss, Rosalind E., 19, 22
Kuenzli, Rudolph E., 7, 25, 36
Kunstgewerbler (Arts and Crafts movement), 3, 8–9

Lange, Helene, 57
Lasker-Schüler, Else, xxv, xxvi, 9, 46, 52, 53–58, 59, 60–61, 63, 64

Die Nächte Tino von Bagdads, 54
Tarub, Bagdads Berühmte Köchin,
 54
Leblanc, Georgette, 22
Lechter, Melchior, 8, 16, 46
Leger, Fernand, 35
Lipps, Theodor, 31
Littauer, Jacob, 71, 73, 80 n.5
The Little Review, 6, 19, 23, 44, 60
Loy, Mina, 5
Luntoski, Adalbert, 86

Maclean's, 126
*Making Mischief: Dada Invades New
 York*, xv, 5, 25, 64 n.2
Makow, Henry, 113, 125, 128 n.3
Mallgrave, Harry Francis, 30, 32, 33
Mann, Thomas, 186, 187
Martens, Klaus, xxv–xxvi, xxxiv n.3,
 9, 38 n.1, 128 n.4
Martynowych, Orest T., 110, 117,
 122–24
McLaren, Angus, 111–12
McLuhan, Marshall, xxxi
mediation, xix–xxii, xxxiii–xxxiv
 and the body, xxx–xxxii, 31 (*see
  also* body, the)
 and gender practice, xxxii–xxxiii
  (*see also* gender performance)
 as migration, xx, xxi, xxv–xxvii
  (*see also* immigration)
 by social-institutional contexts,
  xx, xxi, xxviii–xxxiii, 13
 as translation, xix, xx, xxi,
  xxii–xxv, 71 (*see also*
  translation)
Mercure de France, 53, 78, 146, 147
Meredith, George, 69, 73–74, 77, 81
 n.12, 158, 159

Meyerfeld, Max, 81 n.11
Miller, H.C., 126
Monroe, Harriet, 23
Morris, Paul, xx, xxii–xxv, xxvii
Morton, Desmond, 122

naming, xx, xxxiv n.3, 51, 56, 61, 64,
 119
Naumann, Francis M., 5, 6, 10–11,
 18, 19, 25, 28, 38, 44, 56
Neue Deutsche Rundschau, 73–74, 77
New York Dada (magazine), 18
Nietzsche, Friedrich, 69, 70, 92, 104
 n.16, 148, 149, 164, 165, 182,
 183

Orientalism, xxvi, 24 n.11, 52–61
 and Jewish identity, 54–55
 and poetic imagery, 59–61
 and women's movement (*Die
  Frauenfrage*), 56–57
Oesterheld & Co., 57, 65 n.8, 74, 77

Pacey, Desmond, 124–25
Padolsky, Enoch, 126
parody, 6, 15, 16, 22, 49, 51, 56, 62,
 63
Pater, Walter, 72, 144, 145
 "A Prince of Court Painters," 72
 Marius the Epicurean, 72
Phelan, Peggy, 11
Picabia, Francis, 5, 10–11, 35
Plötz, Else, xx, xxxiv n.3, 38 n.3, 49,
 51, 64, 119 (*see also* Freytag-
 Loringhoven, Baroness Elsa
 von *and* Greve, Else)

Poellnitz, Rudolph von, 73, 77, 80
     n.6
Pound, Ezra, xxxii, 23
Prenowitz, Eric, xxiii–xxiv

Ray, Man, 5, 18, 25, 37, 38, 41, 46
realism, 70, 94, 108–09
Reilly, Eliza Jane, 11
Reiss, Robert, 29, 36, 63
Reventlow, Countess Franziska zu,
     53
Roché, Pierre, 5
Roché, Juliette, 5
Rushdie, Salman, xix–xx, xxxiv
Ryerson Press, 84 n.31, 111, 124

Sawelson-Grose, Naomi, 5, 11, 28
Schamberg, Morton Livingston, 5,
     6, 11, 41
   God (assemblage), 34
Die Schaubühne, 76–77, 83 n.24, n. 26
Scheeler, Charles, 5
Scheerbart, Paul, 54, 55
Schiller, Friedrich, 47, 51, 52
Schmarsow, August, 33
Schmitz, Oscar, 46
Schmitz, Richard, 46
Schwitters, Kurt, 42, 43, 44, 61,
     62–63
Sieburth, Richard, 6
Smith, W.G., 111–12
Spettigue, Douglas O., xxii, xxxiv
     n.3, 28, 36
Spry, Graham, xxx, 126
Stella, Joseph, 5
Stendahl (Henri Beyle), 69
Stettheimer, Florine, 5
Stevens, Wallace, 44, 46

Stobie, Margaret, 113–14, 117, 120,
     125
Stöcker, Helene, 57
Stumpf, Carl, 33
Der Sturm, 42, 53
surrealism, 22, 41, 61, 64
Swinburne, Algernon Charles, 77,
     158, 159
Symonds, Arthur, 148, 149

Theis, Raimund, 75, 76
thick description, xx, xxx, xxxiii,
     xxxv
Thompson, John Herd, 118, 122
Tice, Clara, 5
translation, xix, xxi, xxii–xxv, xxxiii,
     xxxiv, 23 n.3 (see also media-
     tion, as translation)
   Else as translator, 53, 65 n.5
   Greve as translator, xxvii, xxix,
     69, 72–77, 80–84, 85–86,
     133–34, 137, 145
Tzara, Tristan (Sami Rosentock),
     18, 42

Vallette, Alfred, 57
Vallette, Marguerite, 57
Varèse, Edgar, 5
Varèse, Louise Norton, 5
Vischer, Robert, xxxi, 30–31
Vollmoeller, Karl Gustav, 70, 73
Voss, Richard, 47

Wagner, Richard, 51
Warkentin, I.J., 117, 119, 129 n.7
Wells, H.G., 75, 78
Whistler, James McNeill, 73, 77

Wilde, Oscar, xx, xxii–xxv, xxvii,
    xxix, xxv n.6, 35, 54, 61, 69,
    72–73, 76–77, 81, 83, 84,
    85–105, 133–34, 136–87
  The Ballad of Reading Gaol, 83 n.21
  De Profundis, 101
  Intention, 72, 80 n.6, 86, 88, 133
  Lord Arthur Savile's Crime, 134, 186,
    187
  *Phrases and Philosophies for the Use
    of the Young*, 73, 133
  The Picture of Dorian Gray, 72–73,
    77, 81 n.10, 98–101, 146, 147,
    158, 159, 172, 173, 178, 179
  Salomé, 54, 61
  "The Truth of Masks," 90
Williams, William Carlos, xxxii, 7,
    14, 20, 46, 53

Winnipeg General Strike, xxix, 110,
    112–13, 123
Wintergarten shows, 22, 46, 62
Wölffin, Heinrich, 32–34
Wolfskehl, Karl, 24 n.11, 46, 55, 80
    n.2, 83 n.21
Wood, Beatrice, 5
Woodsworth, J.S., 109, 112
  Strangers Within Our Gates, 109, 112

Zabel, Barbara, 11
Zayas, Marius de, 10–11
Zentral Theater, Berlin, 46 (*see also*
    Central Theater, Berlin)
Die Zukunft, 38 n.6, 72, 76